MEASURING SUSTAINABLE DE

Measuring Sustainable Development

Macroeconomics and the Environment

Giles Atkinson
Lecturer in Environmental Policy, London School of Economics and Senior Honorary Fellow, CSERGE, University College London and University of East Anglia, UK

Richard Dubourg
Principal Consultant, ENTEC Ltd and Senior Honorary Fellow, CSERGE, University College London and University of East Anglia, UK

Kirk Hamilton
Environmental Economist, Environment Department, World Bank, USA

Mohan Munasinghe
Distinguished Visiting Professor of Environmental Management, University of Colombo, Sri Lanka and Division Chief for Environmental Economics, Environment Department, World Bank, USA

David Pearce
Professor of Environmental Economics at University College London and Director of CSERGE, University College London and University of East Anglia, UK

Carlos Young
Lecturer at Universidade Federal do Rio de Janeiro, Brazil and Visiting Fellow, CSERGE, University College London and University of East Anglia, UK

Edward Elgar

Cheltenham, UK • Northampton, MA, USA

Published by
Edward Elgar Publishing Limited
Glensanda House
Montpellier Parade
Cheltenham
Glos GL50 1UA
UK

Edward Elgar Publishing, Inc.
6 Market Street
Northampton
Massachusetts 01060
USA

Reprinted 1999
Paperback edition 1999

A catalogue record for this book is available from the British Library

Library of Congress Cataloguing in Publication Data
Measuring sustainable development: macroeconomics and the environment
/Giles Atkinson ... [et al.].
    Includes bibliographical references.
    1. Sustainable development. 2. Economic development—
Environmental aspects. I. Atkinson, Giles, 1969–   .
HC79.E5M4   1997
338.9—dc21   96–39592
                                                                            CIP

ISBN 1 85898 572 2 (cased)
        1 84064 198 3 (paperback)

Printed and bound in Great Britain by
Biddles Limited, Guildford and King's Lynn

Contents

List of figures		vii
List of tables		ix
Notes on the authors		xi
Preface		xiii
Acknowledgements		xv
1	Introduction: The meaning of sustainable development	1
2	Physical indicators	20
3	Resource and environmental accounting	33
4	Empirical measures of sustainable development	69
5	International trade and sustainability	99
6	Ecological economics and indicators	119
7	Social indicators	132
8	Environmental impacts of economywide policies	155
9	Policies for sustainable development	187
10	Towards new measures of progress	201
References		218
Index		241

Figures

1.1	Optimal and sustainable consumption over time	7
2.1	A basic model of environmental indicators	22
2.2	Tunnelling through the environmental Kuznets curve	24
2.3	An environmental pressure index for the Netherlands	26
2.4	Suggested analytical structure of policy-maker information	28
4.1	Net saving versus depletion share of GNP, 1986–1990 average	75
4.2	Genuine savings rates by region, 1980–1990	76
4.3	Genuine savings rates by region, 1980–1990	77
4.4	Investment and saving in East Asia, 1980–1990	78
4.5	Investment and saving in Sub-Saharan Africa, 1980–1990	79
4.6	Savings rates in Chile, 1980–1990	84
4.7	Valuing the costs and benefits of emission reductions	86
4.8	United Kingdom savings rates, 1980–1990	91
4.9	Air pollution damage in the United Kingdom, 1980–1990	92

Tables

2.1	GWP factors of greenhouse gases	25
2.2	Emissions of greenhouse gases in the Netherlands	26
2.3	Health damage from air pollution: the economic costs of air pollution damage to human health in urban areas	30
3.1	Expanded input–output account for natural resources and the environment	35
3.2	A social accounting matrix including resources and the environment	53
4.1	Rental rates for minerals and crude oil	73
4.2	User-cost and net price estimates for a sample of oil producers	82
4.3	Marginal social costs per tonne of air pollutant emitted	88
4.4	Genuine saving as a percentage of GDP in Europe	93
4.5	Air pollution damage as a percentage of GDP	94
4A.1	Genuine savings rates by country	97
5.1	Global resource consumption	106
5.2	Japan: imported resource requirements	111
5.3	United States: imported resource requirements	112
5.4	European Union: imported resource requirements	113
6.1	Falkenmark's water interval by region	124
6.2	Fuelwood availability and sustainable populations in Africa	126
6.3	Crop yield variability in India, 1955–1989	129
7.1	The 1994 human development index	134
7.2	Borda count wellbeing index for top 20 richest countries	140
7.3	The effect on the HDI of varying the elasticity of marginal utility of income	143
7.4	Landholdings, tenure and wage dependence	147
7.5	Hours spent collecting water, 1975–1982	147
7.6	Hours spent collecting fuelwood	148
7.7	A social accounting matrix showing linkages to the environment	153
8.1	Simple example of an action impact matrix	158
9.1	Land conversions, 1979/81–1991	196
9.2	Changes in carbon with land-use conversion	197
9.3	World population projections	198

Authors

Giles Atkinson is Senior Research Fellow at CSERGE, University College London, Gower St, London, WC1E 6BT, and at the University of East Anglia.

Richard Dubourg is Senior Research Fellow at CSERGE, University College London, Gower St, London, WC1E 6BT, and at the University of East Anglia.

Kirk Hamilton is Environmental Economist in the Environment Department, World Bank, 1818 H St, Washington DC 20433, and was Senior Fellow at CSERGE, University College London, Gower St, London, WC1E 6BT, and at the University of East Anglia.

Mohan Munasinghe is Distinguished Visiting Professor of Environmental Management, University of Colombo, Sri Lanka, and Division Chief for Environmental Economics, Environment Department, World Bank, 1818 H St, Washington DC 20433.

David Pearce is Professor of Environmental Economics at University College London and Director of CSERGE, University College London, Gower St, London, WC1E 6BT, and at the University of East Anglia.

Carlos Young is Lecturer at Universidade Federal do Rio de Janeiro, Av. Pasteur 250, Rio de Janeiro, RJ 22290–240 and was Visiting Fellow at CSERGE, University College London, Gower St, London, WC1E 6BT, and at the University of East Anglia.

Preface

Since 'sustainable development' was adopted as an overarching goal of economic and social development by United Nations agencies, by *Agenda 21*, and by many individual nations, local governments and even corporations, it has generated a huge literature. Much of what has been written about sustainable development has generated more heat than light. Politicians prefer that it be vaguely defined. A cynical view of this preference might be that it then permits them to be pursuing sustainable development, almost regardless of what they do. Economists have 'homed in' on a particular interpretation which others find 'monistic' because it fits sustainability into a fairly traditional approach to economic development. Those who prefer 'pluralist' approaches see sustainable development as serving many social goals – a rising standard of living, a particular concern for the poor, a requirement for community participation in decision-making, and so on. We have a great deal of sympathy for pluralist interpretations, but they also tend to obscure many insights from a more directed focus. To this end, we espouse the concept of sustainable development as it has developed in the economic literature, but do our best to identify the social dimensions of the concept as well. Apart from our natural biases as economists, our judgement is that economics has gone further than any other discipline in weaving a consistent 'story' about sustainable development: what it is, what the conditions are for achieving it, what might have to be sacrificed to obtain it, and how it can be measured.

The focus of this book is on the theory and practice of economic development as viewed from the perspective of sustainability. We are not, therefore, overly concerned with detail but rather with the implications of sustainability for the way we view development policy. Our argument is that traditional discussions and analyses of savings and investment at the macroeconomic level can be greatly enriched by integrating the environment into the macroeconomic picture. Simply put, our environment is also capital and we neglect it at our peril. Running it down, or 'mining' natural capital, is a sure recipe for unsustainable economic development. Yet not only do governments neglect this dimension, so, all too often, do international agencies and development banks. They do so without malice, but in ignorance of what well-intentioned policies can do to the natural resource base on which so many economies depend.

We therefore advance the idea of measuring sustainability in a macroeconomic context so that decision-makers can be more alert to the underlying 'true' trends in the economy and to the way in which their policies may affect those trends. The critical concept here is 'genuine' savings, a notion of savings in the economy that nets out the depreciation on all forms of capital, including natural capital. We also advance the idea that the productivity of savings matters: all investment is not equally valuable. As a particular feature of this point of view we also suggest that investing in natural capital is, contrary to so much of the prevailing development paradigm, 'quality' investment.

This book is the outcome of nearly a decade of thinking and writing about sustainable development. The Centre for Social and Economic Research on the Global Environment (CSERGE) has established itself as one of the initiators of measures of sustainability, and the World Bank has taken these measures and developed them into indicators with potential worldwide coverage. We are more than conscious that the actual indicators presented here require improvement. We are convinced that these improvements will come in the next decade, enabling the redirection of development policies to be undertaken.

GA
RD
KH
MM
DP
CY

London, Colombo and Washington.

Acknowledgements

This book is the result of a collaborative effort between CSERGE, London, and the World Bank, Washington, DC. So many of our colleagues have contributed ideas and information that the list would be endless. Particular thanks, however, are owed to John Proops of Keele University for collaboration over the years on sustainability and international trade; to John O'Connor for masterminding the World Bank's efforts to develop databases on which our measures of genuine savings are based, and to Jerry Warford who initiated so much of the World Bank's environment programme.

1 Introduction: The meaning of sustainable development

1.1 The drive for sustainable development

'Sustainable development' has become the catchphrase of the 1990s. Most popularly developed by the World Commission on Environment and Development (WCED) in *Our Common Future* in 1987 (WCED, 1987), sustainable development aims for economic development in the traditional sense of rising per capita wellbeing, coupled with reductions in poverty and inequity, together with the requirement that the 'resource base' of national economies and the global economy should not be depleted. Put another way, the increase in average human wellbeing must not be at the expense of a worsening of the distribution of wellbeing now, or at the expense of the wellbeing of generations yet to come. In the words of the WCED: 'Sustainable development is development that meets the needs of present without compromising the ability of future generations to meet their own needs' (p. 43).

It contains within it two key concepts:

- the concept of 'needs', in particular the essential needs of the world's poor, to which overriding priority should be given; and
- the idea of limitations imposed by the state of technology and social organization on the environment's ability to meet present and future needs (WCED, 1987, p. 43).

'Sustainable development' now figures as a goal in dozens of national environmental policy statements and in the opening paragraphs of *Agenda 21*, the massive shopping list of world actions adopted at the Earth Summit in Rio de Janeiro in June 1992. *Agenda 21* states:

> In order to meet the challenges of environment and development, States decided to establish a new global partnership. This partnership commits all States to engage in a continuous and constructive dialogue, inspired by the need to achieve a more efficient and equitable world economy, keeping in view the increasing interdependence of the community of nations, and that sustainable development should become a priority item on the agenda of the international community. (UNCED, 1992)

But is sustainable development itself a sustainable concept? It appears to hold out the promise of economic development, *and* at least no further degradation of natural environments, *and* a significant improvement in the absolute and relative lot of the poor. This looks like 'motherhood and apple pie': no-one can be against it, but does it mask the realities of the situation?

Many feel that past economic development policies have failed to secure improvements in even average levels of wellbeing. Excluding Nigeria, for example, the annual average growth rate of the economies of Sub-Saharan Africa was *minus* 0.8 per cent per annum between 1980 and 1993 (World Bank, 1995b). As far as poverty is concerned, great strides have been made, yet, out of the 38 poorest countries (for which information is available) appearing in the World Bank's 'Basic Indicators' statistics, 23 of them had negative growth rates of GDP per capita between 1980 and 1993 (World Bank, 1995b). The poorest countries have got poorer. As to the environment, it is only recently that the world of development has come to understand that eroding the natural environment is eroding one form of capital – natural capital – that is critical for future economic development. Development cannot be sustainable unless the resource base is protected and renewed. Finding natural capital indicators is even more complex than finding indicators for progress in development and equity. Those that are currently available suggest a mixed picture of capital erosion. The area of the world that is at least nominally protected from conversion has increased by a factor of three between 1972 and 1990, from 1.6 per cent of the world's total land area to just under 5 per cent. However, carbon dioxide emissions have doubled between 1965 and 1989 (World Bank, 1992c), and tropical forests are disappearing at the rate of some 15 million hectares every year.

The concept of sustainable development now includes economic, social and environmental requirements (Munasinghe, 1993). Embracing sustainable development, then, seems to be a recognition that too many things have gone wrong, and that past development efforts have achieved only part of what should truly comprise human progress. But sustainable development may also be seeking the impossible; perhaps it is an illusion that we can have development, equity and a sound environment all in one package. Sustainable development almost seems to deny that there are tradeoffs among these goals. For others, however, this tripartite goal of economy, ecology and social justice is the very challenge. For them the question is not *whether* sustainable development is achievable, but *how* it can be achieved. Even if we fail, striving for sustainable development may hold out the prospect of a better world for longer than conventional development policies could achieve. But there are prior steps to be taken before we can formulate *policies* for sustainable development. A fundamental step is finding indicators to measure sustainable development, for otherwise it will not be possible to say whether an economy is on or off a sustainable path of economic development. This issue of measurement is the prime focus of this book.

We ask three questions:

- What is sustainable development?
- How can it be measured?
- How can economic policy help achieve sustainable development?

1.2　What is sustainable development?

Defining sustainable development broadly is not too difficult. The difficult issue is in determining what has to be done to achieve it. What is being referred to is sustainable economic development. The term 'sustainable' is not open to much dispute: it means 'enduring' and 'lasting'. So, sustainable development is development that lasts. Economic development could be narrowly defined in traditional terms as real GNP per capita, or real consumption per capita. Alternatively, it could be broadened to include other indicators of development such as education, health and some measure of the 'quality of life,' including human freedom. One such exercise is to be found in the United Nations Development Programme's 'human development index' (HDI) (see Chapter 7). This combines measures of social goals – literacy, life expectancy and GDP per capita – to provide an index of relative achievement, that is, a score which is defined in terms of a country's position relative to other countries.

For immediate purposes, the definition of 'development' does not matter much, although it is a legitimate source of investigation not least because 'development' is a value word that invites any number of interpretations which could proliferate to the point where 'sustainable development' becomes meaningless. The economist would generally prefer to substitute per capita 'utility' or 'wellbeing' as the appropriate focus for sustainability. However, WCED's focus on 'needs' underscores its emphasis on poverty alleviation as the prime objective of sustainable development: needs might be regarded as the minimum level of access to commodities and resources alone beyond which wellbeing or utility has meaning. This at least provides a starting point to an inquiry into the determinants of sustainable development. Defining sustainable development is not the same thing as searching for the necessary and sufficient conditions for achieving it.

The context of sustainable development has always been that of intergenerational equity, as well as intragenerational equity, but the length of any particular sustainability time horizon is of course open to debate. It must be a few generations at least, but it will not be infinity. We might appeal to some 'coefficient of concern' to set some pragmatic limit on how far into the future we should look, say, 100 years. Of course, if individuals now already integrate future concerns into current actions and choices, 'sustainability' is of little concern, since it will automatically be taken care of. But, as Page (1977) observes, the kinds of bequests to future generations that emerge from the existence of 'overlapping generations' reflect what he calls 'selfish altruism', whereby the wellbeing of an individual now (W_0) is determined by consumption now (C_0) and consumption by future generations over some time horizon, that is

$$W_0 = f(C_0, C_1, C_2 \ldots C_T).$$

But a unit of consumption enjoyed by generations 1, 2 … T would most likely have less value than a unit of consumption enjoyed by generation 0 because generation 0 is the arbiter of value. The weighting required to generate this result is in fact the weighting that arises from generation 0's 'time preference', that is, the *discount rate*. If we seek to maximize W_0, we are, by definition, maximizing the wellbeing of the current generation. It can only be by accident, then, that selfish altruism alone would ensure future levels of wellbeing at least equal to those of the current generation.

What is the link between sustainable development and the economist's traditional concept of optimal economic growth? Economists looking at the theory of economic growth have tended to work with utilitarian assumptions. Then an 'optimal' path of future consumption is traced out by setting up the problem in the following form:

$$\text{Maximize} \int_{t=0}^{\infty} U(C_t).e^{-rt} dt, \qquad 1.1$$

where U is utility (wellbeing), C is real consumption per capita, and r is the utility discount rate, that is, the rate at which future wellbeing is discounted. The economic problem is then to maximize the flow of consumption subject to the constraints imposed by the technology available to the economy. r is most often assumed to be greater than zero, even though there is no intrinsic reason for discounting future utility. There may, however, be good reasons to discount future consumption if we can feel assured that future consumption (and wellbeing) will be higher than it is currently. Discount rate issues are discussed further in Box 1.1.

Box 1.1   The discount rate

It is well known that maximization of this present value function can produce paths of real consumption per capita over time which may or may not be 'sustainable' in the sense defined in equation (1.1) (Pezzey, 1989; Page, 1977; Dasgupta and Heal, 1979). The consistency of optimal growth and sustainable growth depends very much on the relationship between the productivity of the resource base and the social discount rate. The higher the discount rate, the more is sustainable development at risk from the deliberate planning of 'optimal' growth. The lower the discount rate, the less is the risk of 'optimal extinction' for future generations (Clark, 1990). For example, discounting is consistent with the sustainable use of a renewable resource as long as the discount rate does not exceed the regeneration rate of the resource. Obviously, for a non-renewable resource, regeneration is zero. However, there is no sustainable rate of consumption when the resource base consists solely of a non-renewable resource in fixed supply. Discounting merely brings forward the day when consumption falls to zero. Hence, the discount rate, or, more simply, the way that individuals and society view the future in decision-making, can have profound implications for sustainable development.

In the economist's perfect world, the market discount rate and the discount rate required for sustainability (that is, the marginal productivity of the capital base) are brought into equilibrium, provided society maximizes some intertemporal welfare function and is operating at the boundary of an intertemporal production possibility frontier (see below). But there are many distortions that are likely to force market rates to be above the 'true' marginal product of capital. The existence of income tax is just one (Baumol, 1968). Another is that the true discount rate is a 'riskless' rate, due to the ability of society in general, through government, to pool the risks of individual projects both across many projects and across the whole population (Arrow and Lind, 1971). We can also argue that the relevant value of the discount rate is that rate which takes the welfare of future generations into account, whereas the value revealed in the market is likely to be more short term in orientation (Howarth and Norgaard, 1990, 1993). That is, we require a societal rate of discount rather than some average of individual discount rates. Alternatively, the wellbeing of future generations can be regarded as a public good as far as members of the current generation are concerned – all will benefit from any single individual's actions to improve future wellbeing. The level of investment and savings will therefore be less under individualistic decision-making than if a collective investment decision were made. This implies that the social discount rate will be below that produced by market forces.

These considerations suggest that an economy could easily be shifted onto an unsustainable consumption path. But the analysis above has also suggested that sustainability can be more guaranteed if the 'true' value of marginal capital productivity could be determined and be used as the actual discount rate. However, if an economy is heavily reliant upon non-renewable resources, this productivity is zero and any positive discounting will result in a consequent tendency to non-sustainability, at least in terms of this resource.

Technically, if welfare is based on consumption, then the appropriate discount rate is the social rate of return as investment given by $SRRI = r + \eta(\dot{C}/C)$. Here, r represents the preference of an individual for consumption today rather than in the future, and may be based on the myopic notion of 'pure' preference, as well as the risk perception that future consumption may never be realized. η is the elasticity of marginal welfare and $\dot{C}/C$ is the growth rate of consumption. The second term $\eta(\dot{C}/C)$ reflects the fact that the declining marginal welfare of consumption and increases in expected future consumption will combine to make future consumption less valuable than present-day consumption, i.e. since we are likely to be richer in the future, today's consumption is more highly valued.

The general consensus is that r is close to zero, usually zero to three per cent, and η may be in the range of one to two. Thus if $\dot{C}/C$ is large (i.e. expected economic growth rates are high), then SRRI could be quite large too.[1] On the other hand, if we consider a long-range scenario in which growth and consumption are falling (e.g. catastrophic global warming in 100 years time), then g could become negative and consequently SRRI may be small or even negative. In this case, with SRRI as the discount rate, future costs and benefits would look much larger in present value terms than if the conventional opportunity cost of capital (say eight per cent) was used, thereby giving a larger weight to long-term, intergenerational concerns. The key point is that it may be misleading to choose discount rates without assuming some consistent future scenario.[2] Thus an optimistic future would be associated with higher discount rates than a gloomy one, which is consistent since the risk of future catastrophes should encourage greater concern for the future.

1. Assuming a consumption-based numeraire for welfare W, we may write $W = W(c)$. Then $b = -[C(d^2W/dC^2)/(dW/dC)]$ and $g = (1/C)(dC/dt)$. Marginal welfare increases with consumption: $(dW/dC) > 0$; but at a declining rate: $(d^2W/dC^2) < 0$. Therefore $b > 0$, so that the sign of the term $\eta(\dot{C}/C)$ is the same as the sign of $\dot{C}/C$. (See Dasgupta and Heal (1979, chapter 10) for details.)
2. For an example, where the discount rate is endogenized and reflects future consumption, see Uzawa (1969).

The optimizing equation (1.1) does not automatically ensure that we also achieve the condition that we have so far assumed for sustainable development – in terms of a path over time of per capita consumption that is constant or rising. Figure 1.1 presents a highly simplified construction in which TT' describes how consumption can be allocated between now (Cc) and the future (Cf). T is greater than T' because there is a positive return on capital investment. SSc and SSf are two alternative intertemporal welfare functions which reflect the desirability of present consumption relative to future consumption (rather than a single-period welfare function which considers the allocation of consumption between individuals of a single generation). SSc is biased towards the preferences of current generations and SSf is biased towards future generations. All points where $Cf = Cc$ must lie on the 45° line, so that strict (intergenerationally) sustainable development requires locating at X, while a more general sustainable development zone is shown by the shaded area. The absolute value of the slope of *TT'* is in fact (1 plus) the marginal product of capital, and the absolute values of the slopes of *SSc* and *SSf* are equal to (1 plus) the relevant rates of time preference. Since the magnitude of the slope of the tangent at X is less than the corresponding value at Y, it follows that the discount rate that needs to be used to achieve a sustainable development consumption path is below the rate that would be used if resources were allocated according to present-oriented preferences. Economic efficiency demands that society move from a point such as A to a point such as Y on the production possibility frontier *TT'*. Sustainable development considerations demand that the move be from A to X where consumption is equalized. The relevant discount rate becomes the marginal product of capital at X, that is, the future marginal product of capital once the intergenerational equity consideration has been built into the maximization problem.

Note that from Figure 1.1, the 'sustainability point' X can be seen to imply a lower level of current consumption (*Cc2*) than the 'optimal' point Y (*Cc3*). If the starting point is A, the efficiency improvement required to shift to either X or Y will be large enough to ensure that both current (*Cc*) and future (*Cf*)

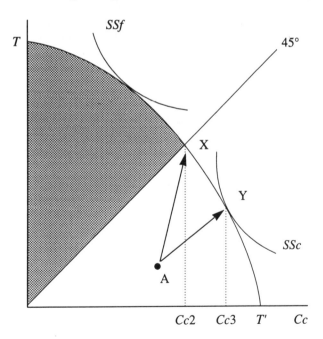

Figure 1.1   Optimal and sustainable consumption over time

consumption increase. However, sustainable development will imply an actual reduction in wellbeing if the starting point is Y. Hence the concern of critics of the idea that policies should aim for non-declining future wellbeing appears to be that these policies will actually work to the detriment of existing generations, in the sense of actually reducing consumption now. We will consider later whether achieving sustainability will mean reducing current wellbeing in actual economies. Before this we need to investigate what it actually means to achieve sustainability.

1.3 The conditions for sustainable development

From the above discussion it appears that a constant consumption path can be achieved by setting the discount rate equal to the marginal product of capital. Contrary to frequent criticisms (for example, Ramsey, 1928; Parfit, 1984; Broome, 1992), discounting can actually be consistent with sustainable development, a result demonstrated in the literature of the 1970s, even if the language was not quite the same (for example, Page, 1977). This resulting 'maximin path' (Rawls, 1971) was first suggested as a criterion for intragenerational justice (for example, distribution within a particular generation), but became widely used to show how economies holding wealth in the form of a non-renewable natural resource could distribute the gains from using up this resource now, to all generations. For example, Solow (1974) showed that an economy with two factors of production (produced capital and a non-renewable resource) could achieve a constant level of real consumption over time if the Hotelling efficiency rule were satisfied and certain alternative conditions were met:

- the elasticity of substitution between natural and produced capital is greater than unity (that is, natural capital is technically inessential to production, so there is no need to substitute for its depletion in production); or
- the elasticity of substitution is equal to unity (natural capital is *essential* but it is possible to use produced capital as a substitute), and the share of produced capital in output is greater than that of natural resources; or
- technological progress increases the productivity of the natural capital stock faster than the discount rate depletes it.

Hamilton (1995) shows that of these conditions, it is the elasticity of substitution requirement that is crucial. If this elasticity is less than one then sustainable development in terms of constant consumption is not feasible. Development will not be sustainable, given fixed technology, and consumption will eventually fall to zero. If, on the other hand, the elasticity is greater than one, that is, the resource is inessential to production, then constant consumption can be achieved. However, the level of consumption under this programme is not maximal. Only if the substitution elasticity is *exactly* equal to one – as with Cobb–Douglas technology – will consumption be both constant and maximal. The extent of knowledge regarding the magnitude of this elasticity for resources and environmental assets is discussed below.

Hartwick (1977, 1978a) showed that, for an elasticity of substitution equal to one, achieving a constant level of real consumption over time required as a 'rule of thumb' that the rents from the exploitation of essential non-renewable resources be reinvested in produced capital. Now known as 'Hartwick's rule', this suggests that sustainable consumption is feasible, in principle anyway, even if there is an initial reliance on non-renewable resources. Hartwick (1978b) extended the model to consider the role of renewable (living) resources. The rule has been generalized to the case of heterogeneous consumption goods and produced capital goods (Dixit, Hammond and Hoel, 1980), and of outputs of pollution and environmental amenities (Stiglitz, 1979; Mäler, 1991).

Achieving sustainable development is not the same thing as maintaining the total value of stocks of both produced and natural assets – this point is made in Hamilton (1995). The changing value of assets typically involves two factors, price changes (capital gains or losses) and volume changes. From the point of view of sustainability, the key point is that the change in the real value of assets (that is, the change in volume times a constant price) should not be negative in aggregate. As will be elaborated in Chapters 3 and 4 of this study, this change in the real value of assets is in fact an expanded measure of saving – 'genuine' saving – that is key in the theory and practice of green national accounting.

Of course, changes in non-renewable and living resources are not the only natural assets of interest in the pursuance of sustainable development. Environmental assets, such as clean air and water, are also pertinent. These assets directly enter the utility function of individuals as an additional argument to the level of consumption. Therefore, a generalized Hartwick 'rule of thumb' is concerned with the achievement of constant utility rather than constant consumption *per se*. In investigating this, it is useful to distinguish between stock pollutants (for example, carbon dioxide, CO_2) and flow pollutants (for example, sulphur dioxide).

Hamilton and Ulph (1994) show that for the former – 'the CO_2 problem' via burning of fossil fuels – a generalized Hartwick rule says that investment should equal the change in the resource stock *plus* the change in the atmospheric stock of CO_2. Each should be valued at its shadow price which in the case of CO_2 is the marginal social cost of CO_2 emissions. For resources, the correct shadow price is the unit resource rent *net* of the optimal carbon tax. It is important to note that this is a departure from the usual Hartwick rule in two ways. First, changes in the stock of CO_2 should be explicitly taken into account in determining investment requirements. Second, fossil fuel resources are less valuable in a greenhouse world as use of these resources leads to 'pollution' in the form of climate change. However, it is acknowledged that this analysis does not take into account the risks of catastrophic impacts of climate change that underlie theories of strong sustainable development examined below.

For flow pollutants, Hamilton and Atkinson (1996) show that investment requirements need to be further augmented to take account of the cumulative impacts of emissions of these pollutants. For example, cumulative exposure to particulate matter (PM_{10}) can lead to impacts on individual human wellbeing via adverse effects on human health.

Hence, there is a clear rationale for expanding the conventional Hartwick rule to take account of the wider range of environmental assets. This is a point that we expand upon in more detail in Chapters 3 and 4 when we investigate the underlying theory of green national accounting and the measurement of genuine savings.

Thus far we have assumed constant population and technology. But clearly, a falling capital stock can sustain growing per capita consumption if the productivity of capital rises because of technological change. It is likely that such change occurs through the act of investment itself (Scott, 1989). It also turns out that technological change is absolutely crucial when depreciation of produced capital – that machines become less productive as they grow older – is acknowledged. With fixed technology it can be shown that a combination of a non-renewable resource and depreciating produced capital will inevitably lead to unsustainable development (that is, declining consumption in the long run) (Hamilton, 1995). This result holds regardless of the aforementioned arguments about substitutability. Sustainability, then, requires some form of technological progress to offset the effects of this depreciating produced capital stock. Yet, many economists argue that not only will this flow of technological change be forthcoming but that such progress is so pervasive as to annul much of the investment requirements implied under a (generalized) Hartwick rule (Nordhaus, 1995). Yet most of these claims rely on a notion of technological progress that is exogenous (that is, determined outside of the economic system) and is thus analogous to 'manna from heaven'. However, increasingly a new focus has been on *endogenous* technological change (see for example, Romer, 1990; and Barro and Sala-I-Martin, 1995). In these theories the creation of new technology uses scarce resources that could otherwise be employed elsewhere in production (and thus do not just 'fall' on the system like 'manna from heaven'). Recognition of these opportunity costs of developing new technologies could go some way in dampening some of the more overoptimistic claims made. Undoubtedly though, a thorough inquiry into the impact of technological change upon prospects for sustainable development is required.

The interaction of technological progress and population change is also worthy of investigation. A basic proposition is that technological change can potentially sustain per capita consumption even in the face of increasing population. Unfortunately, if the rate of technological progress is less than the rate of population growth, falling per capita consumption ensues, even assuming (as most growth models do) full employment and a larger labour force that will increase output.

It has been argued that population change acts as a stimulant, not a deterrent, to modernization and technological progress (Boserup, 1981). Some other evidence seems to point in the direction of a negative relationship between per capita wellbeing and population growth (World Bank, 1984; Kelley, 1988).The effects of rapid population growth on natural resource availability generally may well outweigh the impact of technological progress on agricultural output, the original subject of the Boserup thesis (Lele and Stone, 1989). Nor is all technological change benign, its full implications being beset with uncertainties and surprises (Faber and Proops, 1991). But there are other restrictive conditions that are necessary to achieve the sustainability results of the Hartwick–Solow models. The main concern is the required feasibility of capital substitution in production. In common language, it must be comparatively easy to replace natural capital with produced capital. The Hartwick–Solow models achieve this via the Cobb–Douglas production function, which has a constant and unitary elasticity of substitution, so that the marginal productivity of natural capital tends to infinity as the stock is depleted to zero. Constant elasticity of substitution (CES) functions with a less than unitary elasticity, such as the zero substitution 'Leontief' function, do not permit this result (Varian, 1993). Hence, the crucial question is not the form of the production function *per se*, but rather the feasibility of capital substitution, and in particular the point (if one exists) at which these substitution requirements cease to be met as natural capital stocks decline. Actual empirical evidence concerning the degree of substitutability is at best ambiguous (Berndt and Field (eds), 1981).

But if there is some substitution between natural capital and produced capital either in production or in consumption, then fears of sustainable development as an instrument for depressing current and immediate future standards of living are generally, but not totally, lacking in foundation. Any 'costs' of sustainable development are as likely to result from inefficiently-formulated environmental policies as from the sustainability goal *per se*. Indeed, while the theoretical analysis has tended to become somewhat preoccupied with constant consumption paths, sustainable development is perfectly consistent with rising incomes and consumption. The modification is that, as far as possible, the benefits of growth (that is, higher levels of wellbeing) should be sustainable – rather than, say, a particular rate of growth. While that may seem to add little to what the growth models of the 1970s produced, the fact is that the criterion for deriving optimal policies – of maximum aggregate net present value – has been absorbed into policy thinking without the necessary caveats about the potential for non-sustainability. To spell it out, achieving a sustainable development path will imply a reduction in current wellbeing only if that flow of wellbeing cannot be reproduced for each successive generation. This will be the case where the current flow of wellbeing is being created by running down natural assets without saving or reinvesting for future consumption.

So the critics are right to draw attention to a potential tradeoff between future and current wellbeing. The issue then becomes one of the relative importance of 'sustainability' versus the other objectives of society. Perhaps the sustainable development literature does often read as if the sustainability objective must be met first regardless of the costs it might impose in terms of sacrificing other objectives. As Nordhaus (1992, p. 11) puts it: 'All of the complications arise because the sustainability criterion reifies a particular objective (the non-declining development vector) and demotes all other objectives below that one'.

But it is more likely that the literature is simply emphasizing sustainability because it has been neglected in policy circles in the past. Sustainability has been neglected in favour of 'short-termism'. In turn, that neglect arises from the widely-shared belief that sustainability was not in doubt in the past. The need for thinking about sustainability has emerged only now that apparent global environmental risks exist which could reduce the wellbeing of future generations. To get sustainability 'on to the agenda' then, it is necessary to give it a high moral profile.

The extent to which we should worry about sustainable development thus depends on two things:

- the seriousness of any tradeoffs between sustainability and other social goals; and
- the seriousness of any risk to sustainability.

It is fair to say that the advocates of sustainable development have not so far sought to look at the costs and benefits of sustainability. This failing may have been partly generated by one of the messages of the Brundtland Report, namely, that we can have economic growth and environmental quality without any apparent tradeoff. On the seriousness of the risk, the evidence is surely mounting that some societies are increasingly financing consumption out of capital decumulation, and that identifying this non-sustainability would not have come about but for the search for sustainability indicators.

1.4   Strong sustainability

One of the implications of the past literature on what we now call sustainable development is the possibility of achieving sustainability through substituting produced capital for natural capital along a growth path. In empirical terms this could refer to the depletion of non-renewable resources or the using up of potentially renewable resources for which substitution possibilities are evident. But the issue is not the services of resources that contribute to human wellbeing in easily understandable terms. In reality, natural capital provides multifunctional services. Economists have not so far achieved much success in taking into consideration all of these multiple functions, despite considerable progress in valuing them using the concept of total economic value (TEV) (see Box 1.2). The concept of TEV helps create the links between economic analysis and ecological concerns. Thus, TEV embraces use and 'non-use' values. Use values relate to direct uses made on the environmental asset (for example, timber or rattan from a tropical forest) and to indirect use values such as the forest's function in protecting watersheds, regulating micro-climates, and maintaining diversity. It is these indirect use values that come closest to defining ecological functions, although how far they embrace the wider life-support functions of environmental assets is still debated. Non-use values relate to concerns (and hence willingness to pay) for the conservation of environmental assets even though no use is made of the asset. Arguably, non-use values pick up some of the indirect use values, that is, what appears to be a non-use value is really an appreciation of the wider life-support functions. Non-use values may also reflect valuation *for* the asset as well as *of* the asset, effectively capturing some at least of what others call the 'intrinsic' value of the asset.

Box 1.2   Total economic value

The schema below shows the composition of 'total economic value' (TEV).

TEV comprises use and non-use values, the former relating to some direct use made of the resource and the latter arising even though individuals make no use of the resource, or intend to make use of it. Non-use value is also known as passive use value or existence value. Non-use values may have many 'motivations', raising from a concern for the resource in itself, some feeling that the resource has a right to existence, or some sense of stewardship. To some extent, therefore, existence value may capture part of the 'intrinsic' value of a resource, the value in the resource as opposed to the value of the resource to some individual.

Use values are divided into current and potential use. Current uses include direct use, for example, the exploitation of a resource for its output – timber from a forest, say – and indirect services such as the carbon storage or watershed functions of a forest. There also exists an option value relating to the value of maintaining the resource intact for the eventuality of future use.

The concept of TEV points towards the fact that it is the receiving capacity of natural environments (for example, absorptive capacities for carbon and trace chemicals) and the supply of biological diversity that give the greatest cause for concern. Ecologists tend to see these as primary characteristics of the natural world, for which there are no real substitutes. In essence, these are the life support systems as we know them. If this is correct, then the natural resource scarcity literature does not help us in determining the sustainability or otherwise of current consumption paths. We have no idea of the elasticity of substitution for the resources that impinge on this particular set of sustainability questions. A different approach is called for: 'strong' sustainable development. The basic insight of the sustainability literature – the constant capital rule – still applies. Now it implies an extra constraint requiring the maintenance of natural capital stocks, as a separate, non-substitutable category of assets.

This change of emphasis can be justified for a number of reasons. First, some ecological assets would seem to be essential to human wellbeing even if they are not essential to human survival – the experience of space and amenity, for example. Much of the substitutability debate has been interpreted as a dispute over the appropriate specification of the production function (Ruttan, 1991). Natural capital also provides services that are of direct consequence to human wellbeing such as amenity (Krautkraemer, 1985). The estimated value of natural capital loss, for purposes of determining the required amount of compensatory investment, will then include the direct loss in utility or wellbeing from that loss (Beltratti, 1993). The magnitude of these additional compensations is determined by the extent of substitutability in the utility function. In this respect there is an apparent 'loss aversion' that arises when certain natural resources are depleted (Kahnemann and Tversky, 1979). It is significant that the resources that appear to produce this phenomenon take the form of amenity and wildlife rather than copper and aluminium. Essentially, this loss aversion suggests non-substitutability in utility functions. Contingent valuation studies have repeatedly shown discrepancies between people's willingness to pay for increases in the supply of environmental services, and their willingness to accept reductions in those services, which cannot be explained by income effects (Gregory, 1986). This in turn has been argued to reflect an 'endowment effect' whereby there is a vested interest in maintaining the status quo with respect to environmental assets (Knetsch, 1989; Knetsch and Sinden, 1984).

Second, since natural capital has to be interpreted widely, many assets are essential to human survival, at least in the longer run. The basic biogeochemical cycles – such as the carbon cycle, the hydrological cycle and the nutrient cycle – provide an example (Schulze and Mooney, 1993). There is considerable uncertainty about the way in which natural capital stocks work. As such, we do not understand the full workings of ecological systems. Uncertainty is always a reason for being cautious, unless society can be deemed to be indifferent to risk or positively to welcome it ('risk neutrality' and 'risk loving'). Indeed, this uncertainty lies at the foundation of the precautionary principle whereby decision-makers do not wait for full scientific certainty before making decisions. The existence of uncertainty indicates that the scale of effects from loss of natural capital is unknown, particularly where thresholds are thought to be present at which ecosystems collapse catastrophically with little prior warning. Witness the divergent views about the effects of global warming. Furthermore, when natural capital assets are lost, it may not be possible to recreate them. This is the problem of irreversibility. Once lost, such assets are gone for ever. Natural capital will thus comprise two types of assets – one whose loss will be technically irreversible, and the other, feasibly irreversible. As an example of the former, extinct species cannot be recreated. Global warming, however, is very likely to be feasibly irreversible, that is, the conditions for technical reversibility are unlikely to arise in practice (because of growing population and economic growth).

The combination of irreversibility and uncertainty should make us more cautious about depleting natural capital (Dasgupta, 1982). What this adds up to is a 'constant natural capital' rule. There is, however, a legitimate debate about which natural capital assets are to be included. It seems clear that it could include biodiversity and the basic biogeochemical cycles that support life. It is also clear that it should not embrace many of those assets that we traditionally term 'natural resources' – metals and energy, for example. But in between is the hazy and uncertain area of resources that may serve critical functions (phytoplankton) and those that appear in both the critical and (in)essential categories (coal as an abundant resource, and as a source of global pollution). There are close similarities with the 'safe minimum standards' rule of Ciriacy-Wantrup (1952) which requires a cautious approach to conservation, that is, conserve unless the social costs of conservation are very high (Bishop, 1978, 1992).

What is the appropriate unit of analysis in the implementation of strong sustainability constraints? Obviously there is no single answer to this. Maintaining the natural capital stock intact could imply various levels of analysis. For instance, it does not seem unreasonable, at least in principle, that capital substitution should be no less feasible between capital stocks which are distributed spatially, or even through time, than between stocks of different types of capital (Dubourg and Pearce, 1996). One way to make such considerations operational might be via the implementation of shadow projects (Klaassen and Botterweg, 1976). Accordingly, any portfolio of investment projects that damage the environment should be offset by projects that compensate for this damage. This overcomes the almost practical impossibility (and likely theoretical inefficiency) of imposing the constraint that no single project should inflict environmental damage. It is a programme level constraint. In turn, the shadow projects approach can be implemented continuously, or over some extended time horizon (Barbier, Markandya and Pearce, 1990).

1.5   A summary on sustainable development

While much of the discussion in this chapter has been technical, the main findings can be summarized in non-technical language.

- A definition of sustainable development is non-declining human wellbeing over time. Any society wishing to pursue intergenerational justice defined in these terms must develop in such in such a way as to minimize those activities whose costs are borne by future generations. Where such activities are unavoidable, due allowance must be made for compensating future generations for the costs imposed.
- At its very weakest, a sustainability rule is a requirement that the overall capital stock does not decline. The idea of maintaining an 'overall capital stock' is linked to the concept of 'weak sustainability' in which the overall stock is what matters and substitution between the components of the stock is assumed to be possible (and desirable).
- The weak sustainability rule does not encapsulate many crucial concerns about sustainable development. Essentially what is being argued is that some components of natural capital are unique and that their loss has uncertain and potentially irreversible effects on human wellbeing. In effect, the required compensation to future generations is far more specific than that implied by the weak sustainability approach. Natural capital provides numerous functions which contribute directly and indirectly to human wellbeing, but little is understood of the precise contribution of these functions. Strong sustainable development emphasizes that there is a minimum requirement for the maintenance of at least parts of the natural capital stock. Given a combination of strong sustainability characteristics then, on this view, it is the current stock that should be conserved. Ideally, this refers to 'critical' natural capital – natural capital that is essential to human survival – but it is apparent that the actual process of delineating critical capital is by no means an easy task.
- The difficulties of defining critical natural capital suggest a more precautionary approach to the maintenance of natural capital, where precaution cannot be at any cost. The 'safe minimum standards' principle argues in favour of conservation of natural capital unless it incurs 'substantial' or 'unacceptable' cost. The meaning of substantial and unacceptable, however, remains imprecise.
- Finally, while the theoretical literature on sustainable development has tended to emphasize intergenerational concerns, reference back to the WCED definitions makes it clear that a prime focus is on 'need' and hence on poverty alleviation. We address these issues in Chapter 6 when we look at poverty indicators.

1.6   Outline of the book

The remainder of this book takes the general definition of sustainable development given above and shows how various kinds of indicators can be developed and used to determine whether or not an economy is on a 'sustainable' path of development. This task begins in Chapter 2 with a discussion of physical indicators of sustainability.

Chapter 3 introduces the topic of resource and environmental accounting. Various methods of adjusting the conventional system of national accounts (including social accounting matrices), to account for environmental effects, are discussed. The novel 'genuine savings' approach developed here builds on the concept of 'green national product' (that is, a revised measure of GNP taking into account increases and decreases in environmental services and resources). However, we argue that green national product is not so helpful as the genuine savings concept. Rates of change in green product, for example, could be higher or lower than rates of change in conventional GNP – with no particular implications for sustainability. Weak sustainability – in which the focus is on the overall stock of capital – is treated in the context of the genuine savings rule.

Because weak sustainability aggregates all forms of capital, a single numeraire is needed, and we show how money units serve this purpose in Chapter 4. Genuine savings are computed, for a large number of representative countries, as the level of savings in an economy net of the level of savings needed to cover the depreciation on capital assets. Capital assets include in this case non-renewable natural resources such as oil and gas, renewable resources such as forests, fisheries and other biological resources and mixed renewable–non-renewable resources such as groundwater and soils. If an economy saves less than the level necessary to cover depreciation then it is, *prima facie*, unsustainable in the weak sense.

Chapter 5 looks at the extent to which international trade is implicated in unsustainable development of the global economy and of national economies. The extent to which this claim is justified and the consequent implications for measuring sustainability, are discussed. The chapter examines, in particular, methods to account for transboundary effects (involving both pollution and natural resource depletion), in the measurement of trade flows.

In Chapter 6, we take a closer look at so-called 'ecological indicators' based on the idea that a resilient economy – one with the capacity to 'bounce back' from shocks and stresses – is a sustainable economy. These ecological indicators (as well as the physical indicators discussed in Chapter 2), play a key role in the debate on strong sustainability. The latter focuses on honouring both the savings rule (which reflects weak sustainability), and an additional set of restrictions that at least some critical stocks of natural capital should be non-declining. The dual nature of this rule is important as some advocates of strong sustainability wrongly believe that sustainable development can be secured by having non-declining natural capital assets only. Whereas weak sustainability assumes some substitution between the various forms of capital, strong sustainability denies this substitution – at least for the critical components of natural capital.

What, then, might constitute a reliable indicator of sustainability? Since, for some ecologists, resilience is a function of diversity, it is natural to argue that sustainability can best be measured by indicators of diversity. The focus is on measures of biological diversity, but it is worth noting that this could legitimately be extended to other forms of diversity – perhaps economies might be generally unsustainable if culture, for example, becomes homogenized. Chapter 6 also shows that diversity indicators are, however, problematic as measures of sustainability, since they lack an 'origin' (that is, although it can be established whether diversity is rising or falling, it cannot be ascertained how much diversity is necessary to ensure sustainability).

Chapter 7 reminds us that sustainable development also involves special attention being paid to income distribution and social needs. The various existing measures of progress that incorporate social concerns (including poverty and income distribution), are examined. While welcoming indicators such as the more recently proposed human development index, we show that there are various problems associated with it, as well as other similar measures.

The economic dimension is further elaborated in Chapter 8 with an investigation of the linkages between economywide policies (both macroeconomic and sectoral) and the environment. A key conclusion is that economywide policies (which were not designed to meet environmental objectives, in the first instance) may combine with unaddressed economic imperfections, to cause environmental damage. An approach based on the action impact matrix is outlined, which facilitates the formulation and articulation of policies, projects and complementary environmental measures, to mitigate environmental and social harm. Chapter 8 also examines evidence on the impacts of structural adjustment policies on the environment. In so far as such policies stress short-term adjustment, they may ignore the natural resource implications of those adjustments, which could undermine the basis for long-term development.

In our view, the scope for policy measures that are consistent with sustainable development is substantial, although the implementation constraints are formidable. Chapter 9 takes up the genuine savings theme and shows how policy has to be aimed not just at securing a positive level of genuine savings but also at ensuring that the resulting savings are invested wisely. We have no power to address many of the factors inhibiting the adoption of sustainable development policies, but in some cases the issue is one of a lack of awareness that current policies themselves inhibit sustained development.

Finally, Chapter 10 places the pursuit of sustainable development in the context of development policy. It argues that it is neither desirable to pursue sustainability if current and near-future generations have to suffer privation and infringement of personal liberty in the long run nor rational to treat resources as if they were sacrosanct. Instead, we argue that the first step towards sustainable development is a call for more prudence in the pursuit of development policies that have often been based, in the past, on an ignorance of what development does to the environment and what the environment does for human wellbeing.

2 Physical indicators

2.1 The demand for indicators

While the first chapter emphasized some of the complexities of the concept of sustainable development, it concluded with a simple definition: non-declining human wellbeing over time. Chapter 9 of this book will discuss the policies required for sustainable development. However, any policy regime must be capable of being monitored, if the successes or failures of the policies are to be judged. Ultimately, this means that data concerning the environment, the economy and society must be collected, analysed and made usable to policy-makers.

Monitoring the sustainability of development goes beyond establishing whether the key component of welfare, consumption per capita, is no lower in the current period than it was in the previous period. The critical issues concern the degree to which this consumption entails the consumption of assets (both natural and produced), whether these assets are renewable, whether they have substitutes, and whether the loss of these assets is reversible. Simple indicators of consumption cannot answer these questions. Instead, integrative measures of sustainable development must attempt to embrace these aspects.

The two responses which have been pursued focus on: (1) the development of environment indicators; and (2) resource and environmental accounting. In this chapter we focus attention on the former, while the latter is investigated in Chapter 3. The study of environmental indicators encompasses a wide range of activities from the selection of key indicators to single measures such as an integrated environmental index. However we examine these approaches, we need to identify the criteria for determining good indicators, and frameworks which would provide the building blocks for achieving this goal. Although many currently-used indices represent useful summaries of the state of the environment it is clear that their use as measures of sustainable development is less justified.

Before considering *how* to measure sustainable development, it is important to ask: what sort of information is required, and in what forms, to design and administer policies aimed at achieving sustainable development, over both the short and long term? Information needs for more narrowly-defined policy goals – that is, the work stages on the way to sustainable development – require consideration of such issues as different types of policy-makers, the available information (for example, indicators of environmental quality, state of scientific knowledge) and the efficient collection, analysis and communication of data.

Although we focus here on the information needs of policy-makers, there is nothing unique about the particular sorts of information required by those responsible for the formulation and administration of policy. The way in which they use information may distinguish policy-makers from other economic decision-makers, yet the same information is utilized by many different groups for a variety of purposes which may or may not be related to policy. In fact, one prerequisite for successful policy-making is the efficient dissemination of relevant information to all affected parties.

2.2 Policy-makers and environmental information

Indicators may be defined as aggregates of more elementary data having a significance that transcends that of the individual constituent data. The Organization for Economic Cooperation and Development (OECD, 1993) has established a useful listing of desirable characteristics for environmental indicators.

1. Indicators must have *policy relevance*, which entails that they must:
   - be easy to interpret
   - show trends over time
   - be responsive to changes in driving forces
   - have threshold or reference values against which progress may be measured.
2. Indicators must be *analytically sound*, for example, based on a clear understanding of the goal of sustainable development.
3. Indicators must be *measurable*, that is, no matter how attractive the theoretical construct, if an indicator cannot be measured at reasonable cost, it is not useful.

Decision-makers not only *respond* to the environmental concerns of the public, expert scientific bodies and pressure groups, but also *initiate* environmental action. Therefore, decision-makers should have ready access to an indication of opinion about (a) general environmental concerns, (b) ranking of concerns regarding different environmental issues, and (c) broader social welfare and/or environmental policy objectives. Opinion is a useful indicator of importance, which is relevant to decision-makers. In general, the channels through which constituents' opinions are made known to policy-makers are locally determined. The extent to which, and the means whereby, such opinion is incorporated into policy depends, among other things, on its consistency with the policy-maker's broader objective. There are also problems of the consistency of public opinion with the views of 'experts' where surveys of the former frequently identify risks such as industrial pollution incidents, nuclear accidents, water pollution and oil spills, which experts regard as relatively unimportant.

2.3   A basic model of environmental information

The OECD Environmental Indicators Programme uses a model context for determining the selection of environmental indicators. This model is based on a 'pressure–state–response' framework. As shown in Figure 2.1, in this approach indicators need to reflect:

- *pressures* on the environment (for example, underlying pressures – population change, economic growth, structural change, public concern; proximate pressures – land-use changes, waste emissions);
- the *state of the environment* itself (for example, ambient pollution concentrations, amounts and concentrations of waste in the environment);

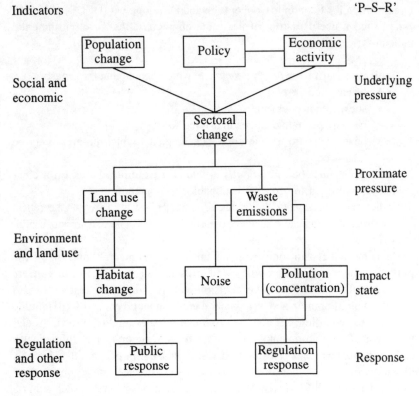

Notes
P – Pressure.
S – State of the Environment.
R – Response.

Figure 2.1   A basic model of environmental indicators

• the *response* of society in terms of government policies, ameliorative measures undertaken by individuals and business, social response in terms of environmental activism, and so on.

Figure 2.1 shows one such model of indicators. While several types of indicators fit into this model, one particular category consists of indicators of environmental efficiency. These are broad magnitudes that link environmental measures to economic activity. Thus, a measure linking energy consumption to GDP would be a surrogate for an environmental efficiency measure of energy use. Energy production and use have well-known environmental impacts. Any reduction in the amount of energy per unit of GDP is a reduction in environmental impact per unit of economic activity. Note, however, that this measure of efficiency is consistent with an increase in the *absolute* level of environmental impact. This is because gains in efficiency can be outweighed by the absolute growth of GDP. Environmental efficiency measures the extent to which the underlying change in the economy reveals 'decoupling' of economic activity and environmental impact. Efficiency gains may come about 'naturally' – that is, as a result of the evolution of the economy – or as a result of deliberate policy measures (environmental regulation, for example). Since disentangling the sources of efficiency gain can be complex, policy decision-makers need guidance on such a decomposition of causal factors.

Environmental information has been combined with economic statistics (for example, GDP) to examine the relationship between environmental quality and economic development between countries and over time. These are known as environmental 'Kuznets curves'. A Kuznets curve is named after Simon Kuznets who hypothesized a relationship between economic growth and income distribution, in which distribution worsened initially with growth, but improved later as growth continued. Environmental economists have borrowed the term to apply to the relationship between income and environmental quality, the argument being that as economic growth occurs so environmental quality tends to get worse at first, but then gets better – along the path ABCDE shown in Figure 2.2. The state of environmental damage reflects the consumer willingness to pay (or demand) for environmental quality.

Various statistical tests of the environmental Kuznets curve have been carried out (see Grossman and Krueger, 1994; Grossman and Krueger and Laity, 1994; Grossman, 1995; Seldon and Song, 1994; Panayotou, 1993). A review by Pearson (1995) suggests that inverted U shapes exist for the traditional air pollutants such as Total Suspended Particulates (TSP), NO_x and SO_x, and lead, and for access to sanitation and clean drinking water. Flores and Carson (1995) argue that the Kuznets curve literature is consistent with income elasticities of demand for the environment less than unity. However, Kriström and Riera (1996) cautions against the use of Kuznets curves to derive such a conclusion since the

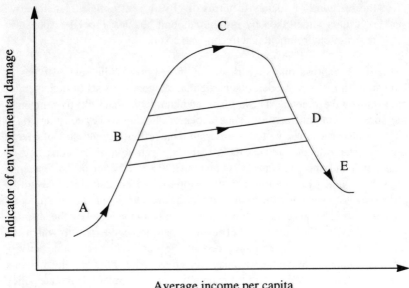

Source: Munasinghe (1995)

Figure 2.2   Tunnelling through the environmental Kuznets curve

curves obviously embody many factors affecting environmental quality, other than just the 'demand' for environmental quality. Munasinghe (1995) argues that the developing countries could learn from the experience of the industrialized world, and use appropriate policies to 'tunnel' through the Kuznets curve along the path ABDE in Figure 2.2 – thus avoiding the peak of environmental damage.

2.4   Aggregate physical environmental indicators

Indicators of the state of the environment have been reported for some time in the developed countries, in the form of air quality indices, water quality classifications, and so on. Munasinghe and Shearer (1995) review the status of biogeophysical indicators of sustainability from a scientific view point. The current emphasis has shifted, however, from these *descriptive* indicators to *performance* indicators. Performance indicators measure, in effect, the percentage deviation of current environmental conditions from some threshold or goal set by environmental policy – thus providing both the means to aggregate individual measures with respect to a given theme (for example, total toxic load), and the means to aggregate within and across themes by adding up the percentage deviations.

The preeminent example of highly aggregated environmental indicators is provided by the work of Adriaanse (1993) of the Netherlands Ministry of

Housing, Physical Planning and Environment and Hammond et al. (1995). This work has concentrated on the development of environmental policy performance indicators, specifically designed to measure progress towards meeting targets set by Dutch environmental policy. Indicators are developed around a number of themes and it is these that provide the basis for weighting and combining disparate physical measures into an integrated indicator. Dutch policy sets sustainability targets for each theme, typically based on the assimilative capacity of the environment.

The themes that have been developed in the Netherlands are: climate change, acidification, eutrophication, dispersion (of pesticides, toxins such as cadmium and mercury, and radioactive substances), disposal (of solid waste), and disturbance (from odour and noise). For each theme a number of physical measurements are combined according to their contribution to the particular environmental problem. This is best explained with an example.

Carbon dioxide is one of many greenhouse gases (GHGs) that contribute to global warming. Each gas can be assigned a 'global warming potential' (GWP) in relation to the predominant gas, carbon dioxide (CO_2). This global warming potential is a function of the particular physical properties of the gases concerned, in terms of their effectiveness in trapping long-wave radiation and thus warming the Earth, and of their residency time in the atmosphere. The GWPs of the main greenhouse gases relative to CO_2 are shown in Table 2.1.

Table 2.1 GWP factors of greenhouse gases

Substance	GWP Factor
CO_2	1
CH_4	12
N_2O	290
CFC–11	3,500
CFC–12	7,300
CFC–113	4,200
CFC–114	6,900
CFC–115	6,900
Halon–1211	5,800
Halon–1301	5,800

Source: Adriaanse (1993).

These global warming potentials are the basis for an integrated greenhouse gas emission indicator in 'carbon equivalents' (Ceq). Quantities of emissions for each gas are weighted by their GWP and the result summed to produce the results in Table 2.2 for the Netherlands in the 1980s and early 1990s. This indicator becomes a *performance* indicator when these emissions in Ceq are compared with policy targets for the Netherlands in terms of the stabilization of greenhouse gas emissions.

Table 2.2   Emissions of greenhouse gases in the Netherlands (m tonnes Ceq)

Year	CO_2	CH_4	N_2O	CFC + Halons	Total
1980	172.000	10.320	11.600	92.369	286
1981	165.000	10.423	11.600	92.000	279
1982	152.000	10.527	11.600	91.500	266
1983	152.000	10.633	11.600	89.500	264
1984	161.000	10.739	11.600	85.800	270
1985	166.000	10.846	11.600	82.000	271
1986	170.000	10.955	11.600	72.760	265
1987	177.000	11.064	11.600	59.792	260
1988	180.000	11.175	11.600	49.141	252
1989	182.000	11.287	11.600	40.816	246
1990	186.000	11.400	11.600	34.811	244
1991	185.000	11.514	11.600	31.132	239

Source: Adriaanse (1993).

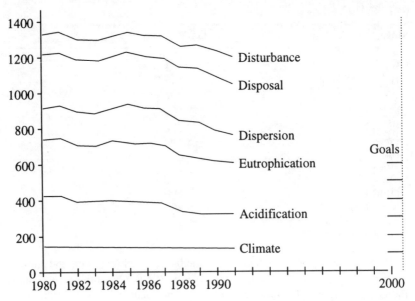

Figure 2.3   An environmental pressure index for the Netherlands

Figure 2.3 shows the integrated environmental pressure index for the Netherlands over the period 1980–91. The cumulative index had reached a level of 1,195 by 1991, falling from a peak value of 1,346 in 1985. Because there are six component themes, the target for the cumulative index is 600. The obvious implication is that the index must fall by one half over the period 1992–2000. Eutrophication and disposal of solid waste are the themes farthest from their target values in 1991.

Constructing aggregate environmental indicators in this manner involves one weighting scheme, based on contributions to particular problems such as acidification, out of many possible schemes. These indicators tend not to be closely coupled to economic phenomena nor, to date, do they deal with questions of the supply of natural resources.

2.5 Environmental indicators and socioeconomic impacts

In the Adriaanse approach, environmental performance is measured in terms of changes in environmental pressures towards predefined policy goals. The extent to which unsustainability can be defined as increasing pressure depends on a host of complex factors. For example, can increasing pressure on a particular environmental asset be compensated by a reduction in pressure on some other environmental asset? Moreover, it may be that increasing environmental pressure can be compensated by investment in alternative forms of wealth as discussed in Chapter 1. Adriaanse (1993) implicitly assumes substitution between performance of his themes in deriving an aggregate indicator. Within themes, pressures are aggregated according to their damage potential (for example, global warming potential, acidification potential and so on.) Yet, as we saw, the attribution of equal weighting of distances to goals across themes begs the question as to whether a less arbitrary method can be found for evaluating the relative contribution of, say, greenhouse gases and acidifying pollutants to total environmental pressure and hence degradation.

In many of the following chapters, we argue that an approach that merits significant attention in the environmental indicators debate is based on the socioeconomic impacts of environmental pressures. Specifically, this requires an emphasis on the social cost of environmental damage in *monetary* terms. Decision-makers require such information in order to gauge the *importance* of environmental damage generally, or of a specific environmental issue. For example, some valuation is based on the derivation of physical quantity of damage from 'dose-response' studies (for example, soil erosion causes a loss in crop output; air pollution resulting in increased mortality and morbidity) combined with prices for these damages based on valuation techniques. Valuation procedures are well developed, even though they are controversial in some cases. In particular, many forms of damage will be non-marketed (for example, the decrease in welfare from pollution-induced health impairment).

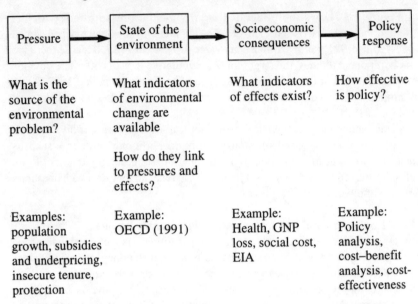

Figure 2.4   Suggested analytical structure of policy-maker information

We investigate the scope for including social costs in measures of sustainability in more detail in Chapters 3 and 4. An advantage of this approach is that it allows the treatment of resource depletion and environmental degradation in a consistent manner.

However, three points are worth making in the context of this chapter. First, environmental performance indicators should reflect the possibility for marginal damage to be increasing over time. For example, because of the accumulation of GHGs in the atmosphere, the marginal social cost per unit emitted will be increasing. Hence, an improvement in environmental performance may not be associated with a decline in socioeconomic impacts. Second, emphasizing the evaluation of social costs of environmental degradation implies that performance goals should be determined with reference to optimal pollution levels. It is unlikely that the goals set for the 'sink' indicators, in the Dutch work, are based on such notions. Finally, the analytical framework for indicators is augmented and adapted by this emphasis on socioeconomic impacts. Figure 2.4 describes how the pressure–state–response framework should in fact be one of 'pressure–state–impact–response'.

Why are social cost estimates an important component of policy-maker information?
The answer depends partly on who the policy-maker is. Environmental management is pervasive to government policy: energy sector planning has

environmental impacts, as have, for example, transport, housing, agriculture and regional policy. Most importantly, the management of the economy has environmental impacts: environmental degradation has a direct economic cost (in terms of forgone business activity and GNP) as well as an indirect economic cost in terms of sacrificed human welfare. Thus, the management of the economy must be seen not only in terms of narrowly-defined economic objectives, but also in terms of its indirect impact on the environment. Social cost estimates are important in that they serve to translate environmental degradation into terms that finance ministers, the business community and others can relate to.

2.6   The health cost of environmental damage

Environmental indicators, which are closely related to the social cost of environmental damage, are the basis for relating environmental statistics to socioeconomic statistics. The OECD approach mentioned earlier is useful in assessing the impact of various pressures on environmental systems and the policies devised to alleviate such pressures. If we can identify levels of pressure/environmental stress associated with social costs, then we will be in a position to develop policy benchmarks and targets, as well as means of monitoring the impact of particular policies. Take a simplified example, that of the health implications of atmospheric pollution. Ambient air quality and exposure of a population to pollution must reach a certain level before widespread detrimental health effects become evident. If this level is known, an estimate of the associated costs, in monetary terms, can be made for the impact of given levels of pollution on the health of the population.

The basic equation underlying these estimates can be written:

Total Economic Cost of Pollutant = Change in Ambient Concentration
* Risk Factor * Stock at Risk
* Unit Economic Value

A growing body of epidemiological studies is identifying substantial economic costs (that is, high-risk factors) from urban air pollution. Mortality from chronic obstructive pulmonary disease (COPD) and acute respiratory infections (ARIs) appear substantially higher in developing countries than in developed countries. COPD rates in developing countries may be twice those in the developed world, and ARIs nearly five times. The China/US ratio for COPD is 5 times. Overall damage costs will be mainly determined by the size of the population or stock at risk (for example, human populations) and the unit economic values used to value symptoms and 'statistical life'. In principle, unit economic values should reflect the associated monetized values of losses in social wellbeing inferred from studies of individual valuations of morbidity and mortality risks. On the other

Table 2.3   Health damage from air pollution: the economic costs of air pollution damage to human health in urban areas

Coverage	Mortality cost $m	Morbidity cost $m	Total health cost $m	Cost per capita $
Cairo (1) (all exposure, PM only)	186–992	157–472	343–1,464	38–161
Jakarta (2) (all exposure, PM, lead, NO_x)	138	82	220	27
Mexico (3) (all exposure, lead, PM, ozone)	480	590	1,070	63
Bangkok (4) (benefits of 20% reduction in lead, PM, SO_x and ozone)	429–2,785	317–353	746–3,138	97–402
Santiago (5) (benefits of package of measures)	8	96 or 112	104 or 120	22-25

Sources
(1)   Estimates of mortality and RADs taken from Chemonics International and Associates (1994). Value of statistical life taken to be $2.25m × GNP per capita Egypt/GNP per capita USA = $62,021. RADs valued at daily GNP per capita of $1.75 per day. Population taken to be 9.08 million. Estimates of hospital admissions valued at $260; minor restricted activity days and days or respiratory symptoms valued at $0.4, asthma attacks valued at $2.5.
(2)   World Bank (1994b). Value of statistical life of $75,000 and population at risk of 8.2 million. Morbidity effects include RADs, outpatient visits, hospital admissions, respiratory illness among children, asthma attacks and respiratory symptoms.
(3)   World Bank (1994d). Bangkok population of 7.67 million assumed. Value of statistical life of $336,000 based on compensating wage differentials in Bangkok for risky occupations.
(4)   Margulis (1992). Value of statistical life of $75,000 assumed based on human capital approach. Population of 17 million assumed.
(5)   World Bank (1994c). Estimates are based on dose-response functions for mortality and morbidity converted to work days lost, each work day being valued at US$9.55. Population of Santiago taken to be 4.8 million. Control costs for this package of measures were estimated at $60m, so that, even without considering other pollutants, the benefits of reduced PM_{10} exceed the costs of control. Other benefits arise form the associated control of ozone, NO_x and SO_x. Alternative estimate for NO_x in 5.1.c assumes NO_x is credited with half the benefits of avoided ozone pollution damage.

hand, the monetization approach causes some problems of political acceptance because of a confusion between valuing 'statistical lives' and the 'value of life' itself. Whatever the latter means, it is not what economists measure when they produce indicators of values for statistical lives which are, in reality, aggregations of individuals' willingness to pay for reductions in risks of mortality. If money units are found to be too controversial, then numbers of predicted premature mortalities can be used. The problem with non-monetary indicators is that there are morbidity effects as well as mortality effects and 'numbers of restricted activity days', or 'hospital visits' cannot be added to indicators of mortality. Other approaches have tended to focus on the costs of pollution-related illness in terms of the economic output that is lost during absence.

Table 2.3 presents estimates of total damage costs in developing economies. However, the components of these totals suggest two air pollutants stand out in terms of damage: particulate matter and lead. The exact manner in which particulate matter may cause health damage is not known with any certainty, but statistical association with respiratory illness and premature death is strong. Health damage caused by lead shows up in the form of reduced IQ scores in children, hypertension in adults (mainly males), coronary heart disease and mortality. Tropospheric (low-level) ozone may rank as a significant health-damaging pollutant while nitrogen oxides and sulphur oxides are generally revealed to be of limited relevance for health damage. A major weakness of the air pollution damage work has been the focus on outdoor pollution. Remarkably few studies have measured indoor air pollution. Fewer still make a distinction between ambient concentrations and exposure. The two differ in that exposure depends on human behaviour in the presence of ambient pollution – how long an individual stays in one place, for example. Adding up the total population of the world and expressing it as 'person hours', about 25 per cent of all person hours are in the developed world, and 75 per cent in the developing world (simply reflecting the respective populations). Sixty-eight per cent of all developed-country person hours are spent indoors in urban environments, and 21 per cent are spent indoors in rural environments, leaving only 11 per cent of time in the outdoors. In the developing world the proportions are 70 per cent and 30 per cent, respectively. In other words, the major part of an individual's time is spent indoors, not outdoors.

2.7 Conclusions: priorities for information needs

While many currently-used indices represent useful summaries of the state of the environment, it is evident that their interpretation as measures of sustainable development is less clear. For example, policy-maker information is contingent upon our understanding of what sustainable development means – that is, non-declining human wellbeing over time. A minimal condition for supposing that development will be sustained is that a nation's capital assets should be at least maintained – this argues for attention to be paid to indicators of natural assets and changes in these assets. Environmental information must therefore focus on: the 'state of natural capital', that is, the *state of the environment*; *trends* in the state of the environment over time, that is, absolute trends and trends in *environmental efficiency*; factors giving rise to past, current and future environmental change, that is, indicators of *pressure on the environment*; measures of *environmental performance*; and measures of *importance* for *damage done.*

3   Resource and environmental accounting

It is abundantly clear that policy-makers cannot make direct use of typical environmental data that are voluminous, difficult to aggregate and not connected to other policy variables. One response to this (already presented in Chapter 2), has been an increasing emphasis on the development of environmental indicators, as evidenced, for example, by the work programme of the OECD. A second response, based on resource and environmental accounting, represents a particular way to summarize and aggregate data – one that can be especially powerful when indicators of environmentally sustainable development are desired.

The 'holy grail' of indicator development is the integrated environmental index, a number whose upward or downward movements indicate whether, and to what extent, overall environmental quality is increasing or decreasing. This is unlikely to be realized for many reasons, not least the lack of a scientific basis for combining divergent physical measurements of environmental conditions. A better model is provided by economic indicators, where a small number of indices (GNP or GDP growth, unemployment rate, inflation rate, and so on), based on coherent theory, characterize the state of the economy.

While the GNP growth rate is often viewed as the integrated economic indicator *par excellence,* no economist would argue that it alone is sufficient to summarize economic performance. To give just one example, robust economic growth at a given point in time can be the result of consumer spending, export growth or public or private investment; the consequences of these different sources of growth for the development path of the economy will be quite distinct.

3.1   Varieties of environmental accounts

Many countries have been developing concepts and methods of resource and environmental accounting ever since the policy focus began to shift towards achieving sustainable development and away from dealing with environmental concerns as a collection of individual issues. The report of the Brundtland Commission in 1987 has much to do with providing the impetus for this work, and the adoption of Agenda 21 in particular, at the Earth Summit in 1992, has provided further stimulus. Agenda 21 explicitly called for the establishment of integrated environmental and economic accounts as a complement to the UN System of National Accounts (SNA), and urged national offices preparing economic accounts to undertake this work.

The first question in assessing the use of resource and environmental accounts as integrative measures of sustainable development is why accounting approaches have gained favour among policy analysts and national statisticians. There are three basic answers to this: (i) many types of accounts embody an accounting identity, and so it is possible to bracket what is being measured with known precision; (ii) accounting encourages comprehensive approaches to problems, since accounts with partial coverage are of limited use; and (iii) placing resource and environmental information in an accounting framework offers at least the possibility of linkages to economic accounting systems, especially the SNA.

While accounting approaches have these advantages, there are also limitations. It is generally difficult to introduce a high degree of spatial detail in accounts. And as Alfsen (1993) notes, accounts are better suited to measuring quantity rather than quality, although this is not an insurmountable problem.

Resource and environmental accounts are being developed in a variety of different forms. The first category is *natural resource accounts* where the emphasis is on balance sheet items, the opening and closing stocks of various natural resources, and the flows that add to and subtract from the balance sheet position – these accounts are in quantities and (possibly) values, and may or may not be linked to the SNA through the national balance sheet accounts. Next there are the *resource and pollutant flow accounts* that typically embody considerable sectoral detail and often are explicitly linked to the input–output accounts, a part of the SNA – these accounts are therefore de facto satellite accounts in physical quantities. The *environmental expenditure accounts* are, obviously, measured in values and, as a breakout of existing figures in the SNA, can be viewed as classical satellite accounts. Finally, *alternative national accounts aggregates* are self-explanatory – no countries are planning to alter their standard national accounts to reflect resources and the environment, beyond what is in the 1993 revision to the SNA (United Nations, 1993a), but alternative aggregates, for example, for national product and wealth, are being considered.

The first step towards standardizing this multitude of accounting approaches is provided by the UN Integrated System of Environmental and Economic Accounting (SEEA) (United Nations, 1993b). The SEEA is designed to be a *satellite* account to the System of National Accounts, in that it is an adjunct to, but not a modification of, the core accounts. The SEEA is highly complex, involving disaggregation of the standard accounts to highlight environmental relationships, linked physical and monetary accounting, imputations of environmental costs, and extensions of the production boundary of the SNA.

An accounting scheme related to the SEEA is given in Smith (1994) and is shown in Table 3.1. The quantities (in physical units) are shown in double boxes while values (in monetary units) are in single boxes. Thus, Table 3.1 embodies natural resource accounts, resource and pollutant flow accounts and environmental protection expenditure accounts. The potential and prospective uses of the different categories of accounts are expanded upon in the following sections.

Table 3.1   Expanded input–output account for natural resources and the environment

3.1.1   Natural resource accounts

As just noted, natural resource accounts generally have a balance sheet flavour, with their emphasis on opening and closing stocks, in quantity and values, of natural resources including both commercial natural resources and non-commercial or environmental resources. As such, resource accounts form the basis of the expanded national balance sheet accounts in the revised SNA. The principal policy and analytical uses of these accounts include:

- *Measuring physical scarcity.* The origins of natural resource accounts lie in the 1970s when the physical scarcity of crude petroleum seemed to present a threat to economic development. Resource accounts permit the calculation of crude scarcity indicators such as the reserves to production ratio, which gives the remaining years of resource supply at current extraction rates. However, it must be recognized that physical scarcity and economic scarcity are not the same thing, and that it is the latter that represents the constraint on development. Measures of physical scarcity can be important for critical materials, and may be an important input into such policy questions as determining the need to maintain strategic reserves of particular materials.
- *Resource management.* Again, one of the concerns when resource accounts were first established in the 1970s was that there was excessive exploitation of natural resources. What constitutes 'excessive exploitation', however, is a question lying outside the accounts – it is certainly an economic concept, considering efficiency conditions such as the Hotelling rule in resource economics. But there are physical constraints as well, such as the fact that excessive pumping of crude petroleum from a given deposit will decrease the total amount ultimately available, as the oil reserves lose contiguity. Given a criterion for excessive exploitation, resource accounts can provide the empirical evidence for it. A variety of policy remedies can then be explored, including tenure arrangements and royalty schemes.
- *Balance sheet of the resource sectors.* The existing national accounts are substantially incomplete with regard to the resource sectors because the values of natural resource assets are not measured. This affects the analysis of economic performance for these sectors, which in turn affects government policies with regard to the natural resource sectors.
- *Productivity measurement.* This is related to the previous point. Because the balance sheet of the resource sectors does not measure the value of resource assets in the standard national accounts, the measure of productivity in these sectors is distorted, which in turn then distorts national measures of productivity. Productivity comparisons between resource-rich and resource-poor countries are also affected by this gap.

- *Portfolio analysis and management.* Measuring natural resources in the national balance sheet implies that governments can work with a measure of total wealth in examining policies for sustainable development – see the section on alternative national accounting aggregates below (section 3.1.4). The balance of natural versus produced assets in this measure of total wealth then becomes an important indicator as governments consider development options. This approach becomes even more powerful if human capital is estimated and brought into the balance sheet.
- *Valuing depletion.* A value for resource depletion is a simple by-product of the stock-flow accounting making up a natural resource account. Current measures such as net national product do not value the depletion of natural resources. The liquidation of important components of national wealth therefore does not have any effect on standard measures of economic performance. The policy implications of accounting for depletion are discussed below under 'alternative national accounting aggregates'.
- *Effects of environmental degradation.* By building living natural resources such as forests and fisheries into a resource account, and ultimately into the national balance sheet, one of the economic effects of deteriorating environmental quality can be measured as damage to these resources. This can be an important input into policy decisions concerning the optimal level of pollution abatement and control for pollutants such as SO_2 emissions or emissions of toxins into water.

Natural resource accounts, and their counterparts in the national balance sheet accounts, can therefore have wide use with regard to resource management policies and broader environmental policies.

3.1.2 Resource and pollutant flow accounts

Resource and pollutant flow accounts are generally conceived as physical extensions to the (monetary) input–output (I/O) accounts. For each production and final demand sector in the I/O tables these accounts associate a physical flow of natural resources, typically as inputs such as energy to production processes, and a physical flow of wastes and emissions in the form of SO_2, NO_x, biological oxygen demand (BOD), and so on. With links to the I/O tables these accounts lend themselves naturally to policy modelling. Examples of policy uses include:

- *Measuring the incidence of environmental regulations and taxes.* Models based on flow accounts can be used to estimate the impact (on output and profits, for example) of existing and prospective regulations and taxes with regard to the environment. Measuring the burden of policies is an important element of policy design.

- *Estimating emission tax rates.* Where market-based instruments are being considered as a policy option, computable general equilibrium models using pollutant flow accounts can be used to estimate the approximate size of a tax. An example would be a CO_2 emissions tax, required to achieve a policy goal, the limitation of emissions to 1990 levels by the year 2000, as many nations have committed themselves informally under the Framework Convention on Climate Change.
- *Efficiency of resource use.* One important determinant of the burden that production activities place on the environment concerns the efficiency of use of natural resources. Resource flow accounts can be used directly to measure these efficiencies in different sectors, or overall per unit of GDP, and models can be constructed to examine the effects of different policies on efficiency of use. 'Energy analysis' as widely carried out in the 1970s was one example of such policy use.
- *International trade.* Both resource use and pollution emissions can be linked to the level and structure of international trade through I/O-based models. This provides the link between trade policies and the pollution burden associated with a particular structure of trade; for instance, countries that export raw and semi-finished materials will typically incur a large burden of air emissions associated with energy use. This approach can be used for both current analysis and prospective modelling.
- *Structural change.* As in the case of linkages to international trade, resource and pollutant flow accounts in combination with I/O models can be used to explore the ramifications of structural change in the economy. This provides a link between development and industrial policies and their likely effects on the environment.
- *Macro models.* Tying resource and pollutant flow accounts to the standard macroeconomic models governments use for projections would permit the reporting of environmental effects (in terms of resource throughput and pollution emissions) as a standard component of the output from such models. Consideration of environmental effects could then become as routine as consideration of balance of payments effects when policy analysts produce projections.
- *Dispersion and impact models.* Whichever modelling approach described above is employed, the calculation of pollution emissions is the required input for 'downstream' models of dispersion and impact. Once impacts on health, living resources, produced assets and natural ecosystems have been estimated, valuation of these impacts becomes possible. This implies that the *net* benefits of policies with regard to trade and development, for instance, can be estimated, which could lead to adjustments of such policies in order to maximize benefits.

Of the accounts under consideration, resource and pollutant flow accounts clearly have links to the widest variety of policy issues. These linkages to economic policy domains should engender the simultaneous consideration of environmental policy options.

3.1.3   Environmental expenditure accounts

Environmental expenditure accounts generally consist of detailed data on capital and operating expenditures by economic sectors for the protection and enhancement of the environment. The accounts may or may not include detail on the type of pollutant controlled or the environmental medium being protected. The prospective uses of these accounts are fairly straightforward:

- *Measurement of the total economic burden of environmental protection.* By measuring explicitly what is only implicit in the standard national accounts, environmental expenditure accounts permit macro-level consideration of whether the costs of environmental protection are commensurate with the benefits.
- *Distribution of sectoral costs.* Environmental expenditure accounts also permit policy-makers to gauge the sectoral distribution of the costs associated with environmental regulations and taxes, an important consideration with regard to equity.
- *Measurement of unit abatement costs.* If the survey vehicles used to collect data on environmental expenditures also collect data on the amount of abatement achieved, it is possible to estimate average unit abatement costs. These costs then become a basic input to the estimation of abatement cost curves, widely used in policy modelling, and the valuation of environmental degradation from emissions.

It should be noted, however, that measuring environmental expenditures is a subject fraught with definitional and measurement problems. To give just one example, it is now often the case that firms are introducing new production technologies that jointly increase productivity and decrease emissions – in such cases there may be no meaningful way to establish the 'environmental' expenditure.

3.1.4   Green national accounts

The United Nations System of National Accounts sets the international standard for national accounting, including the definitions and methods of measuring GNP. As the measure of the total product of an economy in a given period, GNP is the principal statistic used by decision-makers, development planners and the press to gauge economic progress. The SNA has been widely criticized for its failure to account for the environmental side-effects of economic activity. The system was designed to measure the flows of income and product as transactions in the market. This firm linkage to observable activities is one of the strengths of the SNA, but also one of its limitations: when the concern is with effects *external* to the market system, as is typical of many environmental problems, then the SNA becomes a less useful guide to the welfare consequences of human activities. As resources deplete and pollution accumulates as a by-product of economic activity, the national accounts present only a pale reflection of these phenomena.

'Greener' national accounting aggregates attempt to overcome many of these deficiencies in the standard national accounts, to ensure that the correct policy signals are sent to decision-makers in both the economic and environmental spheres.

Much of the impetus for defining new green national accounts aggregates can be traced to Hicks's (1946) concept of income: true income is that income in excess of asset consumption. By defining assets more broadly than in the SNA, to include both marketed and non-marketed natural resources, green approaches to accounting offer the possibility of bringing the environment into the mainstream of economic discourse.

Before describing the different approaches to green accounting in the literature, it is valuable to examine the ways in which natural resources and the environment are reflected in the existing national accounts. This breaks into two parts: commercial natural resources, where there is a market price, and environmental resources, such as clean air or wildlife, which lie outside the market system.

While commercial natural resources are measured directly in the accounts, in the sense that the value added associated with their exploitation is measured in national income, the economic value of these resources as assets appears only implicitly. The value of a subsoil resource deposit or standing forest as an asset is related to the flow of economic rent that results from its exploitation; for a given resource deposit this rent is measured as the difference between the market price of the resource and the full marginal cost of its extraction/harvest, including normal returns to capital. So resource rents show up as a portion of operating surplus for the resource sectors, but are not explicitly measured. Consequently the value of economic depreciation of a resource deposit as a result of exploitation is not measured either, which means that resource depletion does not enter into the calculation of net product, NNP or NDP. While the guidelines for the balance sheet accounts in the SNA[1] call for the valuation of subsoil or standing natural resources, the change in value of these assets from year to year is recorded as a reconciliation item, and so again does not alter net product estimates.

Environmental resources are measured more indirectly in the accounts. To the extent that there is a commercial activity associated with an environmental asset, such as tourism or hunting, then the value added in this activity appears as part of national product. But the underlying asset, the pristine lake or wilderness, is not valued explicitly. When environmental quality deteriorates, the effects show up indirectly in a variety of forms: loss of tourism industry income (as the lake is polluted, for instance); lost productivity of agriculture and living natural resources; increased repair and maintenance costs for buildings and other assets damaged by pollution; increased costs of inputs when water, for instance, must be cleaned prior to use in productive activities; increased health expenditures and lost productivity as a result of increasing morbidity and mortality; and diversion of resources from other valuable employment when accidents, such as oil spills, need to be cleaned up. All these effects are there in the accounts, but not directly and identifiably.

One aspect of government resource policy does show up directly in the accounts: since commercial resources are frequently government owned, with the right to exploitation being leased, governments attempt to capture resource rents through royalty schemes, and these royalties are measured explicitly in the accounts. But broader environmental policies appear only indirectly. Whether through regulation or market-based instruments, policies aimed at abating pollution and preserving ecosystems affect the level of intermediate expenditures and the mix of investment between environmental protection facilities and conventional productive assets. The values associated with market-based instruments will show up in the accounts, as indirect taxes in the case of pollution taxes, or as investments (and corresponding assets in the balance sheet accounts) in the case of emissions permits.[2] Growth rates in national product are affected implicitly by environmental policies.

If there is a common thread running through the literature on green accounting, it is that use of the environment and natural resources represents asset consumption, and that one of the key problems with standard national accounts is that this is not reflected in the measures of income and product. Moreover, this literature is concerned with making explicit what is currently only implicit in the accounts with respect to natural resources and the environment.

With this as background, some notation is required in order to describe the various approaches to constructing green national accounts aggregates:

ES   environmental services
ED   environmental damages
DE   defensive expenditures
IR   invested resource rents
RD   resource discoveries
DEP depletion of resources
NFA net financial assets
TA   tangible assets.

What follows is a brief description and assessment of the main lines of thought on environmental national accounting. Three basic identities are presented below, followed by notes explaining and evaluating the key points. It is useful to summarize the approaches according to whether they are intended to alter GDP (gross national product as conventionally defined), NNP (conventional net national product), or national wealth (denoted NW) as measured in the national balance sheet accounts, including a measure of natural wealth. gGNP, gNNP and gNW are the new green aggregates:

$$gGNP = GNP + ES \pm ED_1 - DE - IR$$
$$gNNP = NNP + RD - DEP - ED_2$$
$$gNW = NFA + TA_H + TA_N.$$

Here ED_1 and ED_2 represent different approaches to valuing environmental damage. We consider the component parts of these expressions in sequence:

ES   Peskin (1989) advocates augmenting GNP by a measure of *environmental services,* viewed chiefly as waste disposal services, which are provided free of cost by the environment. However, to the extent that producers use these services without paying for them, then it is arguable that their value already shows up in profits and therefore in GNP.

ED_1 *Environmental damages* can be either added or subtracted. Peskin views the negative externalities associated with producers availing themselves of the services of the environment as a deduction from GNP.[3] Harrison (1989) takes the opposite tack: since gross product includes the consumption of assets by definition, conventional GNP is understated because it does not measure the consumption of environmental assets. Note that this would require the estimation of a dollar value for total environmental deterioration, including that which was prevented as a result of current abatement expenditures.

DE   *Defensive expenditures* are expenditures on environmental protection undertaken by households (Juster, 1973) and governments (Herfindahl and Kneese, 1973). It is argued that environmental expenditures by households do not increase welfare but merely preserve the status quo (for example, not getting sick from environmental deterioration) and that government environmental protection expenditures (for example, on waste management) are essentially intermediate in character.

IR   El Serafy (1989) calls for the deduction of hypothetically *invested resource rents* from GNP, arguing that true income from a non-renewable natural resource is that constant stream of income that can be obtained from investing a portion of the rents from exploitation in a fund (a suitable programme will ensure that rents in excess of the portion invested will be identically equal to interest on the fund at the point of exhaustion). Hartwick and Hageman (1993) show that this is equivalent to valuing the change in the present value of the resource stock as a result of its exploitation – that is, it is a true user cost.

RD   Turning to the measurement of net domestic product, Repetto et al. (1989) reason that in order to maintain consistency between product and wealth accounts, augmented to include natural resources, the full value of natural *resource discoveries* should be added to net product in the period in which they are made. Hartwick (1990) developed a model in which discoveries are similarly added to net product. Weitzman (1976) showed formally that an unanticipated resource discovery does indeed increase the amount of sustainable product and income, but by less than the full value of the discovery in the period it was made.

DEP   *Depletion* of natural resources is the major adjustment to net product suggested by Repetto et al. (1989). Depletion is valued as the total of resource rents taken in the accounting period (the 'net price' approach) or, in the case of soil erosion, as the present value of forgone production. Repetto notes that the Hotelling rule, that resource rents in an efficient market will increase at a rate of change equal to the interest rate, will yield this valuation of resource depletion. The United Nations (1993) suggests valuing depletion using either the user-cost or net price approaches.

ED_2 As an alternative to deducting *environmental damage* from gross product, Bartelmus et al. (1989) suggest deducting it from net product as asset consumption. This asset consumption is valued as the cost of returning the environmental asset to its state at the beginning of the accounting period. Hueting and Bosch (1990) offer an alternative methodology in which environmental deterioration is valued as the costs that would be incurred to achieve sustainable use of the environment (rather than merely preserving its state, as in Bartelmus et al.). UN guidelines (United Nations, 1993) suggest contingent valuation as an alternative basis for valuing environmental degradation, but without discussing how, or whether, this can be applied to the environment as a whole.

NFA   Turning finally to measures of national wealth, *net financial assets* are an important component of total wealth. For an open economy the difference between financial assets and liabilities is equal to either net claims on foreign assets or net foreign indebtedness. The scale of investment of resource rents by the Organization of Petroleum-Exporting Countries (OPEC) producers in Europe and North America indicates the significance of this type of wealth where domestic investment opportunities are limited.

TA_H *Human-made (produced) tangible assets* are the familiar elements of reproducible capital: machinery, equipment, buildings and infrastructure. The Hartwick rule (Hartwick, 1977) states that, under suitable conditions of substitutability, investing resource rents in reproducible capital will permit a non-declining stream of consumption into the indefinite future. Building up human-made assets to match the drawing down of natural resources, thereby preserving wealth, fits the criterion for weak sustainability described by Pearce et al. (1989).

TA_N *Natural tangible assets* are measured by the dollar value of commercial resources (minerals, energy, forests and fish) and environmental resources (natural environments providing non-market services including waste disposal and amenity value). Scott (1956) first suggested expanding the national balance sheet account to include commercial resources. The problems in doing this include defining the appropriate measure of extent (proven reserves, that is, those that can be produced profitably at current prices and costs, would be the correct measure) and, in the absence of markets for publicly-held resource deposits, deriving values for these deposits. Hamilton (1991) argued that total national wealth per capita is a useful measure of sustainability. Pearce et al. (1989) point out that there is limited substitutability between certain critical natural assets and human-made assets, which argues for maintaining the value of at least some natural assets constant or increasing as a condition for sustainability.

This broad range of approaches to green national accounting is reflected in the activities of national statistical offices as well. Hamilton et al. (1994) review the efforts of Brazil, Canada, France, Germany, the Netherlands and Norway to develop new green accounts. The US Bureau of Economic Analysis has opted to concentrate on expanding the national balance sheet through an 'Integrated Economic and Environmental Satellite Account' – in addition, this account breaks out expenditures on environmental protection (Bureau of Economic Analysis, 1994).

There is little unanimity, therefore, in the literature on green accounting. This is a prime motivation for taking a more formal approach to the problem, to which we now turn.

3.2   Formal approaches to green national accounts

By asking a simple question, why we measure both consumption and investment in national product when the economic goal is to maximize consumption,

Weitzman (1976) provided the theoretical framework for a fruitful line of inquiry into the relationship between resources, the environment and national product.

Weitzman's answer to the question was that, if we assume we are on the optimal path of a dynamic competitive economy, then national product measured as the sum of consumption and investment in the current period is, if held constant and the present value taken, just equal to the present value of consumption along the optimal path – he calls it the *stationary equivalent* of future consumption. In an equally appealing interpretation of this same framework, Solow (1986) shows that increases in national product from some assumed initial value are equal to the discount rate times the accumulation of capital from the initial period to the present – national income and product can thus be conceived as the interest on total wealth, which is the Hicksian notion of income.

There is perhaps a simpler interpretation of NNP in the context of this framework: NNP is what a social planner would choose to maximize, subject to certain efficiency conditions, at each point in time in order to maximize the present value of consumption.[4] This is the basic notion that will be exploited in what follows. Some of the prime examples of this approach include Hartwick (1990 and 1992), and Mäler (1991), who look at both resource depletion and environmental deterioration in such a framework.

This section will highlight a series of results, presented in Hamilton (1994a), on what formal approaches to green national accounting say about the proper treatment of natural resources and pollution emissions in the measure of net national product. Technical details are reserved for the Appendix. The issues to be examined include: (i) living resources; (ii) heterogeneous resource deposits; (iii) resource discoveries; (iv) environmental services as a source of utility and an input to production; (v) greenhouse gases; and (vi) household defensive expenditures. This list therefore covers many of the thorny issues raised in the previous section. Rather than developing one grand model that combines all of these separate effects, which is the basic approach of Mäler (1991), a series of independent models is presented.

What these models have in common is that: (a) the present value of *utility*, which is a function of consumption and, in some models, environmental services, is optimized over an infinite time horizon; (b) the discount rate for utility is constant; (c) production is characterized by a fixed neoclassical production function; and (d) the basic dynamic constraint on the system is provided by the national accounting identity (that is, production equals consumption plus investment). The models are highly aggregated, with a single utility function and a single production function yielding a homogeneous output.

3.2.1 *Living natural resources*
Here we assume a living commercial natural resource that grows, is harvested, and is used in production. This yields the same measure of NNP as that derived

in Hartwick (1990), where it is assumed that the resource is consumed (and yields utility) directly. There is a non-zero cost of extraction/harvest of the resource, and its price is equal to its marginal product. To describe this and the following models we define the following symbols:

C consumption
K capital stock (produced assets)
F production
S resource stock
R resource extraction/harvest
p_R resource price
f extraction/harvest cost
f_R marginal extraction/harvest cost
g net natural growth of resource.

The basic accounting identities for this model are: $\dot{K} = F - C - f$ and $\dot{S} = -R + g$. Here the 'dotted' variables indicate the rate of change with respect to time. $\dot{K}$ therefore denotes net investment. By maximizing the present value of utility subject to these accounting constraints, the following expression for NNP results:

$$NNP = C + \dot{K} - (p_R - f_R)R + (p_R - f_R)g.$$

Note that $p_R - f_R$ is just the unit resource rent, price minus marginal cost. We can now interpret this expression to say: net product when there is a living commercial resource is measured as traditional NNP (consumption plus investment), less the value of current resource rents, plus the net growth of the resource valued at its rental rate. Of course the latter two terms collapse to measuring the increase/decrease in resource stocks, valued at the rental rate. In the steady state this would be zero (that is, harvest would equal net growth).

3.2.2   Heterogeneous deposits of exhaustible resources

Where there is a single homogeneous exhaustible resource the maximization problem gives the result obtained by setting g equal to 0 in the preceding expression for NNP. In this case the correct measure of net product is obtained by subtracting the value of current resource rents from conventional NNP.

A more interesting and realistic case is when there are heterogeneous resource deposits, each with their own cost of extraction, but the resource itself is homogeneous – oil would be a good example, where onshore, offshore, light and heavy oil deposits all have different cost structures. We assume there are N such deposits, that an amount R_i is extracted from each, and that f_{R_i} is the marginal and f_i the total cost of extraction from the *i*-th deposit. The problem is then to maximize the present value of utility, subject to the accounting constraints,

$$\dot{S} = -\sum_{i=1}^{N} R_i \quad \text{and} \quad \dot{K} = F - C - \sum_{i=1}^{N} f_i.$$

The value for NNP that results is:

$$NNP = C + \dot{K} - \sum_{i=1}^{N} (p_R - f_{R_i}) R_i.$$

This is a natural extension of the result for a homogeneous resource: here the sum of the rents on each resource deposit is subtracted from conventional NNP to arrive at true net product. To get the accounting correct, therefore, green national accounts will have to track extraction and costs for individual resource deposits when this type of heterogeneity prevails.

The result provides an important alternative to that of Hartwick and Lindsey (1989), who argued that the value of depletion of oil in North America could be measured using unit rents on offshore Arctic oil deposits, that is, that the marginal cost of oil was that of the most expensive source in production. The value of oil depletion calculated in this manner was correspondingly small. The approach suggested by this model is to consider each resource deposit as a separate supplier, with its own level of unit rent (the percentage rate of increase of unit rents must equal the interest rate, the net rate of return on capital – that is, the Hotelling rule must hold). The different unit rents available on the deposits then become analogous to the rents on farmland of varying quality that Ricardo first noted.

3.2.3   Exhaustible resource with discoveries

Hartwick (1990) presented a non-stochastic model of resource discoveries, characterized by a discovery cost function *v* which was related to the amount of resource discovered and the remaining stock of resource to be exploited. The resulting treatment of resource discoveries in the national accounts was the same as that adopted by Repetto et al. (1989), in that discoveries were added to NNP valued at their full rental rate. If, however, the discovery cost function is related to cumulative discoveries, rather than the remaining stock, then a different result ensues. Define:

D resource discoveries
v_D marginal discovery cost.

Now the problem is to maximize the present value of utility subject to the following accounting constraints: $\dot{S} = -R + D$ and $\dot{K} = F - C - f - v$. With this formulation the expression for NNP that results is,

$$NNP = C + \dot{K} - (p_R - f_R)R + v_D D.$$

Net product therefore becomes conventional NNP, less the value of current resource rents, plus discoveries valued at the marginal discovery cost. The latter term can be conceived as a type of investment.

3.2.4   *Pollution emissions and environmental services*

Here the issue is the treatment of the flow of environmental services that both provides direct utility to consumers and is used as an input to production. These services are reduced by pollution emissions and are increased by natural processes of regeneration. Pollution emissions are linked to the level of production and are reduced by abatement expenditures. The new variables are therefore:

X stock of pollution
B flow of environmental services
b marginal cost of abating emissions
e pollution emissions (tied to production)
d pollution dissipation (tied to the stock of pollution)
a abatement expenditures
p_B price of (marginal willingness of consumers to pay for) environmental
        services.

Environmental services B can be conceived as the flow of services provided by some non-market resource such as clean air. The unit of measure is arbitrary and can in fact be proxied by some physical measure, such as an air quality index. The key points about environmental services are that they are natural (that is, non-produced) and not appropriable. The change in environmental services is governed by a pair of simple equations:

$$\dot{X} = e - d \text{ and } B = B_0 - \beta (X - X_0).$$

These equations say that: (i) the rate of change of the pollutant stock is just equal to emissions minus dissipation; and (ii) the level of environmental services is diminished at rate β times the accumulation of pollutant from some assumed pristine stock size X_0 (B_0 is the level of environmental services in the pristine state).

The problem therefore becomes: maximize utility (as a function of both consumption and environmental services), subject to the above equations for environmental services and the accounting identity, $\dot{K} = F - C - a$. What results from the maximization is a measure of economic welfare:

$$MEW = C + \dot{K} - b(e - d) + p_B B = C + \dot{K} + b\,(\dot{\beta}/\beta) + p_B B.$$

In the first expression we see that the marginal cost of abatement is the appropriate way to value the net change in welfare associated with pollution emissions and the regeneration of the environment (associated with pollution dissipation). This expression says that in addition to the value of the *change* in environmental services, a value must also be ascribed to the *level* of environmental services provided – since these are non-produced services and not appropriable, in contrast with natural resources as treated in the previous models, the expression is therefore one measuring welfare rather than a net product concept. Note that $C + \dot{K}$ is traditional GNP less the value of pollution abatement expenditures, so that GNP is still the starting point in measuring welfare.

In the second expression $\dot{\beta}/\beta$ is the rate of change of environmental services, measured in pollution equivalents. This rate of change is valued at the marginal cost of abatement. When emissions exceed the rate at which the environment can assimilate them this term will be negative, representing a net reduction in welfare.

The preceding expressions show that the appropriate 'price' to attribute to pollution emissions is the marginal cost of abatement. Hamilton (1994b) develops a similar approach in which the marginal social cost (that is, the value of the marginal loss of environmental services) associated with emissions is the relevant price. Because these are optimizing models we know that the marginal cost of abatement must be equal to the marginal social cost at the optimum, and that these are in turn equal to the value of the unit Pigovian tax on pollution required to reach the optimum.

3.2.5   The CO_2 problem

How is welfare maximized when an exhaustible resource is the source of a pollution emission that decreases the flow of environmental services? This is the crux of the CO_2 problem where, ignoring deforestation's role in global warming, the exhaustible resource is fossil fuel. The model of extended national accounting combines some features of the previous ones, and adds some unique features.

- Environmental services are governed by the equations of the preceding problem. Underlying this is a model of a stock of carbon dioxide in the atmosphere; this stock is augmented by the emissions from burning fossil fuels and dissipates at some natural rate as the CO_2 is sequestered in the deep oceans. Environmental services are then negatively related to the size of the stock of carbon dioxide in the atmosphere.

- Fossil fuels are assumed to be exhaustible, with no resource discoveries, are costly to extract and are used in production.
- Environmental services provide utility to consumers, but do not enter the production function.
- Emissions are related to fossil fuel use and are decreased by abatement expenditures.

With this as background, the only new notation required is:

be_R marginal cost of abating emissions from an extra unit of resource.

The present value of utility is maximized subject to the equation for the change in environmental services and the accounting constraints $\dot{S} = -R$ and $\dot{K} = F - C - f - a$. The measure of economic welfare that results is:

$$MEW = C + \dot{K} - b(e-d) + p_B B - (p_R - f_R - be_R)R$$
$$= C + \dot{K} + b\,(\dot{B}/\beta) + p_B B - (p_R - f_R)R + be_R R.$$

The first of these expressions says that welfare is measured as traditional NNP, less the value of emissions, plus the value of dissipation of carbon dioxide, plus the value of the level of environmental services, less the value of net rents on fossil fuel extraction. This bears an obvious resemblance to the preceding results. The biggest difference is in the unit resource rent term, which is measured as the price minus marginal cost of extraction minus the cost of abating a marginal unit of carbon dioxide emission. This latter term can be interpreted as a *carbon tax rate*, a Pigovian tax that is required to maximize utility when consumption and environmental services are traded off. So the linkage between resource use and carbon emissions acts to decrease the value of fossil fuel deposits, because of this reduction in the effective unit rents.

The second expression is a simple rearrangement of terms to highlight the fact that welfare is measured as consumption plus investment, plus the value of the level and net rate of change in environmental services, less resource rents, plus the value of revenues from an optimal carbon tax.

3.2.6   Defensive expenditures by households

This model returns to the issue of the treatment of environmental services and ignores resource extraction and use. It is assumed that households benefit from environmental services only indirectly, and that the effects of environmental deterioration can be mitigated through defensive expenditures. This is expressed in the model by making utility a function of consumption and environmental *benefits*, and these benefits in turn are assumed to be function of the flow of environmental services and the level of defensive expenditures. The new notation required for the model is as follows:

Φ environmental benefits
h household defensive expenditures
d_h marginal defensive cost.

To simplify matters, it is assumed that there is a single cumulative pollutant, so that $\dot{\beta} = -\beta e$ describes the change in environmental services. As before, emissions are related to the level of production and are reduced by abatement expenditures.

The present value of utility is maximized in this model subject to the preceding equation for environmental services and the accounting constraint $\dot{K} = F - C - h - a$. The resulting measure of economic welfare is:

$$MEW = C + \dot{K} - be + d_h\Phi.$$

As in the first model of environmental services, the welfare measure starts with conventional GNP then subtracts the value of pollution emissions valued at the marginal cost of abatement. The term that corresponds to the value of the level of environmental services, paralleling previous models, is the last in this expression: the level of environmental benefits valued at the marginal defensive cost, that is, the extra expenditures h required to obtain another unit of environmental benefit Φ – this is obviously related to the notion of using avertive expenditures to value environmental benefits as described in Smith (1991).

If marginal defensive costs increase with defensive expenditures then this expression can be interpreted to say that not only should household defensive expenditures not be deducted from the adjusted NNP measure (as Mäler, 1991, concludes), but in fact these defensive expenditures understate their welfare effects.

3.3   Social accounting, genuine saving and measures of economic welfare

Social accounting matrices (SAMs) are an alternative way to present conventional national accounting data. The economy is divided into sectors and each sector has an account. A SAM is then a square matrix whose rows and columns correspond respectively to the supply and disposition of goods and services. In some cases more specific interpretations can be placed on column and row sums in terms of income and expenditures of these accounts and each cell records transactions between accounts (Round, 1994). In the simplest SAMs there are five core accounts (that is, 'sectors'): (i) production (for example, firms); (ii) factors of production (for example, labour and capital); (iii) institutions (for example, households, government); (iv) saving/ investment, and; (v) rest of the world (transactions with other countries). More complex variations involve further disaggregation of these accounts. In the social accounting literature these matrices have typically been used to examine issues such as the distribution of income. This can be done via a suitable disaggregation of household (institution) accounts (see, for example, Roland-Holst and Sancho, 1992).

With this emphasis on disaggregation, the integration of green national accounting with SAMs offers a way to increase the policy usefulness of resource and environmental accounts. Some statistical offices have already realized this potential – one example being the Dutch Central Bureau of Statistics (CBS) National Accounting Matrix including Environmental Accounts (NAMEA) (see, for example, de Boo et al., 1991). Indeed, this matrix approach has been adopted as one part of the framework for a European Union green accounting programme (see Commission of the European Communities, 1994). Here, we link the formal approaches to green accounting set out in this chapter to a SAM.

The accounting matrix in Table 3.2 describes seven accounts, each representing a distinct sector. Five of these accounts were described above, and we introduce into this simple framework two 'new' accounts, namely resources and environment. Columns and rows correspond to the supply and disposition interpretation given above. Obviously, accounting convention dictates that the sum of the contents in each column is equal to the sum of the contents of each row. Hence, each account – including 'resources' and 'environment' – will have a corresponding residual balancing item.

For example, for the saving account,

$$I + (X - M) + n.g + \sigma.d \equiv S_g + \delta K + n.R + \sigma.e. \tag{3.1}$$

By manipulating this identity a residual measure of genuine saving (S_g) is obtained. Thus, genuine saving is equal to

$$S_g \equiv [I + (X - M) + n.g + \sigma.d] - [\delta K + n.R + \sigma.e]. \tag{3.2}$$

In this case we have an expanded measure of gross saving, the first bracketed term on the right-hand side of the above expression. This is equal to conventional gross saving (that is, investment, I, plus exports, X, minus imports, M) plus the growth of resources (g) valued by the resource rent (n) and the dissipation of environmental degradation (d) valued at the marginal social cost of emissions (σ). Put another way, the natural ability of resources to regenerate and of

Table 3.2 A social accounting matrix including resources and the environment

	Production	Factors	Institutions	DISPOSITION Saving	Rest of the World	Resources	Environment	TOTALS
Production		NNP	C	I	X			Total disposition of goods and services
Factors	NNP							Net disposition of goods and services
Institutions		NNP				NRP	NEP	Disposition of welfare
Saving	δK		S_g			$n.R$	$\sigma.e$	Total disposition of saving (investment finance)
Rest of the World	M			$(X - M)$				Total disposition to rest of the world
Resources				$n.g$				Gross Resource Product
Environment			$p_B B$	$\sigma.d$				Gross Environmental Product
TOTALS	Total supply of human-made goods and services	Net supply of human-made goods and services	Supply of welfare (MEW)	Total supply of saving	Total supply to the rest of the world	Total supply of resources	Total supply of environmental benefits	

S U P P L Y

53

environments to assimilate waste are components of saving. S_g can be interpreted as a measure of sustainable development (see Pearce and Atkinson, 1993; Hamilton, 1994a; Hamilton and Atkinson, 1995).

In order to derive a measure of economic welfare (MEW), we have to look more closely at the institutions account. Summing the column, MEW is

$$C + S_g + p_B B \equiv MEW.$$

This has three components. Consumption expenditures (C) are the starting point for any measure of economic welfare (see for example, Nordhaus and Tobin, 1973). Genuine saving is an enlarged expression for net asset accumulation as described in (3.1) above. The final expression on the left-hand side of (3.2) is a measure of 'environmental output'. This is distinct from environmental expenditures for it is a measure of the level of services provided by the environment itself. These are benefits (B) that are conferred to households (that is, institutions) and are valued at household marginal willingness to pay (p_B) (Hamilton, 1994b). We investigate this measure in more detail below. In summary, our MEW is equivalent to consumption plus genuine saving plus the value of environmental services.[5] Depending on the size of $n.R$ it is plausible that the value of MEW will exceed that of NNP (or GNP).

Another perspective is obtained by summing across the contents of the institutions' account:

$$MEW \equiv NNP + NRP + NEP.$$

Hence, conventional NNP is only one subset of MEW. This also supports Hamilton's claim that green measures of income are distinct from the measurement of economic activity in the production account (for example, NNP or GNP). Here, MEW encapsulates welfare measured in the institutions account and includes net resource product (NRP) and net environmental product (NEP). In principle, we could envisage a measure of gross economic welfare, for example, inclusive of the value of resource depletion and environmental degradation. However, apart from keeping to the spirit of the distinction in the existing accounts between gross and net output, it is doubtful that such an aggregate would serve much purpose.

That welfare measures are fundamentally about net flows is also reflected in the row and column sums in Table 3.2. In the institutions account these refer to the disposition and supply of welfare (or at least the value of welfare-generating goods and services) respectively. However, gross terms do emerge in both the resource and environment accounts. For example, the row sums correspond to measures of gross resource product and gross environmental product. Nevertheless it is more instructive to look in detail at the net counterparts to these measures. In the case of the resource account, rearranging the row-column identity, yields NRP,

$$n.g = NRP + n.R$$
$$\Rightarrow NRP = n(g - R).$$

This is simply the value of natural growth (which is zero in the case of a non-renewable resource) minus the value of depletion. Hence, NRP is equivalent to the net rent and so does not include the costs of extraction such as payment to labour and the return on produced capital used in extraction.

Similarly, net environmental product can be defined:

$$P_{BB} + \sigma.d = NEP + \sigma.e$$
$$\Rightarrow NEP = p_B B + \sigma(d - e).$$

NEP is thus equivalent to the value of environmental services plus the value of the net rate of change in environmental quality. This is analogous to the expression in Weitzman (1976), $F = C + \dot{K}$, where F is net output of an economy and $\dot{K}$ is net capital accumulation. The first quantity on the right-hand side of these last two expressions is a measure of how much output is currently consumed, while the second is a measure of net accumulation. It follows that expression (3.2) can also be interpreted in this way.

3.3.1 Policy uses

While the uses of green accounting have often been poorly defined (Hamilton et al., 1994), the presentation of this information in SAM form increases the policy usefulness of these accounts:

- by emphasizing the detail of green accounts, thereby reducing the tendency in some of the empirical literature to devote attention solely to changes over time in simple aggregate measures;
- by emphasizing the productive aspects of resources and environment, that is, growth of resources and dissipation of pollution. This is necessary if our flow accounts are to be linked to wealth accounts (balance sheets) such that policies for sustainable development can be evaluated. Moreover, by stressing the components of a measure of genuine saving, the means by which investment is financed is highlighted. Hence, the row sum of the savings account can also be thought of as measuring the finance of investment (see, for example, Hamilton and O'Connor, 1994). In effect this indicates the extent to which sales or liquidation of assets are being exchanged for other assets (for example, sale of resources to finance

investment in produced assets). The residual, S_g, tells us how much of saving is genuine, that is, not made to offset loss of other assets;

- by modelling of linkages between environment and economy. In turn, this framework could form the basis for subsequent analysis and modelling of policy changes. Examples of these linkages could be the disposition of social costs of pollution by household income distribution (disaggregation of the institution account) and the supply of pollution from abroad (disaggregation of the rest of world account). A further linkage of interest – which we have not sought to model in this chapter – is the 'supply' of social costs by industry (production account). Of course, additional information would need to be brought to bear if the modelling of these linkages is to be made possible (for example, the spatial distribution of pollution). The point is that extended SAMs as set out here and elsewhere (for example, NAMEA) offer a flexible structure for organizing this information and in doing so provide a basis for responding to policy questions.

3.4   Conclusions from the formal approaches to green accounts and welfare measurement

This set of independent models provides useful guidance in thinking about the relationship between national accounting and the natural environment. All of the results take conventional GNP as the starting point, which should be encouraging to national accountants, and then suggest a number of adjustments to better measure true income or welfare. Because environmental services are unproduced and are not sold through markets, the adjusted net product measures that result in the models involving environmental services are best interpreted as welfare measures – an explicit value for the flow of environmental services is a feature of each of these models.

For exhaustible natural resources the adjustments to standard GNP are to:

- deduct current resource rents (valued as price minus the full marginal cost of extraction);
- deduct the sum of current resource rents (for heterogeneous deposits);
- treat discovery expenditures as investment.

For living resources the adjustment to GNP is to:

- add the net natural growth of resources, valued at the rental rate (where harvest exceeds natural growth this will be negative, while it will be 0 in the steady state).

For environmental services, add the value of the flow of environmental services (as measured by households' marginal willingness to pay) to conventional GNP and then:

- deduct abatement expenditures;
- deduct pollution emissions, valued at the marginal cost of abatement;
- add environmental regeneration, also valued at marginal abatement cost (in the steady state these terms would be equal and so would cancel);
- note that marginal abatement costs will equal marginal social costs at the optimum.

For fossil fuels whose use leads to CO_2 emissions, begin with GNP, add the value of the flow of environmental services (how to value this will be discussed below) and the rate of change in these services, and then:

- deduct abatement expenditures;
- deduct resource rents;
- add the value of the carbon tax.

For household defensive expenditures, start with conventional GNP, deduct pollution emissions valued at the marginal abatement cost and then:

- deduct abatement expenditures;
- add environmental benefits, valued at the marginal defensive cost.

3.4.1 A comparison with current national accounting practice
To put these results in context, it is valuable to compare them both with how the national accounts deal with these issues currently and with the proposals that appear in the literature on green national accounting.

Exhaustible resources   The results presented here suggest that standard national accounting is incorrect in not deducting resource depletion in addition to depreciation of produced assets in arriving at NNP. The basis of valuing this depletion, current resource rents, appears to favour the approach of Repetto et al. (1989). However, most practical attempts to measure resource rents end up deducting the average, as opposed to marginal, cost of extraction from the market price to arrive at unit rental values, as Hartwick (1990) notes. But the deviation from what is theoretically correct may be small if the following is assumed: (i) there are a number of resource deposits with distinct extraction costs, as assumed in model 3.2.2; and (ii) for any given resource deposit, the difference in extraction cost between the first and last units produced over the accounting period is small. The net price method of valuation featured in these models, in contrast with the user-cost approach of El Serafy (1989), is purely a result of the optimality inherent in the models. A key efficiency condition in the models is the Hotelling rule, that unit resource rents have a percentage rate of increase equal to the net marginal product of capital – under these conditions it is simple to show that the user cost equals the current resource rent (that is, the net price).

Discoveries of exhaustible resources   Our results are at variance with both Repetto et al. (1989) and Hartwick (1990). While these authors value discoveries at the full rental rate, the model presented here suggests marginal discovery cost as the true basis of valuing discoveries.[6] In this respect it is at least similar to the treatment in the standard national accounts, where most exploration expenditures are treated as investment – however, this implicitly values discoveries at the average, as opposed to marginal, discovery cost (the average discovery cost is equal to the total cost of exploration, including 'dry holes', divided by the amount discovered).

Living resources   The results differ again from the SNA, suggesting that the excess of net natural growth over harvest for commercial species should be added to NNP, while any excess of harvest over growth should be subtracted from NNP, with both being valued at the current rental rate. This difference arises from the treatment of resources as productive assets in the models. The model results agree with the approach of Hartwick (1990).

Environmental services   The results are completely outside of the bounds of the SNA, by valuing the services provided by non-market assets. The general thrust of the formal approach is that the value of environmental services should be added to conventional GNP, while net environmental damage, as given by the value of pollution emissions less the value of regeneration of the environment, should be subtracted. This is broadly similar to the suggestion of Peskin (1989), but differs in many details concerning the basis of valuation and the use of *net* environmental damage in the models – in particular, if environmental quality were improving then the models would increase the welfare measure, in much the same manner as any excess of the net natural growth of living resources over harvest would increase NNP in the model for living resources.

CO_2 emissions   In dealing with fossil fuels as both an exhaustible resource and a source of CO_2 emissions, a novel element in the results is the suggestion that the value of a carbon tax should be measured as part of NNP. In this respect the model is in agreement with the SNA, since pollution taxes in the SNA would show up as indirect taxes and therefore in value added. Of course the results

indicate that it is the value of an optimal carbon tax, one that just balances the marginal costs and benefits of cutting emissions, that should be added to NNP.

Household defensive expenditures   The results suggest that marginal defensive costs (avertive expenditures) can be used to value environmental services. Household defensive expenditures should not be deducted from adjusted NNP.

Valuing environmental damage   Turning to the general question of valuing environmental damage in the accounts, the results are at variance with the proponents of expenditure-based approaches, such as Bartelmus et al. (1989) and Hueting and Bosch (1990). The models presented value emissions at the marginal abatement cost, which could well vary considerably from average costs, and also value regeneration of the environment (dissipation of the pollutant) at this same rate, which is an element completely missing from expenditure-based approaches. Moreover, expenditure-based methods are implicitly valuing environmental degradation as the average cost of abatement times the amount abated, compared with marginal abatement costs times the amount emitted, as suggested in the formal approach.

Finally, it is important to compare the treatment of resources and the environment in these models with that proposed in the *System of Integrated Environmental and Economic Accounts* (SEEA) described earlier in this chapter. Described by the UN as interim guidelines, the SEEA provides an important standard for international efforts in environment and resource accounting. The guidelines for valuing depletion and growth of natural resources are in broad agreement with the model results.

Regarding the valuation of environmental degradation there is a much wider divergence between the models and the SEEA. The problem in discussing the SEEA is that there are five different versions presented in the guidelines, along with numerous variants. One of the key points of the foregoing models, that both the value of pollution emissions and the value consumers place on the level of environmental services must be added as an adjustment to NNP, is not clearly made in the SEEA. Most importantly, the SEEA favours using maintenance costs – the cost of returning the environment to its state at the beginning of the accounting period – as the basis of valuing environmental degradation from pollution emissions. This is in clear contrast with the models, which use marginal abatement costs or marginal social costs to value emissions. In addition, the SEEA ignores the value of natural environmental regeneration.

Maintenance cost approaches have some intuitive appeal, representing the cost of 'keeping capital intact'. Unfortunately there is little theoretical support for this method of valuing damage to the environment. To return to the interpretation of the models presented, the derived adjusted NNP represents what one would choose to maximize at each point in time in order to maximize the present value of welfare in the indefinite future. This will value environmental degradation as the marginal abatement (or social) cost times the amount of pollutant emitted.

3.4.2   Social accounting matrices

Organizing these results in an extended social accounting matrix (SAM) should increase the policy usefulness of green national accounting. SAMs provide a consistent and flexible framework for analysing a range of policy questions such as the financing of investment. In addition, the SAM discussed here offered a number of additional insights into the measurement of economic welfare including the concepts of net resource product and net environmental product.

3.4.3   Measurability

One common criticism of the use of optimizing approaches to explore accounting issues is that the results are all expressed in terms of shadow prices, which typically involve the measurement of marginal costs or marginal product. Whether the formal approaches provide any practical guidance for green national accounting is therefore worth exploring.

When it comes to valuing resource depletion, the key element is the measurement of resource rents, calculated as the market price of the resource less its marginal cost of extraction/harvest. As was mentioned above, the model of heterogeneous resource deposits suggests that a practical method of valuation would be to estimate resource rents on each of the deposit types, where deposits are classified by cost of extraction – this would tend to minimize the divergence between average and marginal extraction costs. This logic could be extended to living resources as well, of course although in this case measuring depletion will be data intensive.

It is in the valuation of environmental services that the most obvious problems arise. The measurement issues fall into several broad classes:

- *Units of measure.* The formal approach does not deal with the question of what is the appropriate quantitative measure for environmental services. It may be that the different types of services need to be proxied, for instance by index numbers of air quality and water quality. Then marginal abatement costs could be expressed in terms of the costs of achieving an incremental improvement in air quality as measured by the index, and the price households would be willing to pay for environmental services could similarly be based on incremental changes in index numbers.
- *Spatial resolution.* With the exception of truly global problems such as greenhouse warming, most environmental problems are local or regional. The optimal amount of abatement therefore could vary significantly with local conditions (these conditions would affect rates of environmental regeneration) or even local preferences.

- *Aggregation.* In principle we want to value all environmental services for a whole country. In practice, if we were valuing on the basis of willingness to pay for these services, we would want to know how consumers value a portfolio of such services relative to other consumption options. Most of the methods used by economists to value environmental amenities (travel cost methods, hedonic pricing, dose-response methods, contingent valuation, and so on; see Braden and Kolstad, 1991) are concerned with specific projects or assets. Determining how to add up values across a portfolio without double-counting will be a challenge.

- *Abatement costs and willingness to pay.* The models require willingness to pay (technically, the ratio of the marginal utilities of environmental services to consumption) and marginal abatement (or social) costs as methods of valuation. Abatement curves typically exhibit sharply increasing marginal costs once significant quantities of pollution have been removed. Marginal abatement curves are seldom observed, and so must be modelled. Demand curves for environmental services may be kinked, so that the marginal willingness of consumers to pay for an extra unit of environmental service may be much lower than the willingness to accept compensation for a unit decrease in environmental service (Knetsch, 1989). Moreover, some means of aggregating willingness to pay for the whole range of environmental services in a nation must be provided which is a formidable problem.

   Away from the optimum there is in general a divergence between marginal social costs and marginal abatement costs. Below the optimum (that is, with too much pollution being emitted) one would expect the social costs to be higher than the abatement costs at the margin. Therefore valuation of pollution emissions based on marginal social costs will be an upper bound, and valuation based on marginal abatement costs a lower bound, on the true value of emissions.

Thus it is possible to be modestly optimistic about the possibility of valuing resource depletion in accordance with the models, and pessimistic about the potential to value environmental services comprehensively in the accounts. However, valuing particular environmental services, such as air quality in cities, should be practicable and should, subject to the usual questions of cost versus benefit, yield useful insights for environmental policy.

One caveat that should be added to this concerns discounting and resource depletion. The models require the Hotelling rule as an efficiency condition and so, as previously noted, value depletion as equal to current resource rents. In practice, there is little evidence for efficient pricing of resources in the ground, for which Adelman (1990) is only one recent piece of evidence. As a practical matter, therefore, it may be advisable to value resource depletion as a user cost with a non-zero discount rate (as in El Serafy, 1989 and Hartwick and Hageman, 1993). This in turn leads to questions of what discount rate to use, although there are strong theoretical arguments for using the social rate of return on investment, the so-called 'consumption rate of interest' (see Dasgupta and Heal, 1979, Chapter 10, and Pearce and Ulph, 1995).

3.4.4 Do green national accounts measure sustainability?

There are important questions currently being discussed on the policy usefulness of green national accounts and, at the level of theory, on whether adjusted accounts can measure the sustainability of economic development.

To turn to the theoretical arguments first, both Asheim (1994a) and Pezzey (1994) have argued that no *instantaneous* measure of green national income can tell us whether the economy is on a sustainable path. Both use a simple model of a non-renewable natural resource and derive the result of our model 3.2 excluding resource discoveries: NNP should be measured as consumption plus investment less the value of resource depletion (where resources are valued at their rental rate). Both show that even if investment in produced assets is greater or equal to the value of resource depletion at a given point in time (that is, a weak sustainability criterion is being met), there is no way to conclude that the economy is on a sustainable path. In fact the optimal path for an economy dependent on a non-renewable resource is not sustainable if the pure rate of time preference, the measure of impatience, is positive – this is a result that goes back to Dasgupta and Heal (1979, Chapter 10).

Perhaps the key point in the theoretical argument, one that should be remembered in discussing green national accounts, is that sustainability is a property of the path the economy is on and not of the state of the system at any given point in time. Thus a path for the economy that optimally depletes a non-renewable resource, where the pure rate of time preference is positive, is not sustainable and adjusted NNP will not measure sustainable income; if the rate of impatience is zero, then the optimal path has rising consumption and so is sustainable. Similarly, if the economy is on a path where investment is identically equal to resource depletion at each point in time and the resource is depleted efficiently (that is, the Hotelling rule applies), then it is sustainable[7] and adjusted NNP does measure sustainable income.

A reasonable approach to the measurement of sustainability is to note the following: any path where investment net of depletion is always negative is not sustainable (see the Appendix to this chapter). This suggests that some sort of savings rule, measuring savings net of resource depletion – what Hamilton (1994a) calls *genuine* saving – can be derived from the construction of green national accounts. However, it is only consistent negative savings that will lead to non-sustainability. The measurement of a negative genuine savings rate at a given point in time is not sufficient to lead to the conclusion that the economy is not on a sustainable path. But the policy prescription arising from measuring a negative genuine savings rate is clear: continuing dissaving is not sustainable and must be rectified.

The first difference of wealth is genuine saving as discussed above. The empirical evidence from savings calculations for a range of countries is presented in the next chapter. But the earlier point bears repeating: *genuine savings are a one-sided indicator of sustainability.* While non-negative genuine savings at a given point in time may or may not be indicative of a sustainable path, consistent negative saving behaviour is not sustainable.

There are two caveats that should be added to this discussion of saving as it translates into investment. First, increases in produced assets are not the only way to increase output in the economy, since alternative management schemes can produce more output from the same capital stock. And second, it is not only the quantity of produced assets that matters but the quality as well; for example, investing resource rents in primary education in a developing country will yield far higher returns than investing them in a 'white elephant' project.

3.5 Conclusions

The accounting approaches presented break down into the broad category of resource and environmental accounting and the narrower class of green national accounting aggregates. While it is clear that natural resource accounts, resource and pollution flow accounts and environmental expenditure accounts all have policy uses, particularly when linked to policy models, these accounts do not on their own provide measures of progress towards sustainable development.

Green national accounting aggregates are by their nature the most highly integrative measures of resource depletion and environmental degradation. The weighting provided for different aspects of depletion and degradation is based on costs and benefits at the margin, and so is consistent with welfare maximization. However, as pointed out earlier, actually measuring these marginal costs and benefits is not simple. In some instances, such as estimating the value that consumers place on the current level of all environmental services, we are still awaiting methodological developments.

The formal approach to accounting, based on models of welfare maximization over the long term, provides consistent guidance for the construction of green national accounting aggregates. Several general conclusions follow from the models: (i) NNP should be adjusted to value both resource depletion and, in the case of living resources, resource growth; (ii) when including the effects of pollution emissions the green aggregate is necessarily a welfare measure rather than an national income measure, although NNP is the starting point; (iii) it is necessary to value pollution emissions, pollution dissipation, and the level of environmental services when adjusting for pollution; (iv) where resource use leads itself to pollution emissions, resource rents should be reduced by the amount of an optimal tax on resource use; and (v) household defensive expenditures should not be deducted from the green welfare measure.

Finally, greener measures of savings and wealth are the most useful indicators of sustainable development. But it must be remembered that these are one-sided measures: only consistent dissaving can be shown to lead unequivocally to non-sustainability; positive savings rates at a given point in time do not necessarily indicate that the economy is on a sustainable path.

Notes

1. The key elements of the System of National Accounts in what follows are the income and expenditure accounts, measuring current flows of economic activity (for example, GDP), and the national balance sheet accounts measuring opening and closing stocks of assets (both financial and tangible) over the accounting period.
2. Because they are assets with market values, tradable emission permits would be measured as intangible assets in the balance sheet accounts.
3. Environmental services are, in effect, positive externalities provided by nature. Peskin is not explicit about whether environmental damage would appear subsequently as a decline in environmental services.
4. This interpretation is based on the fact that NNP can be derived as a transformation of the current value Hamiltonian function of an optimal control problem that seeks to maximize the present value of utility – see Hartwick (1990).
5. Of course, this assumes that the conventional accounts otherwise measure welfare accurately. For example, in a 'sustainable income' type measure, consumption should reflect consumption services (see Atkinson, 1995). Similarly, measures of changes in human capital and the services that these assets provide fall within the sustainable income ambit (see Aronsson, Johansson and Löfgren, 1994).
6. This approach to the problem is corrected in Hartwick (1993), where results the same as presented here are derived.
7. This is the well-known Hartwick (1977) rule. These conclusions are subject to the assumptions about the elasticity of substitution of capital and natural resources explored in Hamilton (1995).

Appendix

As an example of the formal approach to green national accounting, we wish to model a pollutant whose effects are cumulative. The level of the flow of environmental services B is therefore related negatively to the cumulative amount of pollution emitted, X, so that the rate of change of environmental services is given by,

$$\dot{X} = e \text{ and } B_0 - \beta(X - X_0) \tag{3A.1}$$

Here B_0 is the level of environmental service flow from a pristine environment. Production of a composite good is given by neoclassical production function $F = F(K, L)$, for produced capital K and fixed labour input L. This production may be either consumed or invested. Utility is a function of both consumption and environmental services, so $U = U(C, B)$. We first assume no abatement expenditures, so that emissions are given by $e = e(F)$. The model is therefore,

$$\max \int_0^\infty U(C, B)e^{-rt}dt \text{ subject to:}$$
$$\dot{K} = F - C$$
$$\dot{X} = e.$$

Here C is the only control variable. The current value Hamiltonian for this problem is,

$$H = U + \gamma_1(F - C) + \gamma_2 e$$

for co-state variables γ_1 and γ_2, and the first-order condition for a maximum (ignoring the dynamic conditions for the moment) is,

$$\frac{\partial H}{\partial C} = 0 = U_C - \gamma_1 \Rightarrow \gamma_1 = U_C.$$

For the first-order condition to yield a maximum, a necessary condition is that $U_{CC} < 0$, that is, that there be declining marginal utility of consumption.

Note that $\gamma_2 < 0$, since increases in the accumulation of the pollutant decrease welfare. The measure of economic welfare is obtained by transforming the Hamiltonian to yield,

$$MEW = C + \dot{K} + \frac{\gamma_2}{U_C}e + \frac{U_B}{U_C}B. \tag{3A.2}$$

There are several things to note about this expression, beginning with why it should be interpreted as a welfare measure rather than net national product. The terms in emissions e and environmental services B provide the answer: as purely external phenomena they reflect adjustments to utility rather than to market production. This expression should be interpreted as what a planner should maximize at each point in time in order to maximize the present value of utility. The expression U_B/U_C is the price that utility-maximizing consumers would be willing to pay for a unit of environmental service, and so a key component of welfare in this model, as with the flow pollutant, is the monetized value of the *level* of environmental services.

Since γ_2 is the shadow price of the accumulation of the pollutant measured in utils, it is natural to define $\sigma \equiv -\gamma_2/U_C$ as the marginal social cost of a unit of the pollutant, and this will equal the Pigovian tax required to maximize utility. If $p_B \equiv U_B/U_C$ then the expression for economic welfare becomes,

$$MEW = C + \dot{K} - \sigma e + p_B B . \tag{3A.3}$$

Economic welfare is therefore measured as consumption plus investment less the value of an optimal emissions tax plus the value of the level of environmental services.

Abatement expenditures, a, are introduced into this model as the use of current production to reduce the level of emissions, so that the emission function is redefined as follows:

$$e = e(F, a), \ e_F > 0, \ e_a < 0.$$

The maximization problem is now specified as:

$$\max \int_0^\infty U(C, B)e^{-rt}dt \ \text{subject to:}$$
$$\dot{K} = F - C - a$$
$$\dot{X} = e.$$

The control variables are C and a and the current value Hamiltonian is as specified above. The first-order condition for γ_1 is again that it should equal the marginal utility of consumption. For γ_2 we now have,

$$\frac{\partial H}{\partial a} = 0 = -\gamma_1 + \gamma_2 e_a \Rightarrow \gamma_2 = \frac{U_C}{e_a} \tag{3A.4}$$

It will be useful in what follows to define $b \equiv -1/e_a$; this is just the *marginal cost of pollution abatement.* Transforming the Hamiltonian into consumption units, we therefore derive,

$$MEW = C + \dot{K} - be + p_B B. \tag{3A.5}$$

Expression (3A.4) implies that $b = -\gamma_2/U_C$. The marginal cost of abatement is identically equal to the marginal social costs of emissions and to the value of the optimal unit emissions tax. Given that $\gamma_1 > 0$ and $\gamma_2 > 0$, a necessary condition for the Hamiltonian to produce a maximum of utility is $e_{aa} > 0$, that is, increasing marginal abatement costs.

Economic welfare, therefore, is measured as consumption plus investment, less the value of pollution, plus the value of environmental services. Note the valuation of pollution in expression (3A.5). While this may appear similar to valuing environmental damage as the current cost of abatement, a moment's reflection shows that this is not so: valuation is based on the *marginal* cost of abatement, and emissions are implicitly held to their optimal value, because welfare is being maximized.

If we consider the accumulation of pollutant X to be a liability in the national balance sheet, then $\dot{K} - be$ is equal to what Hamilton (1994a) calls *genuine saving* – the change in the real value of assets when all assets, including environmental ones, are taken into account. Net national product is therefore derived as,

$$NNP = C + \dot{K} - be,$$

and it is the addition of value of environmental services, $p_B B$, that produces a welfare measure.

Expression (3A.5) can also be written as,

$$MEW = C + p_B B + \dot{K} + \frac{b}{\beta} \dot{B}, \tag{3A.6}$$

so that economic welfare consists of the proximate sources of utility, C and $p_B B$, plus the adjustments required to ensure utility maximization over time, $\dot{K}$ and $(b/\beta)\dot{B}$. Note that $\dot{B} < 0$ for any non-zero production level because pollution accumulates.

Expression (3A.5) yields another interpretation. First, $GNP = F = C + \dot{K} + a$. This implies that

$$MEW = GNP - a - be + p_B B.$$

So we conclude that, in order to arrive at a welfare measure, abatement expenditures should be subtracted from GNP – they become, in effect, intermediate consumption. This is consistent with the notions of Juster (1973) and Leipert (1989). What goes beyond the conclusions in these studies is the subtraction of emissions valued at the marginal cost of abatement and the addition of the value of environmental services.

Negative genuine savings

To show that persistent dissaving leads to unsustainability, we first need to establish the optimal time paths of the shadow prices in the optimal control problem with abatement expenditures. Recall that $\gamma_1 = U_C$ and $\gamma_2 = -U_C b$. From the Hamiltonian function we derive,

$$\dot{\gamma}_1 = r\gamma_1 - \frac{\partial H}{\partial K} = r\gamma_1 - \gamma_1 F_K - \gamma_2 e_F F_K \Rightarrow \frac{\dot{U}_C}{U_C} = r - (1 - be_F)F_K$$

$$\dot{\gamma}_2 = r\gamma_2 - \frac{\partial H}{\partial M} = r\gamma_2 + \beta U_B.$$

Therefore,

$$\frac{\dot{\gamma}_2}{\gamma_2} = \frac{\dot{U}_C}{U_C} + \frac{\dot{b}}{b} = r - \frac{\beta}{b}\frac{U_B}{U_C} \Rightarrow \dot{b} = (1 - be_F)F_K b - \beta\frac{U_B}{U_C} \quad \text{(3A.7)}$$

Expression (3A.7) characterizes the optimal time path of marginal abatement costs. If we assume a fixed labour force L then $\dot{F} = F_K \dot{K}$. Noting that $\dot{e} = e_F \dot{F} + e_a \dot{a}$ and recalling the definition of marginal abatement costs b, we have,

$$\dot{F} - \dot{b}e - b\dot{e} - \dot{a} = (1 - be_F)F_K(\dot{K} - be) + \beta\frac{U_B}{U_C}e. \quad \text{(3A.8)}$$

It is straightforward to show that the rate of change of utility is given by,

$$\dot{U} = U_C\dot{C} + U_B\dot{B} = U_C\left(\dot{C} + \frac{U_B}{U_C}\dot{B}\right) = U_C\left(\dot{C} - \beta\frac{U_B}{U_C}e\right). \quad \text{(3A.9)}$$

Genuine saving in this model is measured as $\dot{K} - be$. Since $C = F - \dot{K} - a$, expression (3A.8) implies that if $\dot{K} = be$ (that is, zero genuine savings) everywhere along the path then, by expression (3A.9), utility will be constant. If $\dot{K} = be - \varepsilon$ for some positive constant ε, and this constant quantity is assumed to be consumed, then expressions (3A.8) and (3A.9) imply that utility will be decreasing; thus efficient pricing of pollution emissions, as given by expression (3A.7), combined with persistent underinvestment will lead to non-sustainability.

4   Empirical measures of sustainable development

This chapter uses 'green' national accounting to present an empirical measure of the extent to which countries, particularly developing countries, are on a path of sustainable development. The core concept used will be that of 'genuine saving' as described in Chapter 3.

Given the centrality of savings and investment in economic theory, it is perhaps surprising that the effects of depleting natural resources and degrading the environment have not, until recently, been considered in the measurement of national savings. This omission may be explained both by the models economists use, which typically rely on gross measures of activity, and by the fact that the System of National Accounts (SNA) ignores depletion and degradation of the natural environment. This is not intended to be excessively critical of the SNA – it measures market activity very well, which is its intent. It is none the less true that the tools which conventional economists use tend to colour or restrict the view of some important issues.

Valuing depletion and degradation within a national accounting framework is an increasingly viable proposition, both as a result of the significant progress made in the techniques of valuation of environmental resources (see, for a recent example, Freeman, 1994) and as a result of the expanding foundation that theoretical developments are placing under the methods of 'green' national accounting (Hartwick, 1990; Mäler, 1991; Hamilton, 1994a). The first application of these savings-based accounting methods to the measurement of net savings appeared in Pearce and Atkinson (1993). This study combined published estimates of depletion and degradation for 20 countries with standard national accounting data to examine true savings behaviour. By this measure many countries appear to be unsustainable because their savings rates were less than the combined sum of conventional capital depreciation and natural resource depletion.

Enlarging the concept of net saving to include the depletion of natural resources is in many ways the most natural alteration of traditional savings concepts. This is because the depletion of a natural resource is, in effect, the liquidation of an asset and so should not appear as a positive contribution to net national product or, by extension, net savings. While minor technical issues remain, the methods of valuing the depletion, discovery and growth of commercial natural resources in the context of the SNA are by now well developed (Hamilton, 1994a; Hill and Harrison, 1994).

More problematic is the valuation of environmental degradation. While UN guidelines for environmental accounting (United Nations, 1993) favour valuing this degradation in terms of maintenance costs (the cost of restoring the environment to its state at the beginning of the accounting period), the latest theoretical approaches (Hamilton and Atkinson, 1995) suggest that the marginal social costs of pollution are the correct basis for valuing waste emissions to the environment.

This chapter presents two sets of empirical estimates of genuine savings rates. After a general description of the savings rule, the first part is concerned with valuing resource depletion and carbon dioxide emissions, in order to measure genuine savings rates, using a consistent time-series data set for the 1980s. The emphasis in this section is on developing countries. The second part presents estimates of the value of air pollution emissions, and the corresponding genuine savings rates, for OECD Europe.

4.1   The savings rule
The following equation adapts the expression for the measure of economic welfare (MEW) from Chapter 3:

$$MEW = C + I - n(R - g) - \sigma(e - d) + p_B B.$$

Here C is consumption, I net investment, n the unit resource rental rate less the value of the implicit pollution tax on production, R resource extraction, g resource growth, σ the marginal social costs of, e pollution emissions, d the natural dissipation of pollution, and p_B the willingness of consumers to pay for environmental services B. For non-living natural resources the term in g is zero, while d is zero for pollutants with cumulative effects.

The measure of net national product simply drops the last welfare term from this expression. The intuition behind this is clear: $I - n(R - g) - \sigma(e - d)$ is the value of *net* investment when changes in natural resource stocks and stocks of pollutants, appropriately shadow priced, are included in addition to increments to the stock of produced assets; consumption plus net investment equals net product.

However, while it is important to know what constitutes the sustainable level of national income, this measure is not particularly relevant for policy purposes (as argued in Chapter 3). A shift in the level of national income does not carry a policy signal with regard to sustainable development, while the relative growth rates of sustainable income and traditional GNP, for instance, are liable to give equivocal signals. Given that concerns about sustainable development are fundamentally concerns about the future, this suggests that adjusted measures of savings and wealth are more fertile territory for policy purposes.

The expression for genuine saving follows directly from the preceding:

$$S_g = GNP - C - D - n(R - g) - \sigma(e - d).$$

Here $GNP - C$ is gross saving as traditionally defined, with C being the sum of public and private consumption; gross saving includes the level of foreign saving as well. D is the value of depreciation of produced assets, so that $GNP - C - D$ is conventional net saving. The last two terms in this expression represent the value of net depletion of natural resources and net accumulation of pollutants.

The importance of this measure of genuine saving is that it is a one-sided indicator of sustainability, in that persistent negative genuine savings are not sustainable, as derived in Chapter 3. Note that it is possible to have apparently robust gross saving and negative genuine saving. So while it is easy to calculate gross savings rates from published national accounts data, this may give little indication of whether the economy is on a sustainable path. This reinforces the point made earlier that the tools economists use may bias their conclusions with regard to economic performance.

In the following section we present a set of estimates of the value of resource depletion and environmental degradation for a range of developing countries, expressed in terms of genuine savings rates. What is presented is necessarily limited by the available data. The natural resource estimates span crude oil, the major metallic minerals, phosphate rock and tropical forests. The only environmental pollutant considered is carbon dioxide, the principal contributor to the greenhouse effect. While it would be highly desirable to expand the coverage of other pollutants, data on both the level of pollution emissions and their marginal social costs are lacking in many developing countries; research is under way to build up the relevant data base.

4.2 Resource depletion: measurement issues

The problems in the measurement of depletion and degradation of the environment break down into several distinct pieces: (i) the valuation of resource rents for non-renewable resources; (ii) valuing depletion of tropical forests; and (iii) valuing the marginal social costs of CO_2 emissions. These will be described in turn.

The basic approach to calculating resource rents for non-renewable resources is to subtract country- or region-specific average costs of extraction from the world price for the resource in question, all expressed in current US dollars. World prices were derived from World Bank (1993a) – where data from multiple markets – for example, London and New York – are reported. A simple average of these market prices serves as the world price. The levels of resource rents are thus calculated as:

Rent = World price – mining cost – milling and beneficiation costs
                        – smelting costs – transport to port
                        – 'normal' return to capital.

For crude oil unit rents are estimated as the world price less lifting costs. There are several things to note about this methodology:

- From a theoretical viewpoint, resource rents should be measured as price minus *marginal* cost of extraction (including a normal return to capital). In practice, marginal production costs are almost never available and practitioners (as evidenced by the 'green national accounting' literature) fall back on using average extraction costs. This will tend to overstate calculated resource rents and hence will understate genuine savings.
- Countries may or may not be selling their natural resources (for internal consumption or export) at the world market price, although one would expect that they have every incentive to do so. This methodology, being based on world prices, can therefore be viewed as shadow pricing of natural resources, based on the border-pricing approach of Little and Mirrlees (1974) and Squire and van der Tak (1975).
- Extraction costs are measured at a fixed point in time, 1985 for minerals (Bureau of Mines, 1987) and 1990 for crude oil (Department of Energy, 1994), and held constant over the period 1980–90. World prices vary over time, leading to corresponding variations in calculated rental rates.
- Where the extraction cost data were region- rather than country-specific, the regional cost structure was applied to all of the producing countries in the region.
- Rents are generally viewed as accruing to the resource owner for the production of the crude form of the material in question, typically an ore. In practice, most mineral operations are vertically integrated to a considerable extent and so the only price and cost data are for refined forms of the materials. Measuring resource rents as described above for these vertically integrated mineral operations therefore implicitly ascribes any excess returns to capital for the milling and refining stages to the resource rent.
- In some cases, such as for lateritic nickel deposits, the rental rates are negative for at least part of the time. This may represent a situation in which producers actually managed to decrease average extraction costs in line with price movements, a phenomenon that would be masked by the above methodology (if this were so then rents are only *apparently* negative

as a result of the estimation methodology); it may also simply be the case that firms continued to operate, in spite of reduced or negative rates of return on capital, while they were meeting their variable costs and in the expectation of improved market conditions. Negative unit rents are set to zero in the calculations below.

Table 4.1 presents the calculated average rental rates for minerals and crude oil. The coefficients of variation are high for zinc and nickel. The table also shows which cost components, subject to data availability, went into the calculation of rental rates. In most (but not all) cases an explicit rate of return on capital appears as a cost component. Missing cost components lead, of course, to overestimates of resource rents. In line with the formal green national accounting methods of Chapter 3, the country-specific unit resource rents in each year are multiplied by the quantities of resource extraction for each of the minerals in Table 4.1, to arrive at the total value of resource depletion.

Table 4.1   Rental rates for minerals and crude oil

	1. Mean Rate	2. Standard Deviation	
Zinc	0.49	0.32	Mining, milling, smelting, transport, 15% ROC
Iron ore	0.56	0.20	Mining, beneficiation, transport
Phosphate rock	0.33	0.14	Mining, milling, transport, 15% ROC
Bauxite	0.59	0.18	Mining, milling
Copper	0.43	0.16	Mining, milling, smelting, 15% ROC
Tin	0.30	0.13	Mining, milling, 15% ROC
Lead	0.56	0.27	Mining, milling, smelting, transport, 15% ROC
Nickel	0.34	0.23	Mining, refining, smelting
Crude oil	0.74	0.14	Lifting costs

Notes
Rental rates estimated from unweighted pooled data, 1980–1990, excluding negative values.
ROC – return on capital.

For tropical forest resources the situation is much more complicated with regard to the valuation of depletion. The issue is essentially one of land use, with standing forests being one use among many for a particular land area. This suggests that the correct way to value deforestation is to measure the change in land value (which should represent the present value of the net returns under the chosen land use) – this is essentially the result in Hartwick (1992). The formal models of Chapter 3 suggest that, where deforestation is not occurring but harvest exceeds growth, it is the net depletion of the resource that should be valued.

Because there are limited data on rates of harvest and natural growth, the estimates presented below are confined to the valuation of deforestation, based on the latest decadal FAO forestry assessment (FAO, 1993). Since there are virtually no data on the value of forested land before and after clearance, the deforestation is simply valued as the stumpage value of the volume of commercial timber on each hectare cleared. Stocking rates (the volume of commercial timber per hectare) by country are as given in FAO (1993). The stumpage rate is assumed to be 50 per cent of the market price, a crude assumption but consistent with studies such as Sadoff (1992) and Repetto et al. (1989), while market prices are from World Bank (1993b). Deforestation rates are linearly interpolated from the decadal estimates of forest cover given in FAO (1993). Thus, the foregoing description of the valuation of forest depletion suggests that the estimates are quite rough. It should also be obvious that the only values being calculated are commercial, so that the values of biodiversity, carbon sequestration and other losses are not captured.

Turning to the value of carbon emissions, the basic emissions data employed are from the Carbon Dioxide Information and Analysis Center (Marland et al., 1989), covering fossil fuel combustion and cement manufacture. The global marginal social cost of a metric ton of CO_2 is assumed to be US\$20 in 1990, taken from Fankhauser (1994). Global costs are assigned to emitting countries as an extension of the 'polluter pays principle' into the domain of environmental accounting. This practice seems consistent with the notion of genuine saving, in that the value of the external costs of emissions imposed on other countries should be, at least notionally, set aside in a fund to compensate those countries which are negatively affected.

The formal model of carbon emissions from fossil fuels in Chapter 3 suggests that the value of an optimal carbon tax should be deducted from fossil fuel rents, to account for the pollution externality, and that the value of natural dissipation of the carbon stock in the atmosphere should be deducted from emissions. Given that the carbon tax, based on marginal social costs, would be less than US\$5.50 per metric ton of carbon in fuel, and that the mean residency time of carbon in the atmosphere is roughly 120 years, these effects are small and have been dropped from the calculations. Higher estimates of marginal social costs would mean that this assumption should be revisited.

A key missing element in the estimates is any valuation of soil erosion, owing to the lack of comprehensive data sets on either physical erosion or its value. This is an important gap considering the importance of agriculture in most developing countries – for example, erosion is considered to be a major problem in Sub-Saharan African countries in particular. Various studies on the economic costs of soil erosion exist (for example, Bishop, 1990) and there is the prospect of assembling data on a more comprehensive basis.

4.3 Estimates of resource depletion and genuine saving

The basic national accounts data used to arrive at genuine savings rates are as given in the World Bank's *World Tables* (World Bank, 1993c). However, these data do not include the value of depreciation of produced assets. Unofficial World Bank estimates of depreciation, as calculated from perpetual inventory models, are taken from Nehru and Dhareshwar (1993). Each of the data sets employed in this chapter, the *World Tables* data, the depreciation estimates, and the resource depletion and degradation estimates have various gaps in their coverage. The result is that there are 56 developing countries for which complete times series of the basic data exist over the period 1980 to 1990.

The first question to be answered is whether the calculation of depletion and degradation adds substantially to the picture of whether countries are on a sustainable path. This reduces to the question of whether there are countries whose net savings rates (as conventionally defined, gross saving minus the value of depreciation of produced assets) are positive but whose genuine savings rates are negative. This is examined in Figure 4.1. (For presentational purposes, a few countries that had net savings rates less than –10 per cent and/or depletion greater than 40 per cent of GNP have been excluded from this figure.)

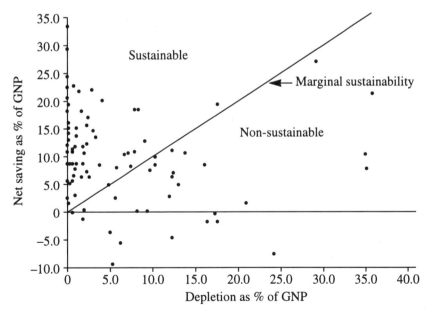

Figure 4.1   Net saving versus depletion share of GNP, 1986–1990 average

In Figure 4.1 the net saving rate (for developed and developing countries) is scatter-plotted against the value of depletion (and CO_2 emissions) as a percentage of GNP, using average figures for the period 1986–90. The line labelled 'Marginal sustainability' is the 45° line – countries falling above this line have genuine savings rates that are positive (since genuine saving is just net saving less the value of depletion and degradation), while those falling below have negative genuine savings rates. While there are several countries that have negative net savings rates, and so are unsustainable even by conventional national accounts measures, there are clearly a considerable number of countries with positive net savings but negative genuine savings. Measuring genuine saving therefore provides useful new information.

Figures 4.2 and 4.3 summarize the genuine savings rates for countries aggregated into regions. Note that the calculated regional savings rates are the net savings for the countries in the sample – they are therefore weighted towards the largest countries (which tend to have the largest absolute amounts of saving or dissaving) and do not estimate or 'gap-fill' for countries in the region but not in the sample. The countries in the sample are presented below in Appendix Table 4A.1.

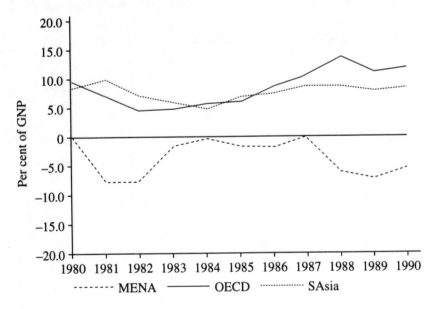

Notes
MENA – Middle East and North Africa.
SAsia – South Asia.

Figure 4.2   Genuine savings rates by region, 1980–1990

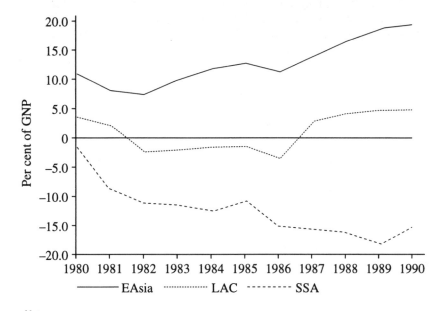

Notes
EAsia – East Asia.
LAC – Latin America and the Caribbean.
SSA – Sub-Saharan Africa.

Figure 4.3   Genuine savings rates by region, 1980–1990

The first thing to note from these figures is that OECD countries and South Asian countries had broadly similar rates of genuine saving through the 1980s – in the neighbourhood of 10 per cent of GNP. To match this, growth in per capita GNP was slightly higher in South Asian countries over this decade, 3.1 per cent compared with 2.3 per cent in OECD countries (World Bank, 1994c). So the savings figures and the growth figures tell a basically consistent story for these groups of countries.

The next point to note is that the countries of the Middle East and North Africa, basically the oil exporters, were marginal and sometimes substantial dissavers. However, this is a result both of oil constituting a substantial portion of economic activity in these countries and of the fact that resource rents are not discounted in the calculation of depletion. While the theoretical models suggest that this is the correct valuation of depletion, the results of the models are the product of optimization, so that unit resource rents are assumed to increase at the rate of interest (for example, the Hotelling rule). The effects of relaxing the Hotelling assumption in calculating the value of crude oil depletion are presented below.

The sampled countries of Latin America and the Caribbean were marginal dissavers during the years of the debt crisis (1982–86). This largely reflects a dip in the gross saving rate over these years, so there is no strong evidence that these countries stripped resource assets in order to pay off debts (although the linear interpolation of the deforestation estimates would mask this effect in the case of forest depletion). From 1987 onwards there is a marked improvement in savings behaviour.

The most striking contrast in genuine saving rates is between East Asia and Sub-Saharan Africa, a contrast that is also vividly reflected in growth rates in per capita GNP. East Asia was consistently the strongest region in terms of any measure of saving: gross, net or genuine. Sub-Saharan Africa shows a near-steady decline in genuine saving over the course of the decade. The steep drop in genuine saving from 1980 to 1981 reflects Nigeria's transition from a sizeable positive to sizeable negative current account balance. The composition of savings and investment in these two regions is shown in Figures 4.4 and 4.5. In these charts the difference between gross investment and gross saving rates is the ratio of net foreign borrowing (NFB) to GNP. If net borrowing is positive then, obviously, gross investment is greater than gross saving.

In East Asia the declining ratio of depletion (and degradation – recall that this includes the value of CO_2 emissions) to GNP is mirrored by an increase in the

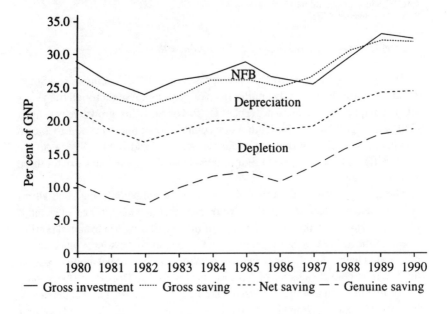

Figure 4.4   Investment and saving in East Asia, 1980–1990

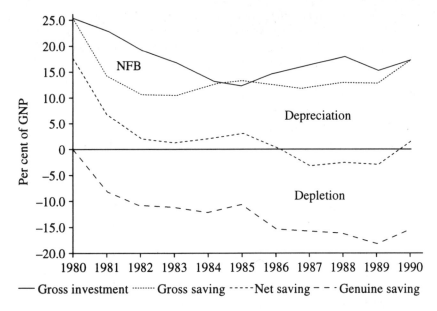

Figure 4.5   Investment and saving in Sub-Saharan Africa, 1980–1990

share of depreciation of produced assets in GNP, with the latter reflecting the effects of industrialization. The falling ratio for depletion reflects a near-constant total value of depletion. This may, again, be an artefact of the linear interpolation of deforestation, an important component of depletion for this region. There is little doubt, however, that the growth in industrial (and service) output in this region is leading to a decline in the relative importance of natural resources.

As noted above, there was a steep drop in all savings rates in Sub-Saharan Africa from 1980 to 1981, reflecting the dominance of Nigeria in the regional aggregate. Net foreign borrowing was significant in the early 1980s. From a net savings perspective, the sampled countries in this region were unsustainable from 1986 to 1989. The effect of including depletion in the genuine savings measure is to sharply accentuate this effect, and to show that the region was not on a sustainable path right through the decade.

Of course, regional aggregates might be a convenient way to summarize the behaviour of countries that are, to a degree, similar in their endowments. It is up to individual countries, however, to design and implement policies for the achievement of sustainable development.

The 'bottom line' in these two figures is clear: there was strong growth in genuine saving in East Asia in the 1980s, while there was strong growth in dissaving in Sub-Saharan Africa.

4.3.1   The Sub-Saharan African experience

The results for Sub-Saharan Africa (SSA) are so striking that they merit a closer examination. Country-level estimates of genuine savings rates for the 1980s are given in the Appendix to this chapter, in Table 4A.1.

In a paper reviewing the literature on long-term development and growth in SSA, Ndulu and Elbadawi (1994) cite the following broad conclusions: (i) SSA has grown more slowly than other developing countries since the mid-1970s; (ii) lower savings rates and levels of human capital have prevented it from catching up with other developing countries; (iii) the policy climate in SSA has not been conducive to sustained growth, characterized as it has been by disincentives to save, overvalued and variable exchange rates, high public consumption, and underdeveloped financial systems; and (iv) the economies of SSA have been subject to elevated levels of external shocks, both economic and physical (in the form of drought and other severe weather patterns), and political instability.

The pattern presented in Table 4A.1 appears to be 'the curse of the mineral-rich' (compare Gelb, 1988). Countries such as Kenya, Rwanda, Burundi and Niger, with relatively few exports of oil and minerals, have the most promising saving performance. On the other hand, resource-rich Zimbabwe exhibited positive genuine savings. As noted earlier, the figures for Nigeria (and the Congo) are probably skewed by the substantial size of the deposits of crude oil. Zambia appears to be the other anomalously large dissaver – while these effects may again be overstated for technical reasons having to do with the valuation of resource depletion, it is also true that the economic policy climate was particularly unfavourable in Zambia for many years.

The sorts of issues raised by Gelb (1988) about the nature and effects of oil windfalls in developing countries are particularly relevant in dealing with this question. Without sound policies, both macroeconomic and with regard to economic development, and prudent allocation of public resources, the effects of reliance upon large resource endowments can be negative for many countries. It would of course be incorrect to conclude from Table 4A.1 that mineral wealth is necessarily a curse. A basic lesson from growth theory is that a windfall increment in wealth will lead to a permanent increase in sustainable income (see Weitzman, 1976). However, growth theory assumes that resources are efficiently priced and that an optimal extraction programme will be combined with an optimal investment strategy. Good policy, therefore, turns resource wealth into sustained increases in income.

The striking result from accounting for resource depletion is the extent of dissaving in most Sub-Saharan African countries. The traditional macroeconomic data and indicators for SSA countries have been uniformly disappointing for two decades, with decline and stagnation being the general picture that results. What the savings approach does is to indicate that the situation *with regard to future wellbeing* is worse than might otherwise be thought. Not only has SSA performed badly by conventional measures, it is clear that the wealth inherent in the resource stocks of these countries is being liquidated and dissipated. Not only have the trends in current indicators been downwards, but total wealth, especially on a per capita basis, has been declining as well.

4.3.2   User cost versus net price

As noted above, there is a potentially important divergence between theory and practice in the valuation of resource depletion. Because the models of Chapter 3 require an efficient time path for resource rents (the Hotelling rule), the change in the present value of a resource deposit as a result of current production – that is, the user cost – is precisely equal to the value of rents on this production – that is, resource depletion valued at its 'net price', the market price less the (marginal) cost of extraction (see Repetto et al., 1989). If efficient resource pricing is not assumed then some non-zero rate of discount should be used in valuing depletion; the formula for the user cost (*UC*) of resource extraction becomes:

$$UC_t = \frac{n_t R_t}{(1+i)^N},$$

where *n* is the unit resource rent (the net price), *R* is the quantity of resource extracted, *i* is the rate of discount and *N* is the reserve life. This formula is in discrete time, rather than continuous time as in the previous chapter. The formula is an adaptation of one in El Serafy (1989) and, as in that paper, implicitly assumes that the product of *n* and *R* is constant over the life of the resource deposit.

This distinction between net price and user-cost methods is not just of theoretical interest: for countries with very long-lived deposits, even small discount rates will yield user costs that are much smaller than current rents. Since it is the user cost that must be reinvested in order to maintain a constant value of capital, this has important consequences for countries' incentives to consume or invest resource rents. Examples of these effects are shown in Table 4.2 for some of the oil producers in the sample of countries.

For this 3 per cent rate of discount the difference between current rents and the user cost is small for reserves–production ratios (*N* in the above formula) less than 10 years. For very large resource endowments, however, such as for Iran and Venezuela in Table 4.2, the user cost of resource extraction is almost negligible.

The choice of discount rate is clearly key in this calculation. While a range of discount rates is possible, growth theory suggests that the social rate of return on investment (*SRRI*) (or consumption rate of interest, as it is sometimes called) is the fundamental discount rate. It is the maximum amount of extra consumption made possible by forgoing a unit of consumption in the current period, and is expressed by the following formula:

$$SRRI = r + \eta \frac{\dot{C}}{C}.$$

Here r is the pure rate of time preference (or rate of impatience, the rate at which future utility is discounted), η the elasticity of the marginal utility of consumption, and $\dot{C}/C$ the percentage rate of growth in per capita consumption. The social rate of return on investment is thus the sum of the rate of impatience and the rate of decline in the marginal utility of consumption associated with an extra unit of consumption. Estimates of the various components of this formula for the UK, reported in Pearce and Ulph (1995), show r to lie between 0 and 1.7 per cent, and η to lie between 0.7 and 1.5. With a long-run growth rate in per capita consumption of 1.3 per cent, Pearce and Ulph estimate a 'best' value of the *SRRI* of 2.4 per cent for the UK, and a likely range of 2–4 per cent. The 3 per cent figure used in Table 4.2 is solidly within this range.

Table 4.2   User-cost and net price estimates for a sample of oil producers

	Average production 1980–90	Reserves	R/P	Depletion: NP	Depletion: UC	UC/NP (%)
Algeria	48.6	1,800	37	6,051	2,024	33
Congo	5.9	110	19	6,051	3,478	57
Indonesia	70.2	726	10	6,051	4,458	74
Iran	110.9	12,700	115	17,617	596	3
Mexico	130.3	6,079	47	1,3451	3,388	25
Nigeria	74.9	2,400	32	9,861	3,825	39
UAE	72.5	1,300	18	11,668	6,868	59
United Kingdom	104.0	535	5	5,727	4,919	86
Venezuela	100.2	8,604	86	11,142	881	8

Notes
R/P – reserves–production ratio, in years.
UC – user cost.
NP – net price.
Depletion adjusted for reserve life, 3% discount rate, 1990.
Figures for production and reserves in million metric tonnes.
Depletion figures in millions of US$.

Another important consideration in the choice of discount rate for valuing the user cost of resource depletion is the fact that the optimal growth path of an economy with an exhaustible resource is not sustainable if the rate of impatience r is positive (Dasgupta and Heal, 1979, Chapter 10). Any positive rate of discounting of utility leads to an optimal path along which utility eventually declines. If sustainability is a goal, this argues for low rates of discounting utility.

The practical consequence of these calculations is that there is at least some argument for adjusting the value of depletion to reflect the size of the resource deposits. This would have obvious consequences for most of the oil-producing states and countries that have long-lived mineral deposits, such as Guyana with its bauxite.

Such divergences between theory and practice represent difficult issues for the practitioner. Given the lack of empirical evidence for efficient resource rents (see, for instance, Adelman, 1990), a low rate of discount in the calculation of resource rents may be preferable to the net price-based calculations presented above. However, the choice of discount rate and the uncertainty of the size of resource deposits (to say nothing about varying resource grades – see Hamilton, 1994c) present new difficulties in practical measurement.

The empirical estimates of this chapter are best viewed, therefore, as a rapid assessment of where the combination of resource depletion and deficient saving may be a significant policy concern.

4.3.3 Human capital and genuine saving

The basic notion behind 'genuine' saving is to measure the change in value of the underlying assets (and liabilities, in the case of stocks of pollutants) upon which welfare depends. The basic contribution of the recent work on environmental accounting, upon which the foregoing estimates depend, has been to establish the proper measurement of natural assets. It is natural, therefore, to consider what other assets could be brought into this framework, and it is obvious that human capital is a missing element. This is the motivation in Hamilton (1994a) for including current expenditures on education in the genuine savings measure.

It may be argued that this is superfluous, given that the returns to human capital are already measured implicitly in GNP. This misses the point, however. The goal of the genuine savings measure is to make explicit the true level of output that is not consumed and is therefore available to provide welfare in the future.

One problem with the standard national accounts from the human capital perspective is that, while capital expenditures on education (for buildings and equipment for instance) are treated as investment, current expenditures, both public and private, are not. From the viewpoint of the creation of human capital it seems clear that these current expenditures should also be considered to be investment.

However, the question of valuing human capital is complex. The literature on this topic (see, for instance, Jorgenson and Fraumeni, 1992) has typically been concerned with valuing the returns to human effort beyond those provided by unskilled labour. As a result, questions of the measurement of the output of the education sector have predominated. This can be simplified in the context of measures of genuine saving by considering the goal just stipulated, to measure the true level of unconsumed output. From this standpoint it is sufficient to include current expenditures on education E as an addition to genuine saving, so that the expression for genuine saving becomes

$$S_g = GNP - C - D - n(R - g) - \sigma(e - d) + E.$$

International data on educational expenditures are fragmentary, presumably owing to the problem of consolidating expenditures by different levels of government. There is also some risk of double-counting because expenditures data typically do not distinguish between current and capital expenditures. Because of this poor coverage, a complete set of genuine savings measures adjusted for education expenditures will not be presented here.

As an example of the difference such an adjustment could make, Figure 4.6 presents the adjusted savings rates for Chile from 1980 to 1990, based on the

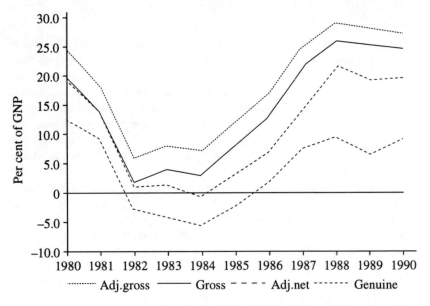

Figure 4.6   Savings rates in Chile, 1980–1990 (adjusted for education expenditures)

World Bank's Economic and Social Database. This figure requires careful interpretation. The curve for 'Gross' saving measures the ratio of traditional gross saving to GNP. The 'Adj.gross' curve adds the share of educational expenditures to the 'Gross' measure. The 'Adj.net' curve then subtracts the depreciation of produced assets share from the adjusted gross curve. Finally, the 'Genuine' saving curve subtracts the share of depletion of resources and the social costs of carbon emissions from the adjusted net curve.

Therefore, the inclusion of educational expenditures in the genuine saving measure improves the picture of saving in each country – in the case of Chile, this amounts to a little less than 5 per cent of GNP, and in most countries it would fall between 2 per cent and 8 per cent of national product. However, as noted when savings measures were introduced above, the effectiveness of these expenditures in fostering economic growth will vary widely. For many developing countries investments in primary education will pay higher dividends than those in higher-profile sectors such as universities. This is a good example of the quality of investment issue that we have identified with respect to the genuine savings rule.

4.4 Valuing air pollution in OECD Europe: preliminary concepts

Valuing pollution emissions in the national accounts will be important both for developed countries and for the most rapidly urbanizing and industrializing developing countries. This section presents the methodology for the treatment of pollution and pollution abatement in the national accounts, and a first attempt to apply this approach for the countries of OECD Europe. The empirical results are presented in the context of the savings rules.

The measure of genuine saving is precisely that presented previously,

$$S_g = GNP - C - D - n(R - g) - \sigma(e - d).$$

Again, $GNP - C$ is gross saving, C the sum of public and private consumption, and D is the value of depreciation of produced assets, so that $GNP - C - D$ is conventional net saving. The last two terms in this expression represent the values of net depletion of natural resources and net accumulation of pollutants. Since the resources analysed here are non-living, the growth term g in this expression is set to zero; since we will assume cumulative effects of air pollutants, the term for pollution dissipation d is also set to zero.

Natural resources are limited to crude petroleum, natural gas and minerals in the analysis that follows, with figures derived from the same data set as in the previous section, with its inherent strengths and weaknesses. While the expression above suggests that marginal social costs σ should be used to value pollution emissions, the formal approaches to green accounting presented in Chapter 3 suggest that marginal abatement costs are another candidate valuation. This will be discussed in more detail below. There is the additional problem in dealing with air pollutants that emit in one country often have an impact upon other countries. This issue will also be explored below.

4.4.1   Measurement

The basic question in valuing air pollution emissions is whether to use marginal social costs or marginal abatement costs as the basis of valuing pollution emissions. Note that this question only makes sense away from the optimum, since it was shown in the Appendix to Chapter 3 that the two valuations must be equal at the optimum.

Turning to the valuation of the costs of pollution, the question of measurement away from the optimum is an interesting one, given that most real economies would not be expected to be operating at the environmental optimum. Figure 4.7 provides a way to think about this issue.

This is the canonical diagram used to derive the notion of optimal pollution. In this figure the horizontal axis refers to reductions in pollution emissions. 'MCA' is the curve for marginal cost of abatement. 'MSC' is the marginal social cost curve, which is equal to the marginal benefit of abatement (MBA). The optimal emission reduction occurs at level '*', while level 'c' represents overpolluting and 'd' underpolluting.

If we assume that the current state of the economy is one of overpolluting, then marginal social costs at level 'a' will provide an upper bound on the value

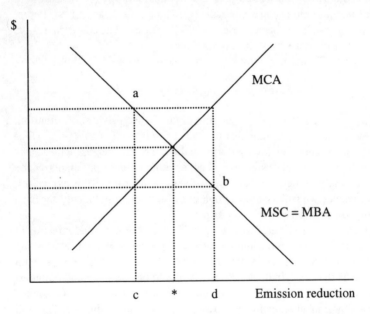

Figure 4.7   Valuing the costs and benefits of emission reductions

of optimal pollution emissions; if the current state is one of underpolluting then marginal social costs at level 'b' will provide a lower bound on the optimal emission value. As long as one is reasonably certain that the economy is overpolluting, therefore, using marginal social costs to value emissions should be viewed as an upper limit estimate and interpreted accordingly in the results of the green accounting exercise. This implies in addition that the deduction for pollution emissions in the welfare measure will decrease as the optimum is approached, which is a desirable property.

Figure 4.7 also makes it clear that using marginal abatement costs to value emissions will not lead to an unequivocal direction of bias in the estimates of the value of pollution. If the economy is overpolluting then marginal abatement costs will be below the optimum, and emissions above; the opposite applies to an economy that is underpolluting.

Data on the marginal social costs of *air* pollution emissions, based on willingness to pay concepts, are increasingly available for developed economies, as are data on the levels of air pollution emissions. One of the challenges for practitioners will be to adapt these marginal social cost figures for use in developing countries, or better, to begin to measure willingness to pay for pollution reductions in these countries. There is a growing literature, reviewed in CSERGE/UNC Chapel Hill (1994), on measuring willingness to pay for forest functions, ecotourism, sanitation, water supply and land degradation in developing countries, but the studies valuing the social costs of pollution *per se* are still quite rare. Data on marginal abatement costs are generally not collected, but models embodying the appropriate technological and economic information to estimate marginal costs are becoming available.

4.4.2 Transboundary pollution

The models of green national accounting presented in Chapter 3 ignored geography for the sake of simplicity, but the question of transboundary pollution is clearly important in the case of air pollution. However, without developing extensions to the formal model, the following line of argument is offered.

First, regarding adjustments to income, an extension of the *polluter pays principle* to the domain of national accounting seems appropriate. In other words, pollution damage caused in country B by emissions from country A should appear as a deduction from income in country A. In practice, this means that the estimates of the unit marginal social costs of pollution in a given country should include all costs, including those in other nations. These unit marginal costs should then be multiplied by the total level of emissions in that country. The argument for this treatment of transboundary pollution in the case of savings rules is, if anything, even stronger. Some portion of a given country's total savings should, *at least notionally*, be set aside in order to compensate the recipients of the pollution emitted and transferred across international boundaries.

4.5 Valuing air pollution in OECD Europe: empirical estimates

We wish to estimate the value of air pollution in Europe caused by carbon dioxide (CO_2), sulphur dioxide (SO_2), nitrogen oxides (NO_x) and particulate matter (PM_{10}). Data on the physical quantity of emissions of key pollutants are relatively easy to obtain in developed countries (see OECD, 1994a). However, these data alone can tell us little about what is economic, in the sense of optimally balancing the costs and benefits of pollution abatement. As the model implies, to achieve this we need to value units of emissions using marginal social costs. Some estimates of the marginal social costs per tonne emitted are shown in Table 4.3. These are drawn from an evaluation of the social cost of fuel cycles within Europe (CEC/US, 1993). The CO_2 estimate is from Fankhauser (1994).

Table 4.3 Marginal social costs per tonne of air pollutant emitted (US$)

	CO_2	SO_2	NO_x	PM_{10}
Health		1,530	470	10,350
Forestry		1,760	1,220	
Materials/ buildings		480	320	320
Climate change				
Total	7	3,770	2,010	10,670

Notes
Values refer to damage caused by a unit of UK emissions across Europe.
No entry indicates 'no effect', or 'not quantifiable'.

Source: CEC/US (1993).

The rows of Table 4.3 are the receptors (that is, receiving agents). These represent the ultimate effects of polluting activities on human health (respiratory problems), forestry (forest death), material and buildings damage (general soiling and corrosion). The corresponding prices indicate the marginal social cost of a tonne of pollutant *vis-à-vis* its impact on each receptor. Note that the figures refer to damages both inside and outside the polluting country.

Before combining these data with information on emissions, the methodology used in the CEC/US (1993) study will be described. The first issue is how emissions of pollutants are traced through to their impacts on receptors, and second, how these impacts are valued. The estimates in Table 4.3 are, in so far as is possible, approximations of marginal social costs and not simply the derivation of average damage costs caused by current emissions. The first point of discussion relates to the scientific part of CEC/US's work, analysing the *incremental* emissions from two hypothetical representative power stations in specific locations in Germany and in the United Kingdom. Incremental emissions are linked to impacts via dose-response functions. Although problems with this approach persist (see Pearce and ApSimon, 1995), with the aid of dispersion modelling techniques the transboundary effects of emissions in particular regions can be accounted for, when combined with data on the relevant population densities and characteristics in the areas where pollutants are deposited. The result is that the dose-response function expresses damage to receptors as a function of emissions: for example, an x per cent increase in emissions of PM_{10} causes y deaths.

The role of economic valuation techniques is to derive an appropriate value of these impacts, which can in turn be used to derive per unit social costs. This aspect of the CEC/US study will be described by receptor. Since the value of human health effects is derived solely with reference to studies using non-market valuation techniques we discuss this in more detail.

- *Human health.* The basis of estimation for health effects is the value of a statistical life (VSL). What is estimated is the willingness of individuals to pay to obtain a reduction in the probability of mortality. For example, if the average amount a person in a particular population at risk would be willing to pay to secure a reduction in the risk of dying by 1/1,000 is $1,000, then under a wide range of circumstances the VSL for that population would be $1 million, that is, the willingness to pay (WTP) divided by the change in risk. It should be noted that such an estimate would not take account of any altruistic motives individuals might have, for example, their WTP to reduce the risk to *other* people. VSL can be estimated by any of three main methodologies: (i) contingent valuation; (ii) wage-risk studies; and (iii) avertive behaviour (see Jones-Lee, 1976, 1989). The first method asks individuals to state their WTP using a range of survey techniques, while the latter two methods infer WTP from actual market behaviour. From an appraisal of available estimates CEC/US (1993) chose a central estimate of the value of a statistical life of approximately US$3.2 million (in 1991 prices). For a critique of this approach, see Broome (1978). Morbidity impacts were not valued; it should be borne in mind, however, that these may be significant (Pearce and Crowards, 1995; Dubourg, 1995).
- *Forestry.* The most obvious economic damage is forgone timber harvest. In addition, carbon sequestration services derived from the growing stock of timber are also lost. Both of these effects are accounted for here. The basis of the assessment of timber losses is the international timber price. The estimation behind the latter forgone benefit is explained below in the description of damage caused by emissions of carbon dioxide (CO_2).

- *Materials and buildings damage.* Estimation of these effects compares the costs of repair or replacement of building materials with and without the corrosion or soiling caused by air pollution emissions. Effects on welfare caused by damage to buildings that form the cultural heritage of a region are not considered.
- *Climate Change.* Climate change will have an impact on receptors such as human health and biodiversity. Using an estimate from Fankhauser (1994) we have accounted for global warming damage in the form of the social costs of carbon dioxide (CO_2) emissions. The absence of adequate time-series data on other greenhouse gases precluded their consideration. Although the mix of greenhouse gases varies from country to country, as a general rule carbon dioxide is the most important in terms of its total contribution to global warming.

Strictly speaking, these estimated damages are specific to emissions from the countries doing the polluting (in the case of Table 4.3, the UK). However, willingness to pay is closely linked to ability to pay. In order to value social costs in additional European countries, the unit marginal values in Table 4.3 are scaled across countries using the simple assumption that marginal valuations depend linearly on differences in income per capita. In reality the valuations in different countries will also depend on factors such as baseline pollution levels, the typical pollution content of a country's emissions and the population density in affected areas. There is ample scope, therefore, to improve these estimates as new data become available. In the case of the climate change problem, Fankhauser's estimate refers to the globalized social costs of CO_2 emissions and hence no adjustment is made to this estimate for different countries.

In addition, while it would have been possible to adopt other receptor damage estimates presented in CEC/US (1993), these would not have been relevant for present purposes. We are interested in those costs which affect future welfare, that is, the effects of air pollution emissions on assets. This is one rationale for excluding from the analysis damage caused directly to crops, since this is a loss of current output and does not directly affect future welfare (as opposed to indirect damage which might be the result of soil acidification that affects output in future periods). Within the receptors chosen, damages can legitimately refer to *either* marketed or non-marketed damages. This is worth stressing because, in the case of damage to marketed assets, it is extremely unlikely that any account has already been taken for these losses in conventional estimates of capital consumption allowances.

Using these prices for pollution emissions, we estimate both the value of the loss of environmental services as a proportion of total output and the measure of genuine saving. The period of analysis is the decade of the 1980s. The values in Table 4.3 are in 1990 prices, so in order translate these to previous years a deflator is required. Since CEC/US (1993) present prices in ECUs, the deflator chosen is an index of European Union (EU) GDP deflators weighted by the ratio of each member's GDP to the EU total. Not surprisingly, this index is dominated by price changes occurring in France, Germany, Italy and the UK. This adjustment does not account for a possibility suggested by Figure 4.7 – since countries typically overpolluted even more in the past, the marginal social costs were likely to be higher than the simple deflation of a 1990 price would suggest. These deflated unit values are scaled by the individual countries' per capita GDP in order to account for differing ability (and willingness) to pay.

4.5.1 Genuine saving in the United Kingdom

Savings ratios for the UK are plotted in Figure 4.8 for the period 1980 to 1990. Shown as a proportion of GDP, these display the successive deductions from gross saving proposed above, with 'Res. net saving' indicating traditional net saving less the value of resource depletion (based on Hamilton, 1994b).

On this measure the UK appears to have persistently undersaved during much of the 1980s. In the period 1980 to 1986 genuine savings rates were between –1.6 per cent and –3.1 per cent of GDP. This is a striking result and shows that, by simply beginning the process of redefining a nation's savings rates to be net of the depletion of non-renewable resources and the value of air pollution, inadequate provision to offset asset loss was made during the 1980s in the UK.

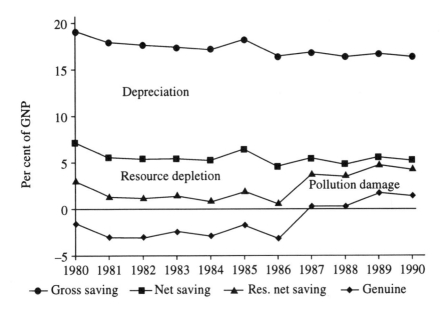

Figure 4.8   United Kingdom savings rates, 1980–1990

Of course, the caveat should be added that these numbers could be refined and that marginal social costs give an upwardly-biased estimate of the value of pollution emissions.

However, there are recent indications that the marginal social costs of PM_{10} emissions could be in excess of the levels used here (see Pearce and Crowards, 1995). These estimates also exclude the value of water pollution – the physical indications are that UK water quality declined somewhat during the latter part of the 1980s. Figure 4.8 also indicates that the gross savings ratio in the UK is less than 20 per cent of GDP for the entire period. This is low relative to the ratios prevailing in other European countries.

The measure of genuine saving indicates that the UK stopped dissaving towards the end of the period. Some of this increase is attributable to a reduction in the value of resource depletion, which in turn is in large part due to the reduction in world oil prices after 1986. Paradoxically, this conveys the impression that, other things being equal, a decrease in the price of oil raises genuine saving. Offsetting this is the fact that the remaining oil reserves are now a less valuable form of wealth, which could conceivably result in a lower level of future welfare. It can be shown that the capitalized value of these increased savings exactly equals the decrease in resource wealth associated with the fall in resource price.

Figure 4.9 displays in more detail the degree to which the value of air pollution damage has changed over the period (note that the curves are not

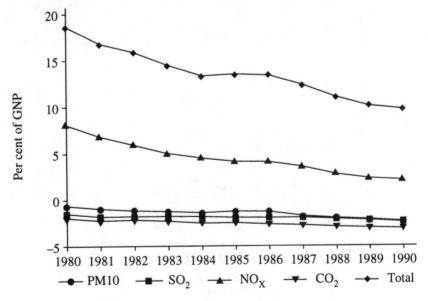

Figure 4.9   Air pollution damage in the United Kingdom, 1980–1990

cumulative). While damage caused by NO_x and CO_2 damages are a slightly declining proportion of GDP, PM_{10} and SO_2 damages fall more dramatically. In the latter case, these costs decrease from 2.6 per cent of GDP in 1980 to 1.5 per cent in 1990. This trend is largely attributable to a 23 per cent fall in the quantity of emissions over that time. In the next section we investigate the extent to which these trends were experienced in other European countries.

4.5.2   Saving experience in the rest of OECD Europe

The calculations in this section are based on the crude scaling, from the UK base of Table 4.3, of marginal social costs by per capita income in the countries of OECD Europe. The earlier caveats about these figures should therefore be recalled.

Table 4.4   Genuine saving as a percentage of GDP in Europe

Country	1980	1985	1990
Austria	11.4	8.8	13.1
Belgium	7.2	5.7	11.9
Luxembourg	8.4	10.3	15.6
Denmark	4.7	7.7	11.5
Finland	8.4	7.3	8.2
France	11.4	5.2	7.9
Germany	8.1	7.5	13.8
Greece	4.1	−3.4	−2.8
Ireland	−3.3	6.3	14.2
Italy	7.5	6.6	7.4
Netherlands	6.0	5.4	13.3
Norway	13.4	5.0	8.5
Portugal	−4.2	3.0	4.4
Spain	4.8	3.4	9.2
Switzerland	2.5	7.3	8.3
UK	−1.6	−1.7	1.4

Sources: Based on gross savings rates from World Bank (1993f) and depreciation from United Nations (1992).

Table 4.4 shows genuine savings rates for 16 European countries. These rates have been increasing in most of these countries, although the experience of Norway appears to one of a fall between the years 1980 and 1985 and a subsequent increase to 1990. Exceptions to this broad trend are (in addition to Norway) France and Greece, while Finland remains largely unchanged. Some of the reasons for increasing genuine saving rates are obvious. For those countries with relatively abundant oil (and gas) resources – the Netherlands, Norway and the UK – the fall in the oil price in the latter half of the 1980s is a significant factor. The key factor in most countries, however, was the decline in the value of emissions, as seen in Table 4.5.

Table 4.5   Air pollution damage as a percentage of GDP

Country	1980	1985	1990
Austria	2.7	1.9	1.2
Belgium	3.1	2.0	1.8
Luxembourg	4.1	3.6	2.0
Denmark	3.7	2.7	1.8
Finland	4.6	2.7	1.8
France	3.3	1.6	1.3
Germany	2.5	2.4	1.6
Greece	7.0	3.7	2.5
Ireland	5.9	4.3	4.0
Italy	4.7	2.6	2.3
Netherlands	2.1	1.6	1.5
Norway	2.5	1.7	1.5
Portugal	8.7	1.9	1.3
Spain	5.1	4.8	2.0
Switzerland	4.9	1.6	1.0
UK	4.7	3.7	3.0

Table 4.5 expresses the value of air pollution emissions as a proportion of GDP, thus giving an indication of the size of these losses across OECD Europe. As in the case of the UK, the picture is one of a declining value of pollution relative to output across the region, because of decreasing emissions of air pollutants during the period. In terms of marginal impacts per unit emitted, Table 4.3 indicated that PM_{10} is the most damaging pollutant. However, the magnitude of the total values of pollution emissions will obviously also depend on the quantity of each pollutant emitted. In this respect, although not shown in Table 4.5, SO_2 is the most significant pollutant over the period. Emissions of this pollutant fall quite steeply in all countries between 1980 and 1990 (as is obvious for the UK from Figure 4.9), probably because of country commitments with respect to the UN ECE First Sulphur Protocol.

Returning to the estimates of net saving in Table 4.4, the large negative net savings ratio indicated for Portugal in 1980 largely reflects the high value of PM_{10} emissions relative to GDP in that year – the return to positive net savings in subsequent periods is owing to the absence of data for emissions of PM_{10} in the years 1985 and 1990. (These data are also lacking for Denmark (1980) and Spain (1980 and 1990).) Table 4.5 shows Portuguese air pollution damages at some 8.7 per cent of GDP. This seems high, with the probable cause lying in the adoption of the estimates of marginal social costs based on UK emissions (weighted for differences in per capita income). We would also expect differences in population densities to play a significant role in explaining differences in these costs; the population density in the UK is about double that in Portugal. Furthermore, the dispersion of pollutants is also a key factor. The consideration of additional factors would go some way to correct this apparent anomaly. Similar comments apply to Ireland and Greece.

Greece exhibits negative genuine savings in 1985 and 1990. In contrast, Ireland shows an apparent increase in genuine savings of 17.5 per cent from 1980 to 1990. This latter finding is largely due to a transition from a relatively low gross savings ratio of 14 per cent in 1980 to 28 per cent in 1990. The former West Germany increases its genuine savings rate owing to a large fall in emissions of SO_2 and PM_{10}. While not part of this analysis, it is noteworthy that the former East Germany emitted PM_{10} at about three to four times West German levels.

4.6 Conclusions

We have argued that the most policy-relevant measure of progress towards sustainable development is the level of genuine savings. Given the complexity of the real world, as opposed to the necessarily simple models used by economists, it is often difficult to say what is the optimal savings rate for a given country. Issues concerning the efficiency and effectiveness of investment, as well as its level, are clearly important. That said, it remains true that savings rules provide useful one-sided tests of sustainability, in the sense that persistent negative genuine savings must lead to eventual declines in welfare.

The omissions in this empirical analysis are many: soils, gold, diamonds, natural gas (outside of OECD Europe), and water pollutants, to name a few. Notwithstanding these omissions, the empirical evidence is that genuine levels of saving are negative in a wide range of countries when the environment and natural resources are included in the savings measure. Negative genuine saving is more than a theoretical possibility, therefore, and the evidence is that many countries, particularly in Sub-Saharan Africa, are being progressively impoverished as a result of poor government policies.

The empirical application of green national accounting suggests that the value of air pollution emissions is a significant percentage of GDP for the countries of OECD Europe. While the use of marginal social costs to value pollution leads to upward bias in the estimates for recent years (assuming countries are overpolluting), there is reason to believe that this is offset at least partially in the estimates for the early 1980s by the higher marginal social costs associated with higher pollution emissions.

Finally, when these pollution value estimates are combined with the value of resource depletion, the resulting genuine savings rates are negative for several European OECD countries and years. This suggests that concerns about the sustainability of development should be taken seriously for developed, as well as for developing, countries. The good news is that pollution emissions are falling. An important question, therefore, is how close these countries are to the optimum level of pollution.

In terms of next steps there are obvious refinements that can be envisioned, including expanding the country coverage of data on willingness to pay for pollution reductions. This is particularly important for developing countries. As countries develop there has been an increasing tendency towards urbanization and the development of problem levels of pollution in these urban areas. The extension of this empirical work into the realm of water pollution will be increasingly important.

There is some evidence from panel data that there is an 'environmental Kuznets curve', that historically there has been a rise and fall in pollution levels as per capita income has increased (see, for instance, Shafik, 1994a and Seldon and Song, 1994). However, there is absolutely no evidence that this was the optimal development path, in the sense that good policies could have increased overall welfare by 'flattening' the Kuznets curve. Valuing pollution emissions and including them in measures of genuine saving will have an important role to play in ensuring that past policy mistakes are not repeated. Placing a value on these emissions will help to provide the information and the motivation for governments to act.

Appendix

This table presents the country-level estimates of genuine savings rates over the decade of the 1980s.

Table 4A.1   Genuine savings rates by country (percentages)

	Average 1980–85	1986	1987	1988	1989	1990
East Asia						
China	11.9	12.1	11.5	12.1	15.2	17.0
Indonesia	−2.3	−6.0	−0.7	1.8	8.1	3.4
South Korea	18.6	25.2	32.1	38.8	34.6	32.7
Malaysia	6.7	−1.1	13.0	13.6	11.1	11.5
Papua New Guinea	−7.9	−4.7	−10.9	−4.0	−9.3	−0.2
Philippines	9.7	5.6	3.5	5.6	7.0	6.2
Thailand	11.6	13.6	15.8	19.7	21.8	23.7
Latin America and the Caribbean						
Argentina	2.5	1.5	4.1	7.7	−3.5	7.3
Belize	9.6	13.3	12.8	12.5	12.8	20.4
Bolivia	−46.2	−49.3	−43.5	−35.9	−35.4	−31.8
Brazil	4.4	3.5	8.8	12.3	15.7	10.4
Chile	−2.9	−2.4	3.4	5.9	3.5	6.2
Colombia	2.1	1.4	4.9	5.4	2.1	2.2
Costa Rica	4.9	14.1	10.3	8.5	7.7	9.4
Dominican Republic	8.6	7.1	9.7	13.8	18.0	13.9
Ecuador	−14.8	−21.9	−14.0	−17.0	−18.6	−19.6
Guatemala	0.7	−1.8	−4.8	−4.1	−2.8	−2.4
Guyana	−26.1	−17.1	−52.6	−51.9	−46.6	−71.7
Haiti	1.9	1.7	3.5	2.4	1.6	2.6
Honduras	−4.8	−1.8	0.2	3.5	−2.3	1.0
Jamaica	−22.4	−17.6	−9.9	0.9	−11.1	−11.7
Mexico	−1.1	−9.1	0.9	−0.8	1.3	2.4
Panama	13.2	11.2	10.7	5.0	−8.9	6.2
Paraguay	5.5	−1.1	−9.1	−2.8	6.6	0.6
Peru	−1.1	−6.4	−3.0	−14.6	−11.2	−11.9
Suriname	−2.7	−15.2	18.6	7.5	3.2	−6.1
Trinidad and Tobago	−9.7	−25.1	−17.4	−25.4	−22.6	−13.7
Venezuela	−13.9	−23.4	−14.7	−15.7	−27.8	−19.1

Table 4A.1   continued

	Average 1980–85	1986	1987	1988	1989	1990
North Africa and Middle East						
Algeria	0.4	–1.0	4.4	–5.6	–5.5	–1.9
Egypt	–11.1	–11.2	–7.2	–2.9	–8.4	–12.1
Iran	–3.9	3.6	0.4	–7.2	–5.6	–3.4
Morocco	4.5	11.1	12.9	11.0	7.4	13.8
Oman	–24.7	–51.3	–22.0	–43.9	–36.7	–27.3
Syria	0.2	–4.0	–6.5	–10.7	–0.5	1.6
Tunisia	0.4	–5.2	3.7	5.7	4.1	7.3
UAE	3.6	–19.1	–2.4	–8.0	–22.0	–23.1
South Asia						
Bangladesh	1.1	0.3	2.8	2.8	1.5	1.7
India	7.4	8.3	9.5	9.7	8.8	9.8
Pakistan	7.7	6.3	8.1	6.1	6.3	5.2
Sub-Saharan Africa						
Burundi	–2.9	–1.5	3.4	–1.4	4.8	1.3
Cameroon	6.1	–3.2	–0.5	–4.3	–9.4	–10.2
Congo	–28.5	–68.7	–36.2	–51.0	–41.6	–44.9
Ivory Coast	–5.8	–9.7	–13.7	–12.9	–16.8	–20.8
Ethiopia	3.0	7.8	6.4	7.4	2.6	1.4
Ghana	–12.4	–3.9	–3.3	–2.3	–2.2	–4.7
Kenya	4.6	6.9	4.5	6.1	3.1	3.3
Madagascar	–13.3	–14.3	–19.0	–19.0	–17.3	–20.2
Mali	–8.9	–4.6	1.4	1.3	2.2	3.8
Mauritania	–13.3	–17.7	–9.5	–2.9	–8.3	–7.7
Niger	2.4	4.6	–5.3	6.0	–3.5	–5.7
Nigeria	–12.8	–23.8	–31.3	–38.0	–41.2	–28.7
Rwanda	7.7	8.3	5.3	5.1	4.2	4.1
Senegal	–12.4	–7.1	–2.8	–0.5	–1.6	3.0
Sierra Leone	–1.5	–6.8	–10.7	–7.6	–9.1	–10.4
Zambia	–36.6	–70.4	–84.5	–96.3	–65.8	–65.1
Zimbabwe	1.8	3.6	3.7	9.7	5.5	4.4

5   International trade and sustainability

The role of international trade in sustainable development has come under recent scrutiny. By relaxing domestic natural resource constraints, international trade allows any particular country to deplete natural assets abroad by importing its natural resource requirements. Rees and Wackernagel (1994), among others, have argued that this is one aspect of the so-called 'ecological footprint' of a country on its trading partners in the global economy: that is, that resources are appropriated from elsewhere in order to satisfy domestic economic activity. One possible pathway is explored in Chapter 8. Basically, any economywide policy (including the liberalization of trade) that enhances economic growth, may lead to greater environmental damage, by magnifying the effects of market, policy and institutional imperfections that already existed in the economy.

Thus far, few attempts have been made to underpin these interactions with a conceptual framework. Yet, the analysis of the connection between domestic economic activity and the use of the environment in countries supplying imports for the domestic market, is uniquely suited to green national accounting. In this chapter, we emphasize this suitability in two ways. First, we use a theoretical accounting model to address the question of international trade and sustainability. We argue that, at least in the specific case of trade in commercial natural resources, the onus is on resource-extracting countries to make provision for the loss of domestic natural assets whether for export or not. Nevertheless, we suggest that an analysis of the degree to which (primarily) developed countries rely on imports of natural resources from (primarily) developing countries may serve other policy uses. Here, we extend another technique used in green national accounting, that of input–output analysis, to examine these interactions.

5.1   'Ecological footprints' and trade
The notion of ecological footprints or appropriated carrying capacity has been articulated in a number of ways. One example has been proposed by Rees and Wackernagel (1994) who argue that the sustainability of an individual country can be viewed in terms of the aggregate land area required to meet the needs of its population. These needs can be expressed in a number of ways, such as the land required to satisfy nutritional requirements or by converting fossil energy into land required to grow the equivalent biofuel (or some amalgam of the two). The contention is that industrialized countries can only meet these requirements by appropriating the carrying capacity of other countries: for example, by importing natural resources. To the extent that these resource-importing countries

are drawing on 'true ecological surpluses' elsewhere – that is, from countries not exceeding their own carrying capacity – this trade will not affect global or regional sustainability. Yet, the claim is that these countries are developing at the expense of their trading partners whose own sustainable development prospects are constrained by the need to appropriate carrying capacity from elsewhere.

Rather than increasing opportunities via mutually beneficial trade, Rees and Wackernagel (1994) contend that a development strategy based on international trade is at best a zero-sum game. In terms of the measurement of this process, the required indicator would measure the ecological footprint of a country *vis-à-vis* its trading partners.

The main role of the 'footprints' notion appears to be the provision of a rhetorical focus for the concerns of those who believe that sustainable development is threatened by the flow of goods and services across international boundaries. The policy implication appears to be that countries should aim for self-sufficiency. That a country may be sustainable by following this route is a possibility. However, it is extremely unlikely that a sustainable level of welfare will be maximized by this strategy.

Attempts to provide a conceptual basis for ecological footprints have attempted to explain mechanisms by which developed countries are overconsuming in supporting their domestic economies (see, for example, Andersson, Folke and Nyström, 1995). Most importantly, we need to define what we mean by overconsumption. One definition is offered by the concept of genuine saving – namely the gross savings rate adjusted for the loss of assets such as natural and produced capital (see Hamilton, 1994a; Pearce and Atkinson, 1993; World Bank, 1995a). Overconsumption can therefore be defined as persistently negative genuine savings. On this basis a country is overconsuming because it is not making adequate provision to offset the loss of assets (including resource depletion and environmental degradation). The question is, how does international trade affect this definition of saving?

5.2   International trade and sustainable development

5.2.1   Transboundary pollution

Emissions of pollutants such as carbon dioxide (CO_2) and sulphur dioxide (SO_2) in any one country can lead to transboundary pollution and the generation of social costs in other countries (in addition to those costs of these emissions borne at home). Of course, this is not international trade as such, although this pollution may be the result of the production of goods for foreign markets. Yet, in one sense, this can be viewed as a type of negative trade inflicting uncompensated damages on affected countries.

Hence, Chapter 4 argued that the value of a country's contribution to climate change – as assessed by valuing that country's CO_2 emissions – should be charged as depreciation regardless of where damage actually occurs. This is an extension of an international *polluter pays principle* to the domain of national accounting. These values should be deducted from measures of economic welfare, green net domestic or national product and, by the same token, genuine savings. In the latter case, the argument for this treatment of transboundary pollution is even stronger. Some portion of a given country's total savings should, at least notionally, be set aside in order to compensate the recipients of the pollution emitted and transferred across international boundaries.

5.2.2 International trade in natural resources

A second type of problem concerns international trade in commercial natural resources, where extraction of a resource in one country is ultimately for use in another country. The alleged importer of sustainability, it is claimed, is any country which imports its resources: for example, the oft-cited example of Japanese imports of timber resources from the Far East. It is argued that while Japan looks sustainable this is achieved at the expense of, say, Indonesia and Malaysia. Similarly, trade in non-renewable resources has also been interpreted in this way. The key question is that while international trade is one proximate cause of the depletion of commercial natural resources does this necessarily imply that measures of sustainability should reflect these trade flows?

The question of sustainability and external trade in natural resources has been explored in models by Asheim (1986) and Hartwick (1994). Both show that if exporters of non-renewable natural resources invest all of the rents on resource extraction in produced capital (the 'Hartwick rule'), then consumption will increase. This contrasts with the closed economy result, where the Hartwick rule produces constant consumption. Hartwick (1994) then shows that investing some amount less than the full resource rent will produce a constant consumption path.

These results depend on the fact that resource prices are determined endogenously in the models and must therefore follow the 'Hotelling rule', that the resource rental rates (which are equal to the resource prices in these models) must increase at a percentage rate equal to the endogenously determined interest rate. As a result there is a terms-of-trade effect that leads to increasing consumption under the Hartwick rule for resource exporters. Hartwick (1994) goes on to develop a partial equilibrium analysis of a price-taking resource exporter. In this model the economy is assumed to have only one activity, the extraction of natural resources, and these resources are wholly exported. For constant resource price and international interest rate, the investment of resource rents offshore leads to constant consumption.

The model of a price-taking resource exporter is extended in Appendix 5.1 to a more complex economy that both consumes and exports natural resources, while engaging in other productive activity. As long as this economy is a price-taker with regard to its exports of natural resources, the investment of total resource rents on both domestically consumed and exported resources leads to constant consumption.

Since resource-exporting countries can be considered to be price-takers for most natural resources, the conclusion from the theoretical models is that persistent negative genuine savings, including the depreciation of produced assets and the depletion of natural resources (whether for export or not) still leads to unsustainable development. There are some notable exceptions to this assumption of price-taking, such as diamonds in South Africa. OPEC has been a relatively unsuccessful cartel when changes in real oil prices are taken into consideration.

The expression of green national accounting questions as an optimal control problem is a familiar aspect of the literature and indeed provides the basis for the theoretical treatment in Chapter 3. Many empirical applications rely explicitly on some control formulation to underpin the revised income aggregates to be estimated (see, for example, Adger and Grohs, 1994; Crowards, 1996). Setting out the initial problem in this way is a useful means of obtaining insights into the welfare effects of resource use (and environmental change) and does lead to an important policy implication in the presence of international trade: each country, developed or developing, needs to ensure that its genuine savings are not persistently negative.

Nevertheless, it is of considerable interest to trace the extent to which economic activity in (primarily) developed economies is dependent on resource imports from (primarily) developing countries. A number of policy considerations can be called upon to motivate further analysis of the extent to which resources are traded across international borders. For example:

a. a given country might be interested as to the extent to which it is responsible for resource depletion elsewhere in terms of whether its trading partners are overextracting or pursuing appropriate compensating investment strategies to secure sustainable development;
b. this extraction may cause external effects in the exporting countries – this motivates some of the work undertaken by the Dutch Central Statistical Office (see, for example, Hueting, Bosch and de Boer, 1992);
c. domestic environmental policies, such as encouraging increased energy efficiency, will have impacts on countries that supply fossil fuel resources;
d. any given resource-importing country may also be concerned about the eventual exhaustion of the resources that it currently imports.

In order to examine the degree to which countries are reliant on imports of resources we need to move to develop an empirical framework to model these flows. One promising policy use of green national accounts is the extension of input–output analysis. For example, resource and pollutant flow accounts are generally conceived as physical extensions to the (monetary) input–output (I/O) accounts. Each production and final demand sector in the I/O tables is associated with a physical flow of natural resources, typically as inputs such as energy to production processes, and a physical flow of wastes and emissions. Characteristically, this technique has been used to analyse domestic environmental issues such attributing industrial waste emissions to final demand sectors.

In the case of international trade, we need to attribute resource depletion to the country where it eventually goes to support (domestic) final demand. In an adaptation and extension of the framework originally used in Proops and Atkinson (1995) we wish to estimate the portion of domestically extracted resources that are either exported *directly* – for example, crude oil – or *indirectly* through embodiment in produced goods destined for markets abroad.

Our framework is set out below, but first it is useful to define two indicators that will be useful in elucidating these issues

1. We denote by N the consumption of *total domestic resource depletion* required to support GDP. This is simply the value of depletion of domestically extracted resources familiar in green national accounting (see, for example, Hamilton, 1994). It is useful to note that N has two components: N_d is domestic resource depletion and N_x is resource depletion exported abroad.
2. The second measure N^* is the *global resource consumption* required to support domestic final demand (that is, consumption plus investment). This includes both domestic natural resource depletion (N_d) and foreign depletion imported directly or indirectly (N_m).

Note, then, that N^* therefore excludes the (total) domestic resources used to produce exports, and includes all of the foreign resources consumed in making up some portion of domestic final demand.

Next we define $[N-N^*]$. A positive dollar value of $[N-N^*]$ indicates that a country's use (that is, consumption) of global resources to support its own domestic final demand is *less* than the total resources it uses (that is, depletes) to support its GDP. In other words, $[N-N^*] > 0$ indicates that the value of domestic resources used to produce exports is greater than the value of imported foreign resource depletion. Examples of these countries are likely to be the oil producers such as Saudi Arabia. Conversely, examples of countries that are likely to have a negative dollar value of $[N-N^*]$ are Japan and the United States.

5.3   Measuring Direct and Indirect International Flows of Resources

As an illustration of this approach we consider a simple two-country global economy (see also Appendix). The basic accounting identities for these countries are:

$$X_{12} - X_{21} + C_1 + I_1 = Y_1$$
$$X_{21} - X_{12} + C_2 + I_2 = Y_2$$

where, Y_i is total output (or GNP); C_i is consumption in country i; I_i is investment in country i and; X_{ij} are the exports from country i to country j.

Relating the imports into each country to the GNP of that country, we define the following import coefficients:

$$q_{ij} \equiv \frac{X_{ij}}{Y_j}.$$

So we can write:

$$X_{ij} = q_{ij} Y_j.$$

Substituting for X_{ij} in the above accounting identities and rewriting in matrix form we obtain,

$$\begin{pmatrix} -q_{21} & q_{12} \\ q_{21} & -q_{12} \end{pmatrix} \begin{pmatrix} Y_1 \\ Y_2 \end{pmatrix} + \begin{pmatrix} C_1 + I_1 \\ C_2 + I_2 \end{pmatrix} = \begin{pmatrix} Y_1 \\ Y_2 \end{pmatrix}.$$

This result can be generalized to several countries giving,

$$q_{ij} = \left[\begin{array}{c} \dfrac{X_{ij}}{Y_j}, \quad i \neq j \\[2ex] \dfrac{-\sum_k X_{kj}}{Y_j}, \quad i = j \end{array} \right]$$

This generalization to several countries permits the calculation of Y in each country based on the domestic final demand $(C + I)$ in all countries.

5.3.1   The global trading economy in 1985

The following empirical application describes the global trading economy in 1985. This is made up of 95 individual countries (OECD – 23; Soviet Union and Eastern Europe – 8; Africa – 23; Central and South America – 18; Middle East – 11; Asia – 11; Oceania – 1). The remaining trading blocs are residual regions, namely: the 'Rest of Africa', the 'Rest of Central and South America', the 'Rest of Asia' and the 'Rest of Oceania'.

Data on the depletion of commercial natural resources and gross national product (GNP or Y) are taken from Hamilton (1995). Trade flows data can be found in OECD (1994a). Our Q-matrix describes trade flows between OECD countries (excluding Iceland and Turkey) – which we denote as OECD–21 – and the rest of the world. Note that this does not describe direct flows of trade between non-OECD–21 countries: for example, between Saudi Arabia and Brazil. Zero entries are therefore ascribed to these portions of the matrix. We would in any case expect such entries to be relatively small and thus make little difference to our estimation of the extent to which developed countries (OECD–21) rely on resources imported from developing countries (non-OECD–21).

Some important caveats to this empirical analysis need to be borne in mind, not least the relatively high degree of aggregation that we have used. Underlying this is an assumption that the value of resource depletion in a dollar of exports is equivalent to the value of resource depletion in a dollar of GNP. This will probably understate resource exports (and thereby imports). It is likely that a greater proportion of the exports of, say, oil producers will be made up of resources. Second, it is also likely that traded produced goods (for example, heavy manufacturing) are more resource intensive than non-traded goods (for example, some light manufactures and services).

Table 5.1 presents the main results of the model for the year 1985. These results are presented in terms of dollar values of $[N–N^*]$ where N is a country's total domestic resource depletion required to support GNP and N^* is the same country's consumption of global resources required to support domestic final demand. For brevity, we might also characterize economies in the following way: (i) countries where $[N–N^*] < 0$ can be defined as net consumers ('importers') of global resources and; (ii) countries where $[N–N^*] > 0$ can be defined as net exporters of resources (to support final demand in the rest of the world).

The results show that countries for which $[N–N^*] < 0$ are primarily from the OECD–21 countries as we would expect. In total, 43 countries share this characteristic. Of these: 17 are OECD–21 countries (and 19 are OECD–23); 4 are from Central and Eastern Europe; 7 are from Africa; 4 are from Central and South America; 2 are from the Middle East; 6 are from Asia; and, finally, 1 is from Oceania.

OECD–21 Japan exhibits the largest negative value of $[N–N^*]$, equivalent to $11,823 million (m). Japan has few resources of its own and hence practically all of the resources that it must consume to support $C + I$ are imported. Indeed, this imported portion of resource consumption (N_m) amounts to some 2.1 per cent of total *global* resource depletion. Similarly, 2.3 per cent of the value of global resource depletion is attributable to supporting the USA's domestic final demand, such that, despite significant domestic resources, the USA's value of N^* exceeds that of N by \$6,715m. Canada too, it would appear, is a net importer of global resources although the degree to which $N^* > N$ is small relative to many of the other OECD–21 countries. Nevertheless, given Canada's considerable commercial natural resources (including oil) this result is something of a surprise.

While our OECD–21 countries predominately consume significantly more global resources to support domestic final demand than they deplete domestically to support GNP, four nations are an exception to this. In the case of Norway and the United Kingdom this position is easily explained by the oil resources owned by these countries. In the Netherlands, with less oil but significant quantities of natural gas, it also appears that $N^* < N$. Finally, resource rich, Australia also depletes more resources to support economic activity abroad than it itself consumes to support economic activity in its domestic economy.

Soviet Union and Eastern Europe   According to our data set, only the former Soviet Union and Romania have significant commercial natural resources in terms of the absolute value of domestic resource depletion. Indeed, the USSR is a large net exporter of resource depletion (just below \$2,100m). Interestingly, net exporters of resource depletion in this region are Romania, Hungary and (former) East Germany. The latter two countries having few resources only marginally fall into this category.

Table 5.1   Global resource consumption: $N–N^*$ *(\$ million)*

Country	$N–N^*$ (\$m)
OECD–21	
Canada	–233.2
United States	–6,715.7
Japan	–11,823.4
Australia	182.8
New Zealand	–112.1
Austria	–462.9
Belgium/Luxembourg	–1,349.0
Denmark	–359.0
Finland	–471.2
France	–4,094.0
Germany	–4,248.2
Greece	–669.8
Ireland	–110.5

Table 5.1   continued

Country	N–N* ($m)
Italy	−4,440.5
Netherlands	1,284.5
Norway	1,779.1
Portugal	−370.3
Spain	−1,949.3
Sweden	−652.6
Switzerland	−662.5
United Kingdom	472.1
Other OECD	
Iceland	−17.2
Turkey	−98.2
Soviet Union and Eastern Europe	
Soviet Union	2,092.6
Yugoslavia	−27.7
East Germany	9.0
Bulgaria	−23.3
Czechoslovakia	−35.2
Hungary	2.7
Poland	−40.2
Romania	127.9
Africa	
Algeria	1,557.6
Burkina Faso	−2.4
Cameroon	435.9
Chad	2.3
Congo	491.8
Ivory Coast	129.7
Egypt, Arab Rep.	648.0
Ghana	7.6
Libya	2,992.6
Madagascar	9.4
Malawi	11.6
Mali	−0.5
Mauritania	29.9

Table 5.1   continued

Country	N–N* ($m)
Morocco	–3.9
Mozambique	–0.4
Nigeria	1,848.1
South Africa	–97.4
Sudan	0.4
Tunisia	102.2
Zaire	272.8
Zambia	123.0
Zimbabwe	–5.6
Rest of Africa	508.6
Central and South America	
Argentina	135.7
Bahamas, The	–22.5
Bolivia	32.4
Brazil	658.3
Chile	91.4
Colombia	78.5
Costa Rica	–2.2
Ecuador	473.3
Guatemala	–8.1
Guyana	5.3
Honduras	13.5
Jamaica	29.9
Mexico	3,011.1
Paraguay	16.4
Peru	250.9
Suriname	15.6
Trinidad and Tobago	246.3
Venezuela	2,294.2
Rest of America	–244.5
Middle East	
Bahrain	25.5
Iran, Islamic Rep.	877.4
Iraq	1,689.9

Table 5.1   continued

Country	N–N* ($m)
Israel	–125.9
Kuwait	1,277.4
Oman	1,272.2
Qatar	998.6
Saudi Arabia	3,800.0
Syrian Arab Republic	46.9
United Arab Emirates	3,365.5
Jordan	–90.0
Asia	
Brunei	607.0
China	361.8
Hong Kong	–176.0
India	–9.9
Indonesia	2,753.7
Korea, Republic	–289.5
Malaysia	867.6
Pakistan	–60.2
Philippines	–40.5
Singapore	–182.0
Taiwan	–170.4
Thailand	46.1
Rest of Asia	13.0
Oceania	
Papua New Guinea	41.2
Other Oceania	–21.3

Africa   Of the 23 countries surveyed, 17 of these are net exporters of resource depletion. The most significant among these are the oil producers. These countries include Algeria, the Congo, Libya and Nigeria. Libya has the fourth largest absolute (negative) dollar value of [N–N*] in our 99-country sample. Similarly, Nigeria and Algeria also rank highly in terms of the dollar value of resources exported in order to support final demand in the rest of world. For the Congo, this magnitude is far lower: $494m. Nevertheless, in terms of the size of Congo's GNP, it can be shown that the proportion of resources exported in order to support final demand in the rest of world is some 24 per cent. (For Libya this value is 12 per cent.)

The depletion of timber resources also figure in the estimation of $[N-N^*]$ for several African countries. Timber exporters include Cameroon, the Ivory Coast and Zaire. In Cameroon, $[N-N^*]$ is equivalent to $436 million. The N_x portion of this – that is, exports of resource depletion – is more than 5 per cent of GNP. In the case of Zaire (and Zambia) the positive value of $[N-N^*]$ is also explained by trade in copper resources.

Central and South America   Again, the most significant positive dollar values are among the oil producers. Hence, Ecuador, Mexico, Peru, Trinidad and Tobago and Venezuela have dollar values of $[N-N^*]$ in the region of $250m (Peru) to just over $3,000m (Mexico). Indeed, the positive Mexican $[N-N^*]$ is the third largest in our sample. Another significant 'net exporter' is Brazil ($[N-N^*] = $658m).

Net importers of resource depletion include, perhaps surprisingly, Costa Rica, although the (negative) dollar value is not significant at $2.2m. These (few) net importers are primarily made up of small island economies such as the Bahamas and many of the countries making the 'Rest' of the region.

Middle East   Not surprisingly, the Middle East is dominated by relatively large positive dollar values of $[N-N^*]$. For example, Saudi Arabia ($3,800m) and United Arab Emirates ($3,366m) rank first and second in terms of those countries where more resources are depleted to support economic activity abroad (or own GDP) than are consumes to support economic activity in its domestic economy. In addition, Iraq ($1,690m), Kuwait ($1,277m), Oman ($1,272m), Qatar ($999m) and Iran ($877m) dominate the 56 countries exhibiting positive dollar values of $[N-N^*]$. Syria and Bahrain have relatively few oil resources but nevertheless remain net exporters, if only marginally so.

Asia   This region presents the most varied of results. Of the 13 countries examined, 6 are net exporters of resource depletion.

The largest dollar value of $[N-N^*]$ is Indonesia ($2,754m). Other large positive values are found for Malaysia, Brunei and China. In the case of Brunei, exported resource depletion amounts to some 16 per cent of its GNP. While Brunei's position is overwhelmingly due to the depletion of oil, for Malaysia, Indonesia and China, $N^* < N$ is also explained by timber and zinc exports.

Asia is characterized by rapidly industrializing economies. Of these countries, Singapore, Hong Kong and Taiwan have little or no domestic natural resources. Not surprisingly, these countries rely on significant imports of resources from the rest of the world to support their domestic economies.

5.3.2   The impact on individual countries

Table 5.2 describes the extent to which a particular country relies on importing resources from the rest of the world to support its domestic final demand. It would also be interesting to find the individual countries from which, say, Japan's reliance on resource imports predominately derives. For example, N_{jap}^* describes the dollar value of resources that Japan uses to support its domestic final demand. In turn, $N_{jap}^* - N_{jap,d}$ describes the value of resources depletion that is imported from other countries. This term, $N_{jap,m}$ can be further disaggregated into individual countries (from our sample) where these imports originated (that is, were extracted). Hence, we will be able to appraise our initial proposition that Japan relies on consuming resources from Indonesia and Malaysia to support its domestic economy.

Table 5.2   Japan: imported resource requirements

Country	Resource exports to Japan ($m)	% of total resource exports	% of GNP of exporter
Imports from			
Brunei	528.0	40.3	13.8
Qatar	679.4	25.0	9.9
United Arab Emirates	2,493.2	23.8	8.5
Oman	1,071.0	23.7	11.4
Malaysia	385.9	10.5	1.2
Indonesia	1,500.2	9.4	1.7
Mauritania	8.4	8.4	1.2
Saudi Arabia	1,861.7	7.8	1.9
Zambia	46.3	7.4	2.0

Source: Atkinson and Hamilton (1996).

Table 5.2 indicates that Japan imports resource depletion valued at $1,500m from Indonesia (equivalent to 1.7 per cent of Indonesian GNP). For Malaysia, this magnitude is somewhat lower at $386m although this still corresponds to some 1.2 per cent of Malaysian GNP. The degree to which Japan relies on imports from Indonesia and Malaysia is large but perhaps not overwhelmingly so. Indeed, in absolute dollar terms, the United Arab Emirates (UAE) and Saudi Arabia have the largest values in column 1 of Table 5.2. For UAE, the resource depletion that it exports to Japan account for 24 per cent of its total resource exports and 8.5 per cent of its GNP. For Brunei these proportions are higher still:

some 40 per cent of Brunei's total exports of resource depletion and 14 per cent of Brunei's GNP.

Tables 5.3 and 5.4 repeat this exercise for both the USA and the European Union (EU). Table 5.3 indicates that the USA imports its resources primarily from countries in South and Central America. In particular, Mexico and Venezuela where the value of resource exports to support the US economy are $2,425m and $1,448m respectively. For Mexico, this amounts to some 10 per cent of total resource exports and 1.4 per cent of GNP. In Ecuador, the value of resource depletion that is required to support the USA's domestic final demand is some 3.7 per cent of Ecuador's GNP and almost 16 per cent of its total resource exports. For the Congo, these proportions are 13.6 per cent and 25.2 per cent respectively.

Table 5.3   United States: imported resource requirements

Country	Resource exports to USA ($m)	% of total resource exports	% of GNP of exporter
Imports from			
Congo	276.4	25.2	13.6
Ecuador	408.3	15.6	3.7
Trinidad and Tobago	208.6	13.6	2.5
Jamaica	23.1	11.0	1.1
Mexico	2,424.8	10.0	1.4
Venezuela	1,447.5	9.3	2.2
United Arab Emirates	369.3	3.5	1.3

Source: Atkinson and Hamilton (1996).

Resource exports from the Congo are also significant for the EU. Indeed, Table 5.4 identifies a number of African countries on which the EU relies for resources to support EU final demand. Most significantly Libya, both in absolute terms and in proportion to total resource exports and GNP. In terms of proportions of total resource trade and GNP, the results for Cameroon (19.6 and 4.2 per cent), Mauritania (21.5 and 3.1 per cent), Zambia (9.5 and 2.6 per cent), Zaire (11.7 and 2.3 per cent) and Algeria (13.3 and 2 per cent) are all notable.

It is interesting to note that direct and indirect international flows of resources are not the only traded form of asset loss. Just as natural resources can be imported indirectly, so too will the depreciation of produced capital be embodied in imports of produced goods. As this also reflects an asset loss, it might be useful to bring this into our analysis. Analogous indicators to N and N^* could be constructed and quantified: that is, D – *total domestic produced capital* *depreciation* required to support GNP; and D^* – *global produced capital depreciation* required to support domestic final demand. Atkinson and Hamilton (1996) calculate that Japan and Germany are both large 'net exporters' of produced capital depreciation. In contrast, the USA and to a lesser extent the United Kingdom are 'net importers'.

Table 5.4   European Union (EU–15): imported resource requirements

Country	Resource exports to EU ($m)	% of total resource Exports	% of GNP of exporter
Imports from			
Libya	2,688.9	29.4	10.4
Congo	195.3	17.8	9.6
Cameroon	352.2	19.6	4.2
Iraq	1,364.6	10.7	3.5
Kuwait	870.1	11.0	3.3
Mauritania	21.6	21.5	3.1
Qatar	205.5	7.6	3.0
Zambia	59.7	9.5	2.6
Zaire	182.5	11.7	2.3
Egypt, Arab Republic	636.2	7.8	2.1
Algeria	1,160.1	13.3	2.0
Nigeria	1,314.2	9.8	1.6
Ivory Coast	98.7	23.8	1.5

Source: Atkinson and Hamilton (1996).

Tables 5.2 to 5.4 demonstrate linkages via resource trade between the USA, Japan and EU and the developing (or industrializing) world. Reference to Table 4A.1 in Chapter 4 indicates that many of these countries have experienced negative rates of genuine saving over the 1980s. What we have argued is that countries are individually responsible for the prudent management of their own assets (in this chapter and in Chapters 3 and 4). This means that demonstrating, for example, that Developed Country A imports significant quantities of resources from Developing Country B does not in turn demonstrate that A is responsible for B's negative genuine saving (if this is the case). Nevertheless, it is interesting to speculate what policy implications might be inferred from modelling resource trade. One mechanism proposed by Atkinson and Hamilton (1996) is via the bilateral aid of resource importers. Developed countries provide significant amounts of development assistance to other countries and may be concerned about its effectiveness when recipients are on an unsustainable path. This in turn raises the question of targeting of at least some of this development assistance: e.g. 'policy-based' loans or grants with conditionality aimed at policy reform, specifically to augment genuine savings (see Chapter 8).

5.4   Conclusions

The argument that international trade in resources is one cause of unsustainable development has been used to support the construction of indicators of sustainability that take into account the fact that developed countries rely on imports of natural resources mainly from developing countries. The extent to which this is the case is said to be indicative of a developed country's ecological footprint. Although this notion has a popular appeal, we have argued that it has yet to be adequately explored as a basis for indicator work. The demonstration of a formal link between sustainable development and resource trade has been investigated in a separate literature using theoretical green national accounting models. There it is proposed that terms-of-trade effects alter the savings requirements implied by the conventional closed-economy Hartwick rule. Nevertheless, we have shown that the attainment of a constant consumption path given for a resource-extracting country is still to be achieved by reinvesting resource rents regardless of whether for export or not.

Yet, the measurement of the degree to which resource depletion is traded internationally can be motivated by other policy concerns (not unconnected to the question of achieving sustainability). In response to this, our empirical computations have measured the degree to which countries rely on consuming global resources to support domestic final demands. Not surprisingly, these countries turn out to be primarily developed nations (or OECD–21) such as Japan, the USA and the majority of EU countries. Our results also permit the identification of those nations upon which resource importers significantly depend. With respect to policy, the extent to which these importing countries are concerned about the sustainability of exporters suggests a possible role for additional bilateral aid in assisting, where needed, the fulfilment of genuine savings requirements, although we have noted some caveats to this argument.

Appendix 5.1   A price-taking resource exporter

As noted above, Hartwick (1994) provided a partial equilibrium analysis of an 'oil kingdom' that only produces oil and invests all of the rents abroad. This model yielded constant consumption assuming a fixed resource price and fixed international interest rate.

To generalize this model, assume that the country is a price-taker for resource exports, that extracted resource quantity R_2 is exported, and that quantity R_1 is used domestically. To make the model tractable we require that the resource be extracted from two distinct deposits of size S_1 and S_2, with extraction cost functions $f_1(R_1)$ and $f_2(R_2)$. The quantities extracted are assumed to be unequal in general, but both must decrease to zero asymptotically in order to exhaust the total stocks of resources over an infinite time horizon. The export price is assumed to be constant at p. The neoclassical production function is $F(K, R_1)$, for produced capital stock K; population is assumed to be constant, so that labour can be factored out of the production function. For utility function $U = U(C)$ and constant pure rate of time preference r, the problem for the social planner is to maximize the present value of utility as follows:

$$\max \int_0^\infty U(C)e^{-rt}dt \text{ subject to:}$$

$$\dot{K} = F(K, R_1) - C - f_1(R_1) - f_2(R_2) + pR_2$$
$$\dot{S}_1 = -R_1$$
$$\dot{S}_2 = -R_2.$$

Here consumption C and resource extraction R_1 and R_2 are the control variables. The current value Hamiltonian for this problem is,

$$H = U + \gamma_K(F - C - f_1(R_1) - f_2(R_2) + pR_2) - \gamma_1 R_1 - \gamma_2 R_2,$$

where γ_K is the shadow price of produced capital and γ_1 and γ_2 are the shadow prices of the resources in their distinct deposits. The first-order conditions for a maximum are:

$$\frac{\partial H}{\partial C} = 0 = U_C - \gamma_K \Rightarrow \gamma_K = U_C$$

$$\frac{\partial H}{\partial R_1} = 0 = \gamma_K F_{R_1} - \gamma_K f_1' - \gamma_1 \Rightarrow \gamma_1 = U_C\left(F_{R_1} - f_1'\right)$$

$$\frac{\partial H}{\partial R_2} = 0 = \gamma_K\left(p - f_2'\right) - \gamma_2 \Rightarrow \gamma_2 = U_C\left(p - f_2'\right)$$

Defining $n_1 \equiv F_{R_1} - f_1'$ and $n_2 \equiv p - f_2'$ to be the unit rental rates, it is straightforward to show that the dynamic first-order conditions for this problem yield the Hotelling rules,

$$\frac{\dot{n}_1}{n_1} = \frac{\dot{n}_2}{n_2} = F_K.$$

Thus, although the unit rental rates need not be equal, their percentage rates of growth must each be equal to the interest rate.

The Hartwick rule for this problem is the standard 'invest resource rents' rule, so that,

$$\dot{K} = n_1 R_1 + n_2 R_2,$$

which implies that,

$$\dot{K} = \dot{n}_1 R_1 + n_1 \dot{R}_1 + \dot{n}_2 R_2 + n_2 \dot{R}_2.$$

Applying the Hartwick rule and the Hotelling rule successively yields,

$$\dot{C} = \dot{F} - \dot{K} - \frac{d}{dt}\left(f_1(R_1)\right) - \frac{d}{dt}\left(f_2(R_2)\right) + p\dot{R}_2$$

$$= F_K \dot{K} + F_{R_1} \dot{R}_1 - \dot{n}_1 R_1 - n_1 \dot{R}_1 - \dot{n}_2 R_2 - n_2 \dot{R}_2 - f_1' \dot{R}_1 - f_2' \dot{R}_2 + p\dot{R}_2$$

$$= F_{R_1} \dot{R}_1 - n_1 \dot{R}_1 - n_2 \dot{R}_2 - f_1' \dot{R}_1 - f_2' \dot{R}_2 + p\dot{R}_2$$

$$= 0.$$

Since consumption is constant under the Hartwick rule, so is utility.

The assumption of a constant export price p may seem unrealistic, but it is a useful way to capture the notion of the country being a price-taker on world markets. It is the endogeneity of the resource price, which is then subject to the Hotelling rule, that leads to the terms-of-trade effect term and rising consumption under the Hartwick rule in the models of Asheim (1986) and Hartwick (1994).

Appendix 5.2 Reattributing resource depletion

As an illustration of this approach we consider a simple two-country global economy. The basic accounting identities for these countries are:

$$X_{12} - X_{21} + C_1 + I_1 = Y_1$$
$$X_{21} - X_{12} + C_2 + I_2 = Y_2$$

where, Y_i is total output (or GNP); C_i is consumption in country i; I_i is investment in country i and; X_{ij} are the exports from country i to country j.

Relating the imports into each country to the GNP of that country, we define the following import coefficients:

$$q_{ij} \equiv \frac{X_{ij}}{Y_j}.$$

So we can write:

$$X_{ij} = q_{ij} Y_j.$$

Substituting for X_{ij} in the above accounting identities and rewriting in matrix form we obtain,

$$\begin{pmatrix} -q_{21} & q_{12} \\ q_{21} & -q_{12} \end{pmatrix} \begin{pmatrix} Y_1 \\ Y_2 \end{pmatrix} + \begin{pmatrix} C_1 + I_1 \\ C_2 + I_2 \end{pmatrix} = \begin{pmatrix} Y_1 \\ Y_2 \end{pmatrix}.$$

This result can be generalized to several countries giving,

$$q_{ij} = \begin{bmatrix} \dfrac{X_{ij}}{Y_j}, & i \neq j \\ \dfrac{-\sum_k X_{kj}}{Y_j}, & i = j \end{bmatrix}.$$

This generalization to several countries permits the calculation of Y in each country based on the domestic final demand $(C + I)$ in all countries. We can rewrite the expression for the output accounting expression in condensed matrix form.

$$\mathbf{Qy} + (\mathbf{c} + \mathbf{i}) = \mathbf{y}.$$

This can be reorganized to give (I is the unit matrix):

$$(c + i) = (I - Q)y.$$

Solving this expression for y, by matrix inversion, gives:

$$y = (I - Q)^{-1}(c + i).$$

Next we define a resource depletion vector – 'v'. This is the product of the resource rent (n) and the extraction rate (R) expressed as a proportion of Y, in any country (see Chapter 3):

$$v_i = \frac{nR}{Y}.$$

Then the depletion of total domestic resources required to support GNP, N, is given by:

$$N = v(I - Q)^{-1}(c + i).$$

An alternative expression allows the calculation of the total direct and indirect consumption of global resources required to support the domestic final demand of each country.

$$N^* = v'(I - Q)^{-1}(c \hat{+} i).$$

6 Ecological economics and indicators

Genuine savings are indicators of weak sustainability. More stringent requirements based on stronger conditions for achieving sustainability will result in a different set of indicators. Indicators of strong sustainability have been suggested by ecological economists. They represent a loosely assembled body of ideas, and in common with other dissenting schools, the most notable unifying theme is a mistrust of neoclassical (environmental) economics, in particular the perceived inability of mainstream economists to integrate ecological imperatives into their analysis. However, some progress is being made in defining ecological economics (see, for example, Perrings, Turner and Folke, 1995). Furthermore, Arrow et al. (1995) identify two core elements of research in ecological economics: carrying capacity and resilience.

In this chapter we focus on the indicators that are suggested by these two strands of work in ecological economics. One broad characterization of such indicators is that they emphasize the maintenance of natural assets as a goal in its own right. In contrast, the focus of Chapter 4 was on the use of natural assets in the context of a maintaining a more general portfolio of assets including produced capital and knowledge. The ground for the preservation of certain natural assets is that they are 'critical' in the sense that there are few or no substitutes for the services that they provide. The problem in selecting appropriate indicators lies in determining exactly which assets are critical. Nevertheless, in Chapter 10 we show how indicators of strong sustainability and genuine saving are, in fact, complementary.

The Dutch environmental performance indicators described in Chapter 2 could plausibly be categorized as a set of strong sustainability indicators: for example, sustainability targets based on assimilative capacity and the measurement of the distance to this goal (Adriaanse, 1993; Hammond et al., 1995). The green national accounting counterpart of this is offered by Hueting, Bosch and de Boer (1992) and is couched in terms of the costs of reaching these goals and was discussed in Chapter 3. However, for the remainder of this chapter we examine in more detail indicators of carrying capacity and resilience. Arguably, these have been the main contribution of the ecological economists to the measurement of sustainable development.

The idea underlying carrying capacity is similar to that of the Dutch work in that the emphasis is on sustainability constraints in the form of, say, assimilative capacity of the environment. The difference lies in the unit of account used, where carrying capacity measures are often expressed as maximum sustainable human populations. Resilience is a more complex concept and focuses upon dynamic linkages between ecology and economy. So far, operational measures are few although one candidate indicator is the loss of biodiversity.

6.1   Carrying capacity

The notion of a carrying capacity is drawn from biology. It states that a given area can only support a given population of a particular species and at this upper limit – the carrying capacity – population will have reached its maximum sustainable level. In order to apply this notion of a saturation point to human populations we have to consider not only the level of population, but also the level of economic activity. Furthermore, the composition of economic output can vary significantly adding a further complication. Inevitably, in developing an indicator of carrying capacity, a number of simplifying assumptions have to be made. Some ambitious attempts have been made to estimate a global carrying capacity, with results indicating that sustainable populations are well below existing population levels or wildly in excess of predicted stationary levels (see respectively, Ehrlich, 1992 and Simon and Kahn, 1984).

More usually within ecological economics, carrying capacity is defined in terms of exceeding limits – to be set by ecological criteria. In moving to actual indicators of carrying capacity we require a more detailed specification of these ecological limits. Usually, these consist of 'sustainability constraints' with respect to commercial or environmental resources, for example, pollution should not exceed the assimilative capacity of the environment; harvest of a renewable resource should not be greater than natural growth. (It is more difficult to think of an appropriate constraint governing the use of non-renewable resources on these terms where growth is by definition zero.) Underlying these constraints is the goal to maintain the stock of *each* resource intact. If the definition of sustainability is non-declining human wellbeing, then what is argued is that human wellbeing is decreased unless *all* specified ecological constraints are observed.

Carrying capacity indicators tend to be extremely pessimistic regarding judgements about technology, that is, the ability of people to expand the carrying capacity of the earth (Cohen, 1995). For example, Ehrlich (1992) speculates that, at industrialized levels of economic activity per capita, the level of global population that would not exceed carrying capacity thresholds is two billion, about one-third of the *current* population. Although the genuine savings rule outlined in Chapter 4 also assumes constant technology, the framework underlying the savings principle does at least allow for substitution between assets. In the carrying capacity schema each asset is to be maintained intact and presumably the scale of economic activity or population is set by whichever constraint is reached first, as suggested by Rees and Wackernagel (1994). This is known as Liebig's Law and implies that,

$$CC = \min CC_i \qquad (6.1)$$

that is, overall carrying capacity (*CC*) is determined by the lowest carrying capacity of each of the *i* assets in the system.

In effect, those who favour carrying capacity indicators are arguing that there is zero substitutability between assets. The difficulties in resolving this argument are well known. Empirically speaking, little is known about what might constitute *critical natural capital*, that is, those environmental assets for which few or no substitutes exist (Pearce et al., 1994). While lack of substitutability may be an appropriate characterization of some classes of environmental assets, it is asking too much to argue that this is true of all such assets. Nor is it the case that limiting factors will remain the same over time (Cohen, 1995).

A variant of this empirical approach to carrying capacity is to link population levels to very simple indicators of resource use. Some commonly-cited examples are land use for food production, fuelwood availability and water use. Various problems are associated with these indicators, such as aggregating the different requirements of a heterogeneous global population, the absence of any specified interactions between various constraints, and possibilities for trade where carrying capacity is defined nationally (Cohen, 1995). Nor do these indicators address the measurement of progress in protecting critical natural assets. One of the only positive comments that may be made in their defence is that they can be interpreted as a first stab at developing poverty or scarcity measures that introduce the notion of sustainable use of resources.

6.1.1 Agricultural output: the carrying capacity of land
The ability of an individual to obtain adequate nutrition can be regarded as a basic need to ensure survival and adequate functioning. Similarly the ability of a nation to provide adequate nutrition for its population might be interpreted in this way. At any point in time population carrying capacity based on food output can be written,

$$CC = \frac{Q_{MAX}}{C_{MIN}} = \frac{qL}{C_{MIN}} \qquad (6.2)$$

where Q_{MAX} is the maximum output obtainable. This is made up of available land that is capable of being cultivated (*L*) and output per unit of land (*q*). C_{MIN} is some per capita food consumption from which individuals derive their calorific requirements defined in terms of required Q/N (where *N* is population).

Using a variant of this simple expression, Rees and Wackernagel (1994) estimate that the world can support roughly a doubling a population from 1992 levels. Such calculations are inevitably crude as they represent highly simplistic descriptions of production potential on cultivatable land. The extent to which policy can be inferred from these indicators is likely to be dubious. For example, even judged on its own merits, any final estimate will be extremely sensitive to the technical assumptions underlying the parameter, Q_{MAX}.

Agricultural production has been subject to significant technological progress bringing into effect a move from shifting cultivation to long fallow periods, to short fallow farming and cropping rotations with organic manuring, to modern intensive monoculture based on high-yield crops and the application of irrigation, fertilizers, insecticides and pesticides (Pearce, 1990). One large empirical study (Higgins et al., 1982) on agricultural carrying capacity calculated three different measures each based on different assumptions regarding technology: (i) low inputs (traditional crops, few inputs, no conservation measures); (ii) intermediate inputs (basic inputs, improved crop varieties, simple conservation measures); and (iii) high input (full use of inputs, improved crop varieties, conservation measures and the best mix of crops).

It may be the case that Q_{MAX} is an unreasonably optimistic view of potential agricultural output (Srinivasan, 1988). In many countries the agricultural sector's terms of trade are distorted because of domestic policies biased towards urban sectors and the protection of markets in the developed world. Such factors are likely to influence farmers' incentives to produce. Furthermore, in this simple calculation, negative environmental feedbacks are ignored (for example, the expansion of agriculture into ecologically fragile areas, soil erosion, loss of crop species diversity).

The assumption that it is *absolute* shortages of food that are responsible for famine, hunger and malnutrition has come under considerable scrutiny. The apparent coexistence of abundant global food supplies with this ongoing suffering has been explained by relative shortages, that is, inequitable distribution of supplies (Sen, 1982; Drèze and Sen, 1987). This inequality in distribution is attributed to 'entitlement failure' – the failure of a right or entitlement to an adequate supply of food, in turn caused by the lack of purchasing power brought about by poverty. The Sen entitlement critique suggests that even a very favourable population carrying capacity can mask relative shortages where the purchasing power of higher-income groups outbids that of the lower-income groups. In areas where even substantial changes in agricultural yields have been outstripped by population growth these tendencies will only aggravate absolute food shortages.

6.1.2 The sustainable use of water resources
While globally abundant, only a tiny fraction of the world's water resources are a usable source of freshwater (World Resources Institute, 1992). Yet even this would be sufficient to meet global demand *provided that it was evenly distributed.* An imbalance of supply and demand can lead to problems across regions,

countries and indeed within countries. Constraints on water availability are therefore local not global.

Precipitation is channelled into groundwater systems and rivers via soil and vegetation. This is known as 'run-off'. Calculating the reliable portion of run-off is complex, where as much as two-thirds can be dissipated (Clarke, 1992). Reliable run-off corresponds to the maximum sustainable supply of water in any period. This *maximum sustainable supply* is defined as precipitation minus (surface and groundwater) evaporation and transpiration (Dubourg, 1992). The general form of a carrying capacity for water resources is basically the same as for agricultural production above,

$$CC_W = \frac{W_{MAX}}{W_0 / POP_0} \qquad (6.3)$$

where W_{MAX} is the maximum sustainable supply, W_0 is total present withdrawal from this flow and POP_0 is the present level of population. (W_0/POP_0) therefore indicates water use per capita: it is present levels of per capita use that we wish to sustain. One operational definition of W_{MAX} is annual internal renewable water resources (net of river flows between countries) as described by the World Resources Institute (1994). This appears to be close to the concept of maximum sustainable supply although measurement is based on average conditions and will disguise seasonal, interannual and long-term variations (Agnew and Anderson, 1992). Falkenmark (1984) has also developed several indicators of water resource scarcity. One such indicator looks at W_{MAX} per capita and within broad bands describes whether particular countries might experience water scarcity problems. This is described in more detail in Table 6.1.

It is important to note that W_{MAX} is likely to be unevenly distributed within countries. The potential for redistribution will depend on spatial substitutability. Diverting water flows is not achievable without fairly major infrastructure investment and hence these requirements are often beyond the budgets of many developing nations. Furthermore, the incremental costs of developing new sources have begun to rise sharply in most countries (Munasinghe, 1992). In view of this, the potential for better management of existing sources is stressed by those who see water scarcity as a problem of poor resource management, that is, current relative shortage as opposed to absolute scarcity (White, 1984). While there is no one particular level of water use associated with a particular level of overall development, improved water resource management is particularly important if a goal is to raise the level of per capita use.

Falkenmark (1984) estimates that in order for Africa to sustain annual levels of water use of 500m^3 per capita, an average water use efficiency of 35 per cent would need to be achieved. (Average water use per capita in Africa was 153m^3

Table 6.1 Falkenmark's water interval by region (annual figures)

Indicator	Comment	Africa	North Africa and Middle East	Asia	North and Central America	South America	Europe	Former USSR states
$W_{MAX} > 10,000m^3$ per capita	Little or no problem concerning scarcity	12	—	8	7	11	5	2
$10,000m^3 > W_{MAX} > 1,000m^3$	Possible general problems	20	3	11	7	1	16	10
$1,670m^3 > W_{MAX} > 1,000m^3$	Possible specific problems: 'water stressed'	4	3	1	1	—	—	—
$1,000m^3 > W_{MAX} > 500m^3$	Chronic scarcity	6	2	—	—	—	—	1
$500m^3 > W_{MAX}$	Water barrier: economic development threatened	1	9	1	—	—	—	2

Note: North Africa and Middle East defined as: Algeria; Egypt; Iran; Iraq; Israel; Jordan; Kuwait; Libya; Morocco; Oman; Saudi Arabia; Syria; Tunisia; Turkey; United Arab Emirates; Yemen.

Sources: Falkenmark (1984) and World Resources Institute (1995).

in 1990.) Where water is particularly scarce and flows between countries via large river systems, there is a potential for conflict arising from competition for these flows (for example, upstream damming) (Alam, 1990). Of course, many countries possess extensive supplies of groundwater or fossil water lying in shallow or deep aquifers thus representing a potentially important source of freshwater, especially in arid regions. However, the rate of recharge is usually extremely low and groundwater stocks can be effectively non-renewable. To the extent that this stock can be treated as a 'mine' of water (that is, little interaction of groundwater with the water cycle), its depletion is amenable to the type of analysis in Chapter 3, depending on the degree of substitution that can be assumed.

6.1.3   Sustainable fuelwood production

The burning of biomass fuels such as fuelwood is an essential source of energy in many developing countries. Fuelwood provides 62 per cent of energy requirements in Africa and 34 per cent in Asia, and in the Sub-Saharan region this figure is sometimes about 90 per cent (Alexandratos (ed.), 1989; Armitage and Schramm, 1989). Combined with high population densities this dependence threatens the continued existence of fuelwood resources and presents some problems in terms of general levels of forest and woodland loss.

Again, we begin with the formula given in expressions (6.2) and (6.3),

$$CC_{POP,f} = \frac{F_{MAX}}{F_0 / POP_0} \qquad (6.4)$$

where F_{MAX} is the maximum sustainable supply of fuelwood. F_0 is current fuelwood demands which, expressed as a ratio to current population, gives current per capita fuelwood use. Again, sustainability in any period is indicated when $F_{MAX} \geq F_0$. If $F_{MAX} < F_0$ then population is unsustainable. F_{MAX} in effect refers to the natural regeneration rate of biomass which in turn represents the sustainable yield at any one time. Natural regrowth will differ for reasons such as species type and climate. For example, regeneration rates will be slow where climatic conditions are unfavourable as in high altitude, mountainous regions as well as in arid and semi-arid areas (Kirchner et al., 1985; World Resources Institute, 1986).

Table 6.2 presents estimates based on FAO data on fuelwood demand (production) and fuelwood supply (regeneration). Obviously, if the ratio of demand to supply is greater than unity, then current rates of harvest must be unsustainable. The carrying capacity estimate simply links this information to data on population levels in 1990 and projected levels in 2000. The estimates also take into account the ecological concern that persistent rates of overharvest will *reduce* the sustainable yield and therefore population, over time. Hence, Nigeria's estimated sustainable population is 138 million in 1990. Yet by the end of the century this is predicted to fall to about 132 million. Because of population growth over that period the estimate predicts that Nigeria's population may well be unsustainable by 2000, at least in terms of a fuelwood constraint. It is worth noting that Nigeria has oil resources but that pressure on fuelwood resources persists owing to the lack of suitable refineries (Armitage and Schramm, 1989). All of the countries described in Table 6.2 are either unsustainable in 1990 or are predicted to be unsustainable by the year 2000. Some of these choices are not surprising, being countries located in typically arid North Africa with few forest resources. Pressure on forest resources in other countries such as Malawi has been well documented elsewhere (see, for example, Pearce and Warford, 1993). The size of this threat in terms of energy use will depend upon the availability of substitute fuels, technological measures that increase the productivity of the scarce resource, for example, more efficient stoves, or sufficient foreign exchange with which to purchase imported refined fuels.

Table 6.2   Fuelwood availability and sustainable populations in Africa (millions)

Country	Sustainable and (actual) population, 1990		Sustainable and (predicted) population, 2000	
Algeria	4	(25)	4	(31)
Burkina Faso	4	(9)	3	(12)
Chad	4	(6)	4	(7)
Ethiopia	37	(51)	36	(67)
Gambia	>1	(1)	>1	(1)
Kenya	14	(24)	14	(31)
Madagascar	16	(12)	15	(16)
Malawi	2	(9)	2	(11)
Mali	8	(9)	7	(12)
Morocco	9	(25)	9	(30)
Nigeria	138	(96)	132	(128)
Senegal	6	(7)	6	(10)
Sudan	21	(25)	21	(33)
Tanzania	16	(25)	15	(33)
Tunisia	>1	(8)	>1	(10)
Uganda	2	(16)	2	(22)
Zimbabwe	10	(10)	9	(12)

Sources: Adapted from Atkinson (1993) and World Bank (1994b).

6.2 Ecological resilience

Many ecological economists have come to interpret sustainability as resilience along the lines introduced by Charles Holling (Holling, 1973). Resilience determines the persistence of relationships within a system and is a measure of the ability of these systems to absorb changes and still persist. In turn the *degree of resilience* of the system determines whether ecological productivity (for example, ecosystem functioning) is largely unaffected, decreased either temporarily or permanently or, in the extreme, collapses altogether, as a result of stress or shock (Conway and Barbier, 1990). *Stresses* are small and predictable changes such as increasing erosion and salinity. However, while small these forces can have large cumulative effects. *Shocks* on the other hand are relatively large, temporary and unpredictable such as, for example, a new crop pest or a rare drought. A system that is unable to respond is, in some sense, unsustainable if the stresses and shocks are themselves not capable of control, or, for some reason, are unlikely to be controlled. In turn, capability of response to stress and shocks is usually, but not necessarily, thought to be correlated with diversity of capital, in the sense of either a wide portfolio of natural and produced assets, or a wide portfolio of natural biological assets (Holling, 1973; Conway 1985, 1993; Common and Perrings, 1992).

A measure of the degree of resilience could be interpreted as an indicator of the *degree of sustainability* of the system. However, it is less clear what this means for the sustainability of human development. In the green national accounting literature this link is provided by models that connect changes in human welfare to resource depletion and environmental degradation. These result in green alternatives to GNP (for example, measures of economic welfare) and lead directly to a notion of genuine saving. Hence, green accounting tells us how resource and environmental issues are linked to sustainable human development. The task for the resilience school is to provide a similar link between changes in resilience and sustainability in this way. Although Common and Perrings (1992) have offered one such possible interpretation based on measures of biodiversity, this preliminary work is not yet suggestive of a set of feasible indicators, although standard measures of species diversity and keystone species are clearly candidates, as we discuss below.

It is clear that resilience is not something that can be observed directly and so the search for indicators leads in the direction of measuring *inputs* that are thought to contribute to resilience, or the *outputs* that are believed to be affected by changes in resilience. Examples of the former are indicators of biodiversity. If resilience is positively related to biodiversity – as Common and Perrings (1992) and Arrow et al. (1995) tentatively suggest – then indices of diversity might be a useful input-based indicator of resilience in ecosystems. The ecology literature offers many such measures (Krebs, 1985) and a useful summary of information about species and habitat diversity is provided by the World Conservation Monitoring Centre (1992).

However, several problems remain. The first of these, as noted above, is that it is not at all obvious how given measures of diversity-resilience map on to sustainability. A related problem is the absence of any clear baseline to assess the degree of sustainability using these indicators. The genuine savings approach in Chapter 4 has a natural measure of the degree of sustainability, since zero genuine saving defines the borderline between sustainability and non-sustainability. Zero or 'low' diversity would appear to qualify as low sustainability on a diversity measure, but there is no obvious scaling involved. Unless our criterion is to be non-declining diversity, at what value of the diversity index does sustainability become threatened?

Even if non-declining diversity (say, from existing levels) is to be our benchmark, there is a second problem of an empirical nature where available data are often constrained to a single point in time, whereas the relevant measure of sustainability is the change in diversity, in addition to the amount of diversity.

Finally, meaningful interpretations of the data, even if they do exist, are often unclear. For example, the appropriate spatial scale of the index is not simple to determine. Are such indicators meaningful on a national scale or relevant to particular ecosystems regardless of national boundaries? It is likely that national measures of diversity may tell us little about resilience or sustainability in general, although they may be useful in giving a preliminary answer to a different question, namely, where to direct conservation funds most effectively (see, for example, Moran et al., 1995).

If we restrict our focus on ecosystems to agricultural systems then a mixture of input- and output-based indicators is suggested. An *output-based indicator* reflecting the loss of resilience in agricultural systems is variability in crop yields. Upward trends in production may be associated with increasing variability of yields from year to year. In the limit, without any counteracting mechanism, these fluctuations might become so extreme that output collapses. A measure of this variability is the coefficient of variation. Thus, one indicator might be changes in the coefficient of variation of crop productivity over time. This is actually a measure of stability (that is, the ability of a system to return to an equilibrium state after a small, temporary disturbance arising from normal fluctuations and cycles in the surrounding environment). In practice, stability and resilience are likely to be closely and positively linked and hence the distinction may not be critical (Pearce and Prakesh, 1993). For example, Hazell (1984) shows that in India, while the annual growth rate of cereal production was 2.7 per cent between 1952/53 and 1977/78, the coefficient of variation (CV) around this trend is 4.5 per cent per annum before 1965/66 and 6 per cent per annum thereafter. Table 6.3 shows estimates of crop yield variability in India for the period from 1955 to 1989. While other (for example, climatic) factors need to be controlled for in the analysis, this period also coincides with the structural shift embodied in the green revolution and reveals that, in all but two cases, greater output has been achieved at the expense of greater variation in yields over time. In the case of coarse cereals and groundnuts this change in variation has been highly significant. Conway (1985, 1987, 1993) has provided a framework for this kind of analysis – agroecosystem analysis – whereby indicators of a number of desirable attributes of the system (for example, productivity, resilience and equity) can be assessed. The extent to which farmers can either insure against loss of income in low productivity years or smooth their consumption by saving a portion of high productivity harvests also requires further investigation.

Table 6.3   Crop yield variability in India, 1955–1989

Crop	CV pre-green revolution	CV post-green revolution	Change in CV (%)
Rice	5.1	7.0	+37
Wheat	7.2	5.8	−19
Coarse cereals	3.5	7.3	+108
Pulses	8.3	8.5	+2
Foodgrains	3.8	5.4	+42
Groundnut	5.5	12.1	+220
Cotton	8.8	8.9	+1
Sugarcane	5.2	4.4	−15

Sources: Pearce and Prakesh (1993); adapted from Ninan and Chandrashekar (1991).

Indicators of diversity as discussed above are not irrelevant to this analysis. One of the principal explanations of the loss of resilience/sustainability in agricultural systems is changes in biological diversity. While there are a number of different definitions of biodiversity (Pearce and Moran, 1994), here we refer to *genetic diversity* (that is, the genetic information contained in the genes of plants, animal and micro-organisms). The significance of genetic diversity is often highlighted with reference to global agriculture and food security. The reliance of the majority of the world's human population is on a small number of staple food species (often high-yield varieties), which in turn rely on supply of genes from their wild relatives to supply new characteristics, for example to improve resistance to pests and diseases (Cooper et al., 1992). Anderson and Hazell (1989) cite statistical evidence for variability induced by genetic uniformity of crops.

Of course, other factors are implicated in this process, not least an increased reliance on artificial fertilizers, pesticides and technology. Perrings (1994) suggests that the need to continually substitute produced assets for natural assets in the form of genetic diversity in agriculture can be seen as a cost of the loss of resilience. As such he suggests that the loss of sustainability of a system can be 'measured by the value of increasing quantities of herbicides, pesticides, fertilisers, irrigation and other inputs needed to maintain output at or above current levels ... [and] ... where output fails, the costs of relocation where soils or water resources have been irreversibly damaged' (Perrings, 1994, p. 39). Here, the weak sustainability aspects of substitutability – produced assets for natural assets – are linked to the strong sustainability consideration of ecological functions and the properties of ecosystems. The key question that future research must answer is the extent to which the substitution option is as effective as in the past.

6.3   Conclusions

We have identified two distinct sets of indicators associated with ecological economics. The first – carrying capacity – is in practice an overly simplistic description of technical constraints and the level of population deemed to be consistent with these constraints. In the ecological economics literature these limits are usually interpreted as either the assimilative capacity of the environment or, for living resources, the sustainable harvest. The question of which of these constraints should be observed on the grounds of criticality is not directly addressed. In practice society is expected to observe all specified constraints with population or human impact to be ultimately constrained by Liebig's Law. Empirical applications have tended to be restricted to questions concerning absolute availability of agricultural production, fuelwood and water supply. Yet to the extent that these indicators are intended to inform policy this is not helped by the total absence of any socioeconomic content to these indicators.

Arrow et al. (1995) also arrive at a pessimistic conclusion regarding this avenue of research in ecological economics. There it is argued that indicators such as those proposed by Vitousek et al. (1986) are better broad-brush measures of human pressure on ecosystems, for example, human appropriation of global ecosystems. However, implicit judgements concerning such a limit may need to be inferred if we are to suggest what levels of ecosystem appropriation are considered to be excessive.

The diversity-resilience/sustainability link seems far less researched, however. Arguments in favour of conserving diversity, as opposed to the stock of biological resources, have been advanced in terms of ethics, aesthetics and economics (Wilson, 1988; Pearce and Moran, 1994). It is widely argued, however, that biodiversity conservation is required for *insurance* purposes, for example, for sustaining output, and in particular agricultural output, in the face of risks to the genetic base of existing output. The argument here is that the risk of system collapse is higher the less diverse the system. If so, then diversity does have a link to sustainable development as many suspect. Problems in measuring this loss in sustainability include the absence of a baseline required to make sustainability judgements and the inadequacy of existing data, restricted as it is to single point estimates.

Output variability or some other indicator related to agricultural production is most relevant to the developing world where agriculture comprises a significant proportion of GNP. In developed countries agricultural output contributes such a relatively small proportion of total output that these indicators are of little strategic importance. Although of course these countries may need to import their food requirements from countries affected by large variability. This may be one form of the 'ecological footprint' of Rees and Wackernagel (1994) discussed in Chapter 5. If pressures on agricultural resilience are increased by both foreign demand for food and modern farming practices, sustainability might be threatened. Meeting these demands has obvious benefits to these countries in the form of valuable foreign exchange, with the possible downside of loss of sustainability in the form of resilience. Moreover, in applying the resilience concept to ecosystems in general, affected 'outputs' will, more often than not, be intangible and non-marketed. Measures such as the coefficient of variation will not be operational. However, measures of resilience have more appeal than the carrying capacity approach in that indicators of biodiversity are stressed as central to the measurement problem and many would now agree that diversity is a critical natural asset (see Schulze and Mooney, 1993). However, as we have seen, practical indicators of biodiversity fall short of what we require to measure sustainability. For these reasons, we argue that resilience, while attractive from an ecological economics standpoint, has, at the moment, little to offer for the development of practical indicators that will help in decision-making.

7 Social indicators

7.1 Social indicators: nature and rationale

In Chapters 3 and 4, environmental sources of human wellbeing were integrated into sustainability indicators based on national accounting aggregates. As yet we have not considered the social dimension of the indicators debate. However, it cannot simply be assumed that conventional indicators of income are adequate measures of *social* wellbeing. In effect, social indicators represent the third broad category of indicators – economic, environmental and social – required to measure sustainability.

Preceding the environmental indicators debate, the 'social indicators movement' enjoyed considerable attention during the 1970s. In common with the development of green accounting indicators, the construction of social measures was intended to provide a counterbalance to measures of economic activity such as GNP per capita. In contrast, social indicators draw on diverse notions of development and are often expressed in heterogeneous units. Hence, a wide variety of social phenomena, such as health and educational status, have been translated into indicators. Indeed, social indices are now an established feature of the family of indicators used to measure development (see, for example, World Bank, 1994c). Even so, social indicators have tended to be judged as the poor relation in this hierarchy. One problem is that they do not fall into any 'neat disciplinary niche' (Baster, 1972). The consequence of this lack of theoretical precision is that it is not possible *consistently* to justify and derive social indicators with the same degree of formality as, say, set out in Chapter 3. In practice, the implementation of social indicators has proceeded on a more *ad hoc* basis as a pragmatic response to the identification of social concerns rather than the implementation of a framework of analysis.

Yet, it is possible to analyse some classes of social indicators within an economic framework based on individual preferences. Indicators measure the extent to which human wellbeing is satisfied and the justification for social indicators is provided where this function is not adequately expressed in national income (Dasgupta, 1989). For example, indicators of life expectancy could be taken to reflect individual preferences for longer life where future experiences carry possible utility. Hence, indicators of life expectancy at birth, and at other times, have become a commonly cited social indicator. In turn, the wellbeing derived from changes in life expectancy will depend on the quality of life, and so social indicators describing these states are justified. On the pragmatic level, the United Nations (1975) suggest that indicators of life expectancy at birth point to the efficacy of policies that raise the general standard of living (described by, say, income per capita) at low levels of development. More detailed inferences require the use of more detailed indicators. For example, the infant mortality rate is defined as the number of live births out of every 1,000 that die during the first year. This indicator not only focuses attention on nutrition and hygiene but also is related to the health of the mother (Dasgupta, 1993).

Other frameworks used to justify social indicators include the 'basic needs' school. The key to this approach is the identification of minimum requirements believed to be justified on either instrumental grounds (that is, to achieve a minimum acceptable level of wellbeing) or some notion of rights of individuals. Hence, 'needs' tend to be defined as absolute as opposed to relative, for example, without explicit reference to fulfilment of needs relative to the average. The concept of basic needs has been particularly influential in the measurement of poverty by providing a definition in terms of an absolute minimal standard of living. Clearly such a definition still begs at least two questions: (a) what we mean by a 'standard of living'; and (b) what we mean by 'minimal'. The idea of a 'minimal' level of consumption or income appears most often in the literature in the form of a *poverty line*. A poverty line tends to be defined in terms of some minimum nutritional requirement to survive, plus some set of basic non-food items.

7.2   Composite indicators

Social indicators become more useful when presented in a composite form involving the aggregation of social data. Of course, composite indicators are not restricted to social measurement. Chapter 2 described composite environmental indicators made up of different environmental themes. Measures of national income are also of composite form by adding together information about a diverse range of goods and services. In such measures monetary values provide the weights by which data can be compared. In social (and environmental) composite indicators some other system of weighting must often be found. A recent revival of interest in social indicators has been caused by one such composite measure – the human development index. In the remainder of this chapter we focus upon this particular index, using it as an example of the problems encountered in the construction of meaningful social indicators. In particular we examine the scope and the desirability of integrating environmental and sustainability concerns into such a measure. Finally, we return to a framework for indicator analysis proposed in Chapter 3, that is, the construction of social accounting matrices.

7.2.1   The human development index

Probably the most celebrated social indicator of development is the *human development index* (HDI) which was introduced in the United Nations

Development Programme's 1990 *Human Development Report* (UNDP, 1990). It has been published annually since then. We classify it here as a *social* indicator, although one of its attractions is that it combines economic and social information. Before looking at the way in which the index is constructed, we report some of the more recent results to emerge.

Table 7.1 shows the rankings that emerge for 1994 for the top ten countries and the bottom five countries. It is easy to see why such rankings excite international attention. Few wish to be bottom of an international ranking, while some will believe that they should be higher up than they are. In the 1990 HDI, for example, the USA was actually 19th, below Spain and Ireland. In 1991 the USA was 7th, a remarkable change in just one year. But the way the index was computed changed during that year: per capita income in excess of the poverty line counted for the first time, favouring those countries with relatively high incomes (see below). Information deficiencies also came to light. The USA was 6th in 1992 and 1993 and 8th in 1994 when the method of computation changed again.

Table 7.1   The 1994 human development index

Country	HDI	Rank	GNP rank – HDI rank
Canada	0.932	1	10
Switzerland	0.931	2	–1
Japan	0.929	3	0
Sweden	0.928	4	0
Norway	0.928	5	0
France	0.927	6	7
Australia	0.926	7	11
USA	0.925	8	1
Netherlands	0.923	9	7
United Kingdom	0.919	10	9
...			
Niger	0.209	169	–21
Sierra Leone	0.209	170	–7
Afghanistan	0.208	171	–2
Burkina Faso	0.203	172	–19
Guinea	0.191	173	–44

Source: UNDP (1994).

The HDI has served to focus some attention away from GNP as an indicator of development bringing in measures of educational attainment and health status. The final column of Table 7.1 shows the difference between the ranking of countries in terms of GNP per capita and the HDI. If the rankings were the same, the differences would be zero. In fact we see that some of the differences are large, particularly as the countries get poorer. But even the 'most humanly developed' country, Canada, would have been ranked 10th on GNP per capita compared with its first place on the HDI. Other countries making ranking improvements under the HDI include Czechoslovakia (up 29 places), Lithuania (up 35), Hungary (up 23), Uruguay (up 20), Columbia (up 41), Sri Lanka (up 38) and China (up 49). Minus numbers mean that the HDI has the effect of bringing a country down relative to a GNP ranking. Countries making significant falls in this respect include Luxembourg (down 15), Singapore (down 22), most of the Arab states, Botswana, South Africa and Algeria.

The index underlying the results in Table 7.1 is constructed as follows:

a. take a set of measures of development, X_1 to X_m where an individual measure might be GDP, some measure of health, and so on;
b. compute a measure of *deprivation* for each individual country as

$$I_{ij} = (X_{ij} - \min X_{ij})/(\max X_{ij} - \min X_{ij})$$

where j is the j-th country and i is the i-th component of the index (health, GDP and so on). Max X_{ij} is then the maximum value that X_{ij} can take, and conversely for min X_{ij}. The way in which the maxima and minima are measured actually changes in the HDI over time, so for the moment we leave their determination to one side;
c. compute $I_j = \Sigma I_{ij}/\Sigma i$, that is, the unweighted average of the components, implying that each component deserves equal weight in an overall index;
d. compute $HDI_j = (1 - I_j)$ as the human development index for country j.

To take an example, let X_1 be life expectancy at birth, X_2 educational attainment, and X_3 GDP per capita. The HDI for a single country, say the Philippines, would be:

$$X_1 = (64.6 - 25)/(85 - 25) = 60/39.6 = 0.66$$

where 85 years is the maximum assumed hypothetical life expectancy at birth; 25 years is the minimum life expectancy; and 64.6 years is life expectancy at birth in the Philippines.

Educational attainment (X_2) is made up of two components – adult literacy and average years of schooling. The maximum and minimum years of schooling are 15 and 0, respectively, and the range for adult literacy is from 0 to 100 per cent. Hence,

Literacy = (90.4 − 0)/(100 − 0) = 90.4/100 = 0.904
Schooling = (7.6 − 0)/(15 − 0) = 0.506

In the 1990 edition of the *Human Development Report*, the schooling component of educational attainment received no weighting, but in 1991 the weights were changed to 0.67 and 0.33 (still in favour of literacy). Hence for our example,

$$X_2 = (0.67 \times 0.904) + (0.33 \times 0.506) = 0.77.$$

Further changes were made in 1995 (UNDP, 1995). First, mean years of schooling was replaced by the ratio to population of all individuals in primary, secondary and tertiary education. To a large extent, this would appear to account for the (sometimes dramatic) changes in 1995 rankings.

The adjustment to income is a little more complex. A relatively undemanding approach might simply impute the per capita incomes into the HDI. However, rather than income, what is measured is the utility of income in dollars, $W(y)$ rather than y, with Atkinson's (1970) formulation chosen for the social welfare function:

$$W(y) = (1/1 − \varepsilon).y^{1−\varepsilon} \quad \text{for } \varepsilon \neq 1$$
$$W(y) = \log y \quad\quad\quad \text{for } \varepsilon = 1,$$

where ε is the elasticity of the marginal utility of income, that is, the percentage change in the utility of income for a small change in the level of income.

The use of this weighting scheme in the HDI has changed over the years. The starting point is a distinction between the income above and below what is defined to be the poverty line (y^*). As it is assumed that income below the poverty line is not subject to diminishing returns the problem is to impute a reasonable value for ε for $y > y^*$. In the 1990 HDI, $W(y) = \log(y)$, that is, ε was effectively set equal to (minus) one, and income above the poverty line y^* was set equal to zero, that is, income above the poverty line did not count. In 1991 this overrestrictive constraint was relaxed. In its place it was assumed that the (absolute) value of ε increases with increases in per capita income, the exact increases to be determined by multiples of the poverty line.

Up to y^*, $\varepsilon = 0$, that is, each unit of income counted equally. For $y^* < y < 2y^*$, ε was set equal to (minus) 0.5. And for $2y^* < y < 3y^*$, $\varepsilon = (−)0.67$ and so on with the general form: if $ay^* \leq y \leq (a + 1)y^*$, then $\varepsilon = a/(a + 1)$. In 1994 the thresholds were changed so that y^* was no longer defined by the poverty line, but by global average income per capita ($5,120). Similarly Y_{max} was no longer equal to the income of the highest country but was set equal to $40,000, while Y_{min} was set equal to $200 as described above. GDP deprivation for the Philippines is:

$$X_3 = (2{,}440 - 200)/(5{,}385 - 200) = 2{,}240/5{,}185 = 0.43.$$

The average of these three indicators is then 0.62, so that the HDI for the Philippines would be $1 - 0.62 = 0.38$ and is ranked 99 in the index for 1992. (All data are from the 1994 *Human Development Report.*) In 1995, the minimum income level was revised downwards to $100 at purchasing power parity.

Once the basic idea of the HDI is accepted, it is capable of a variety of applications and adjustments. For example, the HDI can be calculated separately for men (HDI_m) and women (HDI_f). Despite data difficulties in terms of gender-differentiated incomes, the HDI regularly reports male and female indices. The 1994 *Human Development Report* argues that the ability to disaggregate the index in this way is in fact its main strength. Thus it also computes an income distribution-adjusted HDI. Disaggregated HDIs can not only be computed across countries but within countries as well. For example, HDIs can be compared across different ethnic groups, one region can be compared with another, and so on. Finally, since the 1994 revisions which 'fixed the goalposts', the HDI can now be used to compare progress over time. UNDP (1994) reports that Malaysia, Botswana and the Republic of Korea have achieved an absolute increase in their HDI index of 0.46 over the period 1960 to 1992. Similar major increases of over 0.4 points are made by Tunisia, Thailand, Syria, Turkey, China, Portugal and Iran.

In many respects, the HDI's focus on education and health reflects the 'basic needs' development philosophy (for example, Streeten and Burki, 1978). Although the term 'basic needs' appears now to be outmoded, the philosophy itself lives on. Basic needs emphasizes the role that good (or better) health, education, food, public transport, housing, sanitation and water make to solving poverty problems. The implication is that governments should provide these goods and services before considering the more traditional investments in manufacturing and infrastructure. This process of giving priority to basic services also implies that more traditional policies aimed at stimulating some broad measure of economic growth, such as GNP, were not reaching the poorest in the community. The benefits of growth were not, in other words, 'trickling down'. The debate over basic needs is a longstanding one (and often vociferous; see, for example, Lal, 1983). Its opponents, who are essentially traditional 'growth-first' economists, argue that even countries which have achieved high literacy rates or longevity (Sri Lanka, China) could just as easily have achieved those objectives through growth-first policies, as Korea or Taiwan have done. Moreover, the provision of basic needs implies a government bureaucracy capable of such *dirigiste* policies, whereas the reality is that such bureaucracies sap the growth potential of economies rather than stimulating it, and their cost adds to excessive public expenditure. Proponents of basic needs argue that growth-first may eventually improve the lot of the poor, but not quickly enough, and perhaps not at all. Moreover, by providing basic needs, labour productivity is increased, so that not only is poverty directly addressed in the first instance but a sustainable growth process is enabled as well.

Basic needs can be linked to the genuine savings concept of Chapter 4. First, as we emphasize throughout, the quality of investment financed by genuine savings matters considerably for the development process. If 'basic needs' – or enhancing human capabilities – is formally equivalent to investing in human capital, then sustainability may well best be served by a careful focusing of investment into human capital formation. This does not deny the potential for a tradeoff between short-term gains and longer-term sustainability, however. Second, basic needs emphasizes *some* but not all the environmental variables we discuss. Sanitation, water and energy supplies certainly fit basic needs and also fit environmental priorities. But the basic needs literature rarely discusses soil or forest conservation, yet both may be preconditions of good nutrition and hence human health. As Chapter 2 showed, it is not difficult to extend this idea to air quality: air pollution impairs human health and thus lowers the quality of human capital, and hence impairs sustainability.

The HDI's emphasis on basic needs indicators is therefore interesting in the context of sustainable development. The HDI is a partial attempt to account for descriptive and prescriptive social goals, but all in the context of a single number. While care has to be taken not to infer that only basic needs should be met for an economy to promise sustainability, the HDI at least reminds us of the role of human capital in the longer view of economic development. And human capital should in turn remind us of the need to incorporate environmental factors into the relevant indicators.

7.2.2 Criticisms of the human development index

Numerous criticisms of the HDI have been advanced. Many are discussed at length in UNDP (1993) and some have in fact been answered by the successive changes in the way the HDI has been calculated over the years. The main criticisms can be summarized as follows:

The HDI is relative, not absolute   The major change in the way the HDI has been calculated has been the setting of X_{max} and X_{min} values independently of the maximum and minimum values for countries in the sample. However, the HDI is bounded by unity, that is, the value of the HDI for any country cannot go above a value of one. Yet if a country achieved a value of one, it would not imply that it could not 'develop' further. This would depend on to what extent the independently determined maximum values may eventually be exceeded. Such values can be changed but at the expense of year-by-year comparisons of country performance. Furthermore, as Dasgupta (1993) notes, if the minimum value of X_i was to change, the HDI of all countries would change, even though nothing need have happened in those countries to alter the 'output' of health, education or the 'input' of income.

Dasgupta's proposal is to focus solely on the ranking of countries via an alternative way to aggregate social indicators: a Borda rank. The ranking of a particular country for any given indicator becomes its score for that indicator, for example, a country which is 27th on real income per capita is given a score for income of 27 (or it may be done the other way round: the worst country getting the lowest score). The same procedure is used for other indicators. The scores for each country are then summed, and the totals for all countries are compared, with those with the highest score ranked last, and those with the lowest score ranked first and can be written as,

$$S_i = \sum_{m=n}^{n} S_{im}$$

where S_i is the aggregate score of country i, S_{im}, is the score of country i on indicator m of the n indicators.

Dasgupta (1993) reports a Borda count exercise in which the chosen indicators of real per capita income, life expectancy at birth, infant mortality rate, adult literacy rate, an index of political rights and an index of civil rights are applied to the 48 poorest countries in 1980 (poorest in the sense of GNP per capita). He then computes the rank correlation between the Borda count and the rankings by each of the selected indicators. Interestingly, the Borda count is closely correlated with life expectancy at birth and with real income per capita (the former correlation being a little higher than the latter). If this were to hold true generally, it follows that a *single representative indicator* could act as the surrogate for a *composite indicator* such as the Borda count or the HDI. The other correlations are interesting too: income and life expectancy are quite highly correlated, which might be expected, while literacy and freedoms are poorly correlated, which might not. Note, however, that Dasgupta's rankings are for the poorest countries of the world in 1980. Table 7.2 shows what happens when a Borda count is applied to the top 20 richest countries. Out of the first five countries ranked by GDP, three are also ranked in that group by the Borda count. Of the six lowest GDP countries five are also ranked lowest on the Borda count. But there are some significant shifts in rankings, as with Hong Kong's seventh place (GDP) to 16th place (Borda count); and the upwards shift of Sweden and the Netherlands when assessed on the Borda count. Luxembourg also makes a fairly dramatic shift downwards on the Borda count.

Table 7.2   Borda count wellbeing index for top 20 richest countries

Country	Life expectancy	Mean years schooling	Real GDP per capita (PPP 1991 US$)	Freedom index	Borda score and ranking	
USA	15=	1	1	14=	31	5=
Switzerland	3	7=	2	12=	24	1
Luxembourg	19	16	3	6=	44	14
Germany	15=	7=	4	6=	32	7
Japan	1	15	5	16=	37	9
Canada	6=	2	6	12=	26	2=
Hong Kong	5	19	7	19	50	16
France	11	4=	8	6=	29	4
Denmark	18	13	9	1=	41	12=
Austria	13=	9=	10	4=	36	8
Belgium	13=	11	11	6=	41	12=
Sweden	4	9=	12	1=	26	2=
Iceland	2	17	13	6=	38	10=
Norway	8=	3	14	6=	31	5=
Italy	8=	18	15	18	59	19
UAE	20	20	16	20	76	20
Netherlands	6=	12	17	3	38	10=
Australia	10	4=	18	14=	46	15
UK	12	6	19	16=	53	17
Finland	17	14	20	4=	55	18

Notes and source: Life expectancy, years of schooling and GDP/capita from UNDP (1994); PPP refers to purchasing power parity. Freedom scoring from UNDP (1994). UNDP (1994) does not record a freedom score for UAE (United Arab Emirates), Luxembourg or Iceland; UAE is assumed to be similar to other Middle East states; Luxembourg has been given the same score as Belgium here; Iceland has been given the same score as Norway; mean years of schooling is used rather than adult literacy which tends to be the same for the richest countries. The total score in the last column is then the sum of the scores in each of the composite columns.

   Much therefore seems to depend on what use is being made of wellbeing indicators. If the focus is on the poorest countries, Dasgupta's claim that GDP per capita may be a good surrogate for wellbeing may be correct. For the rich economies this is less apparent, so that if the indicator in question is meant to be *universal* there are continuing attractions to adopting wellbeing measures in their composite form.

   Dasgupta further argues that given the quality of social data for many countries this method of aggregation relying on ordinal ranking is not subject to the distortions that come from systematic biases in the data. If these biases are large then the increased informational content of a cardinal ranking (such as the HDI) will not be significant. To the extent that countries are primarily interested in improving their ranking *vis-à-vis* each other, a composite indicator using the Borda rule should raise the profile of policies aimed at raising social wellbeing.

The HDI is incomplete   Since 'development' is itself a value word it is hardly surprising that many comments relate to the component parts of the HDI. The rationale for selecting education, life expectancy and income is that they reflect capabilities or basic needs rather than ends in themselves; capabilities to lead a better life. They do not measure development as such, but rather the means to development. It remains the case, however, that the selection of these three variables is very much dictated by the desire to find indicators for which data are available. Two obviously missing components are (i) human freedom and (ii) environmental quality. The absence of the latter is particularly relevant to our search for sustainability indicators and we deal with this separately in Section 7.3.2. In fact, human freedom was addressed in the 1991 HDR by adopting the Humana index. This index attaches a value of one to rights protected and zero to freedoms violated. The list of freedoms runs to 40 so a maximum human freedom score would be 40, and the minimum zero. Note that this assumes each freedom is equally valuable. Computing the 'Human Freedom Index' for 1985, UNDP (1991) records countries such as Sweden with scores of 38, Malaysia with a score of nine and Iraq with a score of zero. But no attempt was made to integrate these scores into the HDI. In the 1992 *Human Development Report* the discussion was retained but with the focus being on political freedom rather than human freedom, and without any attempt to identify measures with specific countries. By 1993 the discussion ceased.

Selection of indicators   Given the main component parts of the HDI, could the indicators themselves be improved? There are technical debates about whether life expectancy at birth should be replaced by life expectancy at age one year, or under-five mortality, or infant mortality generally. Part of the debate centres on the extent to which life expectancy is a secondary indicator, itself explained by, for example, child mortality and income. Thus including income and life expectancy 'double-counts', whereas infant mortality and income would not. As UNDP (1993) points out, the problem with infant mortality is that it will not discriminate between industrial countries whereas life expectancy does. Ultimately, indicator choice has to be a matter of judgement as well as requiring a rationale in terms of what it is that is being measured. Despite the correlation between indicators, the HDI may add something to the indicators debate by highlighting outlying countries: for example, those with high per capita incomes but relatively low life expectancy.

Income per capita in the HDI   From Section 7.2.1 the GDP deprivation index in the HDI amounts to the following:

$$X_3 = (y_i - 200)/(5{,}385 - 200)$$

where all values are adjusted for a variable elasticity of the marginal utility of income (ε) as above.

Arguably, despite moving from the more extreme position of UNDP (1991), the income per capita component in the HDI is still accorded too little weight. For example, the first multiple of income per capita over the global mean income per capita yields $143 in terms of utility. The second multiple of mean income yields only $52 and so on. UNDP (1993) reports on this criticism but – despite the appeal of both the underlying premise and ingenuity of the empirical method – has so far failed to provide a justification for the magnitudes of ε chosen.

Of course, there is no easy resolution to such a debate. One alternative is to ask how sensitive is the HDI to changes in the assumptions for the parameter ε. If values are chosen that are less severe than currently used in the HDI then this is equivalent to according income levels above the global average a greater weight in the HDI and hence country rankings.

For example, in the special case where $\varepsilon = 0$ over all income, $W(y) = y$:

$$X_3 = (y_i - 200)/(40{,}000 - 200).$$

While it can be argued that this extreme assumption is unappealing we use it as a comparison with the method used in UNDP (1994).

Although Table 7.3 indicates that the overall changes in rankings are not large it is significant that the main beneficiary of assuming $\varepsilon = 0$ is the USA. Its rank increases seven places from eight to one. Trabold-Nübler (1991) also found this assuming that $\varepsilon = 0.5$ over all income beyond y^*. UNDP (1991) has argued that overall the differences are slight even given such extreme changes in assumptions. Given that some countries clearly benefit from changes in the magnitude of ε and the excitement that is generated by the annual publication of these rankings, further investigation of the extent of diminishing returns to income is desirable. A further attribute of the UNDP values for ε is that income levels are compressed between the industrialized countries in the sample. Differences in the HDI and these countries rankings are largely determined by slight differences in educational attainment and health status. For example, the USA's rank in 1995 was 2 which may indicate an improvement of 6 places on its 1994 rank. Yet this is in no small part due to the different means to estimate educational attainment in 1995.

Table 7.3   The effect on the HDI of varying the elasticity of marginal utility of income

Country	Ranking (a)	Ranking (b)	Difference
Canada	1	3	−2
Switzerland	2	2	0
Japan	3	4	−1
Sweden	4	6	−2
Norway	5	7	−2
France	6	5	1
Australia	7	8	−1
USA	8	1	7
Netherlands	9	9	0
United Kingdom	10	10	0

Notes
Ranking (a) – computed according to UNDP (1994).
Ranking (b) – computed with $\varepsilon = 0$.

7.2.3   Poverty measurement

The other main area where major efforts have been made to develop social indicators is in the measurement of poverty. The reasons for this focus have already been discussed: the widely perceived failure of GNP to indicate what is happening to the wellbeing of the poorest groups, and the desire to develop an indicator that raises the profile of the poor in the development process. Poverty was defined above as the inability to secure even a minimal standard of living. Probably the best set of poverty indices is contained in International Fund for Agricultural Development (IFAD) (1992). The data collected there cover *rural* poverty only, as befits an institution which is concerned with agriculture. It goes without saying that there are many below a poverty line in urban areas as well. The IFAD dataset produces three indicators:

a. the integrated poverty index (IPI);
b. a food security index (FSI); and
c. a basic needs index (BNI).

In addition, it takes the arithmetic mean of these three indices to produce a relative welfare index (RWI). The rest of this section shows how these indicators are estimated and how they have been used.

The integrated poverty index   Two basic measures of poverty tend to be used and both are combined in the IPI. The two measures are the *headcount* index, and the *income gap* index. The headcount index (HI) simply computes the percentage of the population below the poverty line level of income Y^*. So

$$HI = n(Y_i < Y^*)/N$$

where $n(Y < Y^*)$ is the number of people with income Y below Y^*, and N is the total population. HI is a first-order indication of the extent of poverty.

The income gap measure (IG) looks at the 'distance' $Y^* - Y_i$ for each person or household (i) below the poverty line, sums this and expresses the sum as a percentage of all (national) incomes. That is:

$$IG = \sum_{i=1}^{N}\left(Y^* - Y_i\right)/Y.$$

IG adds further information to HI because it can be interpreted as the amount of income needed to overcome poverty in that economy, provided, of course, that extra income was all allocated to those below the poverty line.

The World Bank (1990) estimated the extent of world poverty in 1985 using these two indicators. They used two poverty lines, $275 and $370 per capita per annum (PPP in 1985 prices). People below the lower line were regarded as 'extremely poor', and people below the upper line as 'poor'. Taking the lower line the result was that 633 million people in 1985 were extremely poor, and 483 million people were poor. Adding them together, 1,116 million people were poor or extremely poor, providing some evidence for the widely quoted figure of '1 billion poor' in the world, about 20 per cent of the world's population, urban and rural.

IFAD (1992) estimated that 36 per cent of the world's rural population was below the poverty line in 1988. In terms of the income gap, the World Bank (1990) estimated that just 3 per cent of the developing countries' income would, if allocated to the poor, lift all the poor up to the poverty line, a remarkably small percentage, although in regional terms the figure could be as high as 10–12 per cent for South Asia and India. That 3 per cent, expressed as an absolute sum, would have been about $60 billion in 1985. Sen (1976) combined the HI and the IG indicators to produce a composite poverty index:

$$I_{Sen} = HI\ [IG + (1 - IG)g]$$

where g is the Gini coefficient of household income below the poverty line. IFAD (1992) uses the HI and the IG indicators but combines them with other standard indicators – income per capita, growth rates of income per capita, and life expectancy – to derive an integrated poverty index based on Sen (1976). IFAD's index is

$$IPI = \frac{HI[IGR + (1 - IGR).LER}{(1 + \Delta Y)}$$

where: HI is the headcount index as a fraction; IGR is the income gap expressed relative to the maximum per capita income in developing countries (that is, IGR = [max $Y - Y_i$]/max Y); LER is life expectancy ratio, also measured relative to maximum life expectancy in the sample (that is, LER = [max LE – LE_i]/max LE). Note that the life expectancy ratio is being used here as a surrogate for the Gini coefficient in Sen's formula (presumably on the basis that the two are significantly correlated); ΔY is the growth rate of GNP per capita.

The effect of these normalizations is to constrain the IPI to take values between 0 and 1. To illustrate, consider Mozambique. The data are: HI = 0.65; max Y = \$6,260 (Cyprus GNP per capita); Y_i = \$100; LE = 48 years; max LE = 76 years (Cuba); ΔY = –2.0 per cent = –0.02; to give IPI (Mozambique) = 0.656. Compared with all other developing countries, this IPI score ranks Mozambique as the 26th poorest country in the world. The closer the IPI score is to 1, the poorer it is.

The IPI clearly suffers the same limitation as previous incarnations of the HDI: it is 'anchored' by the performance of those developing countries with the highest income and the longest life expectancy. If the performance of either of those countries should change, the score for the country in question will change. The IPI also has some idiosyncrasies of its own, the main being that the denominator $(1 + \Delta Y)$ appears to be an essentially arbitrary addition to the Sen composite measure. This is also an attribute of the IFAD's food security index (FSI) and its basic need index (BSI). These measures are a mish-mash of legitimate development concerns weighted in an arbitrary manner without due consideration to the simplicity or meaning of the resulting indicator. For example, the health component of the BSI is made up of no fewer than five indicators (that is, physicians per head of population relative to countries with maximum and minimum physicians per head, that is, a normalization which is the same in form as that used in the HDI; infant mortality rate normalized relative to countries with maximum and minimum values; percentage of population with access to health services; percentage of population with access to safe water, and percentage of population with access to sanitation). If some of these indicators are correlated then the resulting measure is unnecessarily complicated. This is compounded by several differences in the methods that are used for normalizing the data. Such problems are carried over into the calculation of the relative welfare index (RWI). Despite attempting to cover considerably more indicators than the

HDI, it is unlikely that the RWI adds any informational content. It may even be that informational content is lost relative to the HDI.

The extent to which an indicator is actually meaningful is crucial for another issue, namely the use to which such an index might be put. As a ranking for individual countries the IPI is certainly interesting in the same way that the HDI is interesting. Yet as the indicator is intended to measure the degree of poverty in countries, it could be used by the donor community to target the poorest countries. IFAD (1992) shows that the difference in ranking between this measure and a simple income per capita measure is substantial, suggesting that a composite indicator such as the IPI could not be replaced by a single representative measure such as income per capita. Whether the IPI has policy relevance over and above this 'targeting' use is not clear.

7.3   Social indicators incorporating environment and resources

Without question, the HDI is probably the most successful modern development indicator. It has attracted enormous attention from policy-makers anxious to change their ranking. It has also served to differentiate between narrow-focused indicators such as GNP and the wider social development-oriented indicators. But it is not without its problems, as we have seen. From the point of view of measuring sustainable development, the absence of an environmental component is a particular concern. Of course, one of the problems with integrating environmental factors into wellbeing and poverty indicators lies with the availability of data. Nor are conceptual issues that determine the selection of indicators straightforward to resolve. Chapter 2 noted that while some environmental indices are key indicators of the state of the environment it does not follow that they can be interpreted as sustainability indicators, as, say, a measure of genuine saving can. A simpler goal is the extension of the simple poverty indicators. We briefly deal with this below, before considering the more ambitious goal of integrating environmental information into the HDI.

7.3.1   Indicators of poverty and environment

Landholdings and tenure   The scattered data on landholdings have been collected together by the International Fund for Agricultural Development (IFAD, 1992). Table 7.4 shows some selected data. The problems with such data are many. First, they are derived from scattered sources and do not emerge from any consistent process of data collection. Comparability across countries is therefore difficult. Second, even if the sources were comparable, the censuses on which they are based are often ten or even more years old. None the less, assembling what is available serves to indicate what is needed if indicators of *capability to escape poverty* are to be developed.

Table 7.4   *Landholdings, tenure and wage dependence*

Country and year of estimate		Gini coefficient of landholding distribution by household, and trend over time (up = more inequality)	Incidence of tenancy: % total landholding (cash rent, sharecropping, etc.)	Dependence on non-wage income (percentage)
Bangladesh	1983/4	0.50 up	23	na
Ghana	1984	0.44 down	14	86
Guatemala	1979	0.72 constant	12	45
India	1976/7	0.55 na	9	na
Nepal	1982	0.59 up 1961–71, down since	13	100
Peru	1984	0.61 down	na	50
Philippines	1981	0.48 na	33	92
Sri Lanka	1982	0.58 na	27	90
Thailand	1978	0.41 na	16	100

Notes: For cautions on comparing data in this table see text. The higher the value of the Gini coefficient, the more inequality there is. Incidence of tenancy indicates percentage of all landholdings covered by a tenancy agreement, in principle. Dependence on non-wage income measures reliance on own production of agricultural and non-agricultural output.

Source: IFAD (1992).

Water availability   Chapter 6 dealt with indicators of water availability as integral components of indicators of carrying capacity. The data used there were

Table 7.5   *Hours spent collecting water, 1975–1982*

Country	Hours per week
Senegal	17.5
Mozambique (dry season)	15.3
India (Baroda)	7.0
Botswana	5.5
Nepal (10–14 yrs of age)	4.9
Nepal (15+ yrs of age)	4.7
Ghana	4.5
Ivory Coast	4.4
Burkina Faso	4.4
Pakistan	3 5
Nepal (5–9 yrs of age)	1.5

Note: In all cases, water is collected by women.

Source: UN (1991).

'macroeconomic' in the sense that they looked at average water availability per capita within a nation. In practice, what matters, of course, is the availability of water to specific regions, that is, 'micro-availability'. A more appropriate indicator in this context might be time taken to collect water from wells and rivers. Evidence on this indicator is growing but is still too sporadic to be used as a comprehensive indicator (see Table 7.5). Note that the studies used for Table 7.5 may cover only small areas of the countries cited. (IFAD (1992) contains more extensive data on hours spent collecting water, covering 25 countries. Unfortunately, the tables nowhere state whether the numbers recorded are per day or per week.)

Fuelwood availability   Chapter 6 also showed methods of integrating fuelwood availability into indicators of carrying capacity use. As with water, time taken to gather fuelwood is a useful indicator of 'poverty of resource access'. Table 7.6 shows some data. They suggest that fuelwood collection may take far more time than water collection, although there are difficulties of comparison since water may have to be collected daily while fuelwood collections may last several days. As far as possible, the data have been averaged to secure a weekly time comparison.

Table 7.6   Hours spent collecting fuelwood

Country	Hours per week	Carrier
Tanzania	56	Women
Niger	28–42	Women
Senegal	28–35	
Nepal	7–35	Adults/children
Ghana	24–28	
Kenya	24	Mainly women
India (Gujarat)	21	
Peru	17	Women
India (south)	12	Women/children

Source: Adapted from Lewenhak (1989).

7.3.2   Sustainability, environment and the HDI

Our interest in social indicators is the result of a desire to account for current distributional concerns. Our examination of the conceptual aspects of sustainable development in Chapter 1 began with the Brundtland Commission's often-quoted definition: 'development which meets the needs of the present without compromising the ability of future generations to meet their own needs'

(WCED, 1987, p. 43). At the same time, the role of the 'essential needs of the world's poor' (ibid.) was also noted, thereby underlining a poverty-oriented approach to measurement. An emphasis on indicators of current social wellbeing suggests that our sustainability criterion ought to prohibit not only current development which was at the expense of the future, but also increases in wellbeing for the better off in society which came at the expense of those who were worse off. This is a rather more specific requirement and may imply at least some connection with the nature of capital ownership, or at least, entitlement. From a distributional perspective, this might serve to underline the importance of human capital (and hence education) to sustainable development, especially since human capital is inherently specific to the individual. Currently, however, it is difficult to say much more. This is undoubtedly a result of the lack of discussion which has so far taken place on the subject of intragenerational sustainability. It might also be the case that distributional issues do not fit so neatly into a formal economic model, precluding the construction of robust and consistent indicators. Yet it is clear that indicators such as the HDI are not sufficient for the purpose of measuring sustainable development and need to be supplemented with complementary indicators or indeed, augmented with 'environmental' components.

The simple indicators described in Section 7.3.1 were very much local indicators. Integrating the environment into the HDI is an altogether different proposition. Again, data difficulties exist, yet just as importantly, conceptual problems also abound. In principle, how would the HDI treat an environmental component? It is worth recalling that each component in the HDI is afforded equal weight. Should environment have equal weight with income, education and health? This is a good test of the extent to which sustainable development really means anything to policy-makers. For if environment is integral to sustainable development and if human development is supposed to be sustainable human development, then environment should be afforded at least equal weight.

In thinking about environmental indicators that could be included in the HDI, it is important to focus on the relationship between the environment and human development. The point of view that will be brought to bear in what follows is based, therefore, on the definition in the 1990 *Human Development Report:* 'human development is a process of enlarging people's choices' (UNDP, 1990, p. 10).

This definition helps to clarify a problem with traditional environmental indicators, particularly those associated with the measurement of pollution emissions or ambient concentrations. There is no unequivocal relationship between human development and such indicators because of the 'typical' pattern of economic development, wherein the poorest countries do not have a polluting industrial base (or excessive use of pesticides and fertilizers in agriculture, for that matter), the newly-industrializing countries typically are polluted as a result of opting for rapid growth, and the richest countries have enough income for other goals, such as a cleaner environment, to be afforded. In addition, it is difficult to generalize these indicators because they are usually associated with a particular locale, topography, weather pattern, and so on. One exception to this, perhaps meriting consideration for the HDI, would be emissions of *persistent* pollutants.

Desai (1994) provides a number of candidate indicators for possible inclusion in the HDI. These are energy use per unit of GDP, water use as a percentage of annual renewable water supplies, and carbon dioxide (CO_2) emissions per capita. The first two indicators would appear to fall foul of the criteria that we have set out above. Energy efficiency tends to trend with the typical patterns of development while the water use indicator is largely determined by such conditions as weather patterns. Chapter 6 showed how this indicator can be viewed as a type of carrying capacity constraint but also revealed the extent to which countries vary in their 'endowments' of renewable water resources. For example, in countries such as Bangladesh and Zambia, this ratio is practically zero while in the arid countries of North Africa and the Middle East it commonly exceeds 100 per cent.

Support can be given for the inclusion of Desai's third indicator, namely CO_2 emissions per capita. The greenhouse warming aspect of environmental change belongs to a class of problems with *long time horizons*, that is, where the rate of regeneration of the environment is very slow. Building an indicator such as per capita emissions of greenhouse gases into the HDI would be highly controversial, because it would immediately penalize all industrialized countries, and because of disagreement with regard to the costs of global warming. Nevertheless, if the judgement is that the costs of greenhouse warming are large, then emission of greenhouse gases per capita is a candidate indicator. The advantage of the CO_2 indicator is that relatively good data exist for a wide range of countries.

Other indicators not considered by Desai (1994) can also be envisaged. *Irreversible* actions are clearly inconsistent with enlarging people's choices, and therefore questions of species loss and protected areas are candidates for inclusion in a green HDI. But there are significant problems to resolve: appropriate measures of biodiversity are required (a significant theoretical problem); and how to weight the loss of different species is not obvious. For protected areas one candidate indicator is the percentage of total land area that is protected (with regard to the Rio target, for instance), but similar questions arise: how to distinguish quantity from quality in protected areas; how to aggregate protected areas (for example, is one hectare as valuable to protect as another?); and how to measure the effectiveness of the protection afforded these areas. Obtaining objective information on effectiveness of protection is particularly problematic.

7.3.3 Genuine savings and the HDI

So far we have considered candidate physical indicators for inclusion in the HDI. We have left the mechanics of how to actually integrate these indicators to one side. Instead our emphasis has been on identifying indicators with a reasonable conceptual basis for inclusion. If sustainability concerns are to be explicitly introduced in the HDI, then genuine savings from Chapter 4 would fulfil many of the criteria set out above. For incorporation into the HDI countries could be ranked according to the size of their genuine savings rate, where positive numbers would indicate countries that are saving for the future, and negative numbers would indicate countries that are consuming their patrimony. This approach is not without problems, since it will say that a genuine savings rate of, say, 15 per cent is 'better' than one of 10 per cent, which has no particular foundation in economic theory. But it does provide a handy index of how provident countries are.

However, it can be argued that including an indicator of sustainability would add little to the HDI. Although the indicators that make up the HDI are selected on the basis that they broadly measure human capabilities or basic needs, the resulting measure remains a mix of diverse indices. This characteristic may be compounded by the introduction of genuine savings into the measure rather than to add seriously to the informational content of the index, which is what policy-makers require. This does not mean that the consideration of an environmental component of the HDI is redundant. Given the unquestionable role of the HDI in raising the political profile of general health and educational policies, it seems fitting that there should be a similar statistical treatment of the environment, including some of the physical variables discussed earlier. Genuine savings could then be considered as a distinct and separate indicator in its own right. However, we should note that Chapter 3 described a framework whereby social, economic and environmental indicators could be considered side by side. It is to this that we turn to now.

7.4 Social accounting matrices revisited

Chapter 3 introduced the notion of social accounting matrices (SAMs) as an alternative way to present conventional national accounting data. There we presented a simple version of this framework to provide a link between green accounting and national accounting. It was noted that SAMs are tools for analysing social concerns in their own right. Chapter 3 also pointed out that approaches linked to national accounts had the advantage of embodying accounting identities. SAMs confer this advantage on the analysis of social concerns. Indeed, it is possible to estimate the national accounts on the basis of a SAM, where the row and column totals of each account represent its total incomings and total outgoings, respectively (Keuning, 1995).

SAMs have a widely established role in the analysis of social concerns, particularly the distribution of income and expenditure or the origins of income. This is achieved via a suitable disaggregation of household (institution) accounts and factor accounts respectively (see, for example, Roland-Holst and Sancho, 1992). Each entry in an aggregate SAM can be viewed as the total of the submatrix (Keuning, 1995) and hence, disaggregation of SAMs can proceed as far as available data will permit. In the Indonesian SAM that has been the basis of a number of detailed studies (see, for example, Keuning, 1995 and Weale, 1991), the 'factors' account is disaggregated to distinguish between for example, farmers, agricultural workers, non-agricultural rural 'rich' and 'poor' and urban 'rich' and 'poor'. The factor incomes of these groups can be systematically analysed and as they are in money terms can be inserted directly into the SNA (Weale, 1991).

Organizing social indicators in accounting terms raises the profile of these indicators relative to economic data, in much the same way as green national accounting has done for environmental indicators. For example, accounts for time use might be constructed from the information in Section 7.3 (see, Pyatt, 1990). These accounts could then be linked to the United Nation's System of Social and Demographic Statistics (SDSS). SAMs can be based either partly or wholly on physical information (Stone, 1977; Weale, 1991). For example, time-use accounts can be described in units of time or the opportunity cost to individuals of undertaking particular activities (Pyatt, 1990). Stone (1977) suggests that in terms of social indicators, measures reflecting composite categories and states – for example, by age, gender – could be linked to the conventional accounts. The unit of account in these cases is human beings as opposed to units of currency. These may be related to the costs of provision of, say, educational services. An advantage of these data is that they can be analysed in terms of stocks and flows. Keuning (1995) has analysed social indicators in both human and currency units within a SAM in order to examine the impacts of economic activity in Indonesia on employment and the distribution of income. One of his conclusions is that the Indonesian oil boom of the 1980s benefited an urban elite via an increase in profits for this category and an increase in the demand for labour for high-skilled urban workers. Our analysis in Chapter 4 examined the degree to which the proceeds of oil depletion were being reinvested for future generations. SAMs also offer a way of bringing current distributional concerns into the frame of measurement. Both approaches are explicitly linked to the national accounts.

Table 7.7 presents a SAM comparable to that presented in Chapter 3. There are three main differences with Table 3.2 because: (i) there is no produced capital depreciation; (ii) intermediate consumption (ImdCon, that is, purchases between firms) is identified as are government transfers (G_T, that is, from government to households); and (iii) resources and environment are not included in the main part of the matrix: that is, not in monetary terms. The environmental account is introduced here along the lines suggested by Weale (1991). E_1 itself might be thought of as consisting of submatrices or accounts of emissions of particular pollutants or environmental problems (or environmental themes along the lines proposed by Adriaanse, 1993). These environmental indicators can be linked to the SAMs data by converting the accounts in Table 7.7 into 'propensities to spend' (Weale, 1991). This is achieved by dividing each account by its appropriate row total, $T_1 - T_5$. Weale then shows that environmental linkages can be ascertained by estimating the matrix, $E_1(T_1)^{-1}$. This shows the impact of 1 unit of a particular type of production on an environmental variable. This should capture both direct and indirect effects of the activity.

Table 7.7   A social accounting matrix showing linkages to the environment

	Production	Factors	Institutions	Saving	Rest of World	Total
Production	ImdCon		C	I	X	T_1
Factors	Y					T_2
Institutions		GDP	G_T			T_3
Saving			S			T_4
Rest of World	M			$(X-M)$		T_5
Total	T_1	T_2	T_3	T_4	T_5	
Environment	E_1					

Source: Adapted from Weale (1991) and Chapter 3.

Keuning and Timmerman (1995) have used this type of analysis to indicate what categories of labour will be affected by environmental policies and the resulting changes in economic structure that occur: for example, by estimating interactions with the factors account, Y and social indicators of educational attainment. In Table 7.7, Y is GDP and can be interpreted as a matrix of different factor incomes that sum to GDP. Keuning and Timmerman find that Dutch males with 'middle-level' education suffer the most as they are most often employed in sectors that contribute relatively highly to pollution.

7.5   Conclusions
Social indicators represent the third category of indicators required to measure sustainable development. Nevertheless, a disadvantage of these measures is that they often have poor conceptual foundations. Yet, such indicators are extremely useful to policy-makers, especially when presented in an appropriate composite form. The most successful of recent composite indicators is the HDI. This measure integrates both social and economic data. Many issues are yet to be

resolved in the construction of this index although it has been highly effective in raising the profile of broad social concerns. As such it seems appropriate for a component to be added to the HDI to reflect environmental concerns. We have made several suggestions in this respect, including measures of CO_2 emissions per capita and amount of habitat protected. Hence, a country whose HDI ranking is decreased by a poor record with regard to the environment may be 'forced' to implement policies to reverse this trend. In terms of measuring sustainable development, a key focus should still be on measuring genuine saving. Yet, it is likely that both this measure and the HDI would suffer by the integration of the two into a single indicator. However, genuine saving can be analysed alongside social concerns via social accounting matrices (SAMs). SAMs also offer the possibility of combining social and environmental indicators with the conventional accounts. This holds the prospect of retaining the aforementioned policy relevance of social data and the provision of a conceptual foundation for subsequent analysis.

8 Environmental impacts of economywide policies

8.1 Introduction

This chapter focuses on how indicators of sustainable development may be used to shape economywide (that is, macroeconomic and sectoral) policies, which in turn affect the environment. Hence, economywide policies are not sustainable development policies *per se* (considered in Chapter 9). However, given the core message of the analysis of sustainability in linking the economy and environment, such policies are surely extremely relevant. For example, one crucial question is the extent to which economywide policies work for or against a goal of sustainable development via indirect impacts on resource use and environmental quality. In sum, policies for sustainable development and the economy as a whole are inextricably intertwined and so it is crucial that they do not pull in opposite directions.

Economywide policies mainly involve a variety of economic instruments, ranging from pricing in key sectors (for example, energy or water) and broad sectoral taxation or subsidy programmes (for example, agricultural production subsidies, industrial investment incentives) to macroeconomic policies and strategies (exchange rate, interest rate or wage policies; trade liberalization, privatization, and so forth). Such policies are often packaged within programmes of structural adjustment or sectoral reform, aimed at promoting economic stability, efficiency and growth, and – ultimately – human welfare. Although the emphasis is on economic policies, other non-economic measures (such as social, institutional and legal actions), are also relevant. It is not unusual for such sweeping measures to have a range of environmental impacts as well.

An analytical and presentational approach based on the action impact matrix (AIM) is presented as a method of prioritizing key economic–environmental linkages and formulating remedial measures to protect the environment. The AIM process could be made an even more effective tool for sustainable development, if it is used in conjunction with some of the other indicators of sustainability discussed in earlier chapters. An AIM that incorporates key sustainability indicators could provide decision-makers with practical benchmarks and trends on which future economywide policies and strategies for sustainable development may be based.

While the focus of this chapter is on economic–environmental linkages, it also includes a discussion of associated social issues such as poverty, income distribution and resettlement. Other key social objectives, such as popular participation, empowerment and the rights of indigenous peoples, fall outside the scope of this discussion. Nevertheless, the generic findings and AIM-based approach presented here could be useful also in systemically identifying a wider range of social impacts, and analysing them – provided that techniques are available for this purpose.

One recurring theme is that the potential for achieving parallel gains in conventional economic, social and environmental goals is often present whenever economywide reforms attempt to improve macroeconomic stability, increase efficiency and alleviate poverty. However, in important cases these potential gains cannot be realized unless complementary environmental and social measures are carried out.

The application of the AIM process (including the key potential role of sustainable development indicators in assessing the environmental impacts of economywide policies and formulating mitigatory measures), is described in the next section. This is followed by a more detailed discussion of actual links between economywide policies and the environment. Finally, the Appendix contains further evidence of the environmental and social impacts of structural adjustment policies adopted during the past decades.

8.2 Integrating environmental concerns into economic decision-making
The systematic integration of environmental concerns into economywide decision-making is a key first step towards sustainable development. The increasing need for such integration is underlined by a recent review of World Bank loan conditions in adjustment operations, which indicated an increase in the number of environmental components included in these loans (Warford et al., 1994). The review covered adjustment lending operations over the period 1988–92 and found that about 60 per cent of the sampled loans explicitly included environmental goals or loans conditionalities addressing environmental concerns in agriculture, forestry, energy, trade and industry. This was up sharply from only 37 per cent during the 1979–87 period. While, the recent loans encompassed a much wider range of policy instruments or sectoral strategies (for example, from energy and resource pricing reforms to institutional capacity building), there is considerable room for improvement in coordinating economic and environmental policies.

The links between economywide policy reforms and the environment can be complex and usually require country-specific analysis. However, while impacts are often too diverse to be comprehensively traced with precision, *many key economywide reforms have specific, identifiable, impacts on a much smaller subgroup of priority environmental problems.* Some of these impacts may be intuitively obvious, and many of them, with some effort, may be traceable. Even modest progress in this regard is helpful because the proper *recognition of the environmental benefits of economywide policies will clearly help build support for economic reforms.* At the same time, *broader recognition of the underlying economic and policy causes of environmental problems can enhance support for environmental initiatives* – in terms of both environmental policies and projects.

The best approach to avoid environmental damage that might arise from economywide policies, would be to identify, prioritize and analyse the most serious economic–environmental linkages, and devise specific complementary mitigating measures, before such economywide reforms are implemented. Where data and resource constraints preclude the accurate tracing of such links (*ex ante*), the preliminary screening and prioritization of environmental issues could be followed by establishing contingency plans and carefully monitoring these environmental problems, to deal with them if they worsen *ex post*. In cases involving more severe environmental degradation (especially where *ex ante* analysis has carefully prepared the ground), special care may be required to orchestrate the timing and sequencing of various economywide policies and complementary environmental measures, to minimize environmental damage.

8.2.1   Action impact matrix (AIM): a tool for policy analysis, formulation and coordination

In the context of the foregoing discussion, economic and environmental analyses and policies may be used more effectively to achieve sustainable development goals, by linking and articulating these activities explicitly. Implementation of such an approach would be facilitated by constructing an action impact matrix (AIM) – a simple example is shown in Table 8.1, although an actual AIM would be very much larger and more detailed (Munasinghe, 1993a). Such a matrix helps to promote an integrated view, meshing development decisions with priority economic, environmental and social impacts. The far left column of Table 8.1 lists examples of the main development interventions (both policies and projects), while the top row indicates some of the main sustainable development issues. Thus the elements or cells in the matrix help to: (a) identify explicitly the key linkages; (b) focus attention on valuation and other methods of analysing the most important impacts; and (c) suggest action priorities. At the same time, the organization of the overall matrix facilitates the tracing of impacts, as well as the coherent articulation of the links between a range of development actions – that is, policies and projects.

A stepwise procedure, starting with readily available data, has been used effectively to develop the AIM in several countries (for instance, Ghana and Sri Lanka). This process has helped to harmonize views among those involved (economists, environmental specialists and others), thereby improving the prospects for successful implementation. First, data from National Environmental Action Plans, environmental assessments, and so forth may be organized into

Table 8.1 Simple example of an action impact matrix (AIM)[1]

Action/policy	Main objective	Impacts on key sustainable development issues			
		Land degradation	Air pollution	Resettlement	Others
Macroeconomic & sectoral policies	Macroeconomic and sectoral improvements	Positive impacts due to removal of distortions Negative impacts mainly due to remaining constraints			
• Exchange rate	• Improve trade balance and economic growth				
• Energy pricing	• Improve economic and energy use efficiency	(–H) (deforest open-access areas)	(+M) (energy effic.)		
• Others					
Complementary measures[2]	Specific/local social and environmental gains				
• Market based	• Reverse negative impacts of market failures, policy distortions and institutional constraints	Enhance positive impacts and mitigate negative impacts (above) of broader macroeconomic and sectoral policies	(+M) (pollution tax)		
• Non-market based		(+H) (property rights)	(+M) (public sector accountability)		
Investment Projects	Improve efficiency of investments				
• project 1 (Hydro Dam)	• Use of project evaluation (cost–benefit analysis, environmental assessment, multicriteria analysis, etc.)	Investment decisions made more consistent with broader policy and institutional framework (–H) (inundate forests)	(+M) (displace fossil fuel use)	(–M) (displace people)	

158

- Project 2
(Re-afforest
and relocate)
- Project N

$(+H)$
(replant forests)

$(+M)$
(relocate
people)

Notes
1. A few examples of typical policies and projects as well as key environmental and social issues are shown. Some illustrative but qualitative impact assessment are also indicated: thus + and – signify beneficial and harmful impacts, while H and M indicate high and moderate intensity. The AIM process helps to focus on the highest priority environmental issues and related social concerns.
2. Commonly-used market-based measures include effluent charges, tradable emission permits, emission taxes or subsidies, bubbles and offsets (emission banking), stumpage fees, royalties, user fees, deposit-refund schemes, performance bonds, and taxes on products (such as fuel taxes). Non-market-based measures comprise regulations and laws specifying environmental standard (such as ambient standards, emission standards and technology standards) which permit or limit certain actions ('dos' and 'don'ts').

Source: Munasinghe (1993a).

159

an environmental issues table that prioritizes these problems, provides quantitative or qualitative indicators of damage, and helps identify underlying economic causes. Second, using information readily available from country economic and sector work, the main economywide policies (current and intended) could be set out in a second table, together with a brief review of the basic economic issues that they address and potential environmental linkages. The information from these two tables is then combined to develop a preliminary action impact matrix (see Munasinghe and Cruz, 1994 for details of this process).

One of the early objectives of the AIM-based process would be to help in *problem identification* – by preparing a preliminary matrix that identifies broad relationships, without necessarily being able to specify with any accuracy, the magnitudes of the impacts or their relative priorities. For example, in Table 8.1, a currency devaluation may make timber exports more profitable and lead to deforestation of open access forest. The appropriate remedy might be to strengthen property rights or restrict access to the forest areas. A second example might involve increasing energy prices towards marginal costs to improve energy efficiency and decrease pollution. Adding pollution taxes to marginal energy costs will further reduce pollution. Increasing public sector accountability will reinforce favourable responses to these price incentives, by reducing the ability of inefficient firms to pass on cost increases to consumers or to transfer their losses to the government. In the same vein, a major hydroelectric project is shown in Table 8.1 as having two adverse impacts – inundation of forested areas and villages – as well as one positive impact – the replacement of thermal power generation (thereby reducing air pollution). A reafforestation project coupled with adequate resettlement efforts may help address the negative impacts. The matrix-based approach therefore encourages the systematic articulation and coordination of policies and projects to achieve sustainable development goals. Based on readily available data, it would be possible to develop such an initial matrix for many countries. Furthermore, a range of social impacts could be incorporated into the AIM, using the same approach.

This process may be developed further to assist in *analysis* and *remediation*. For example, more detailed analyses and modelling may be carried out for the subset of main economywide policies and environmental impact links identified in the cells of the preliminary matrix. This, in turn, would lead to a more refined final matrix, which would help to quantify impacts and formulate additional measures to enhance positive linkages and mitigate negative ones. The availability of simple but accurate indicators of sustainable development would greatly improve the effectiveness of the matrix elements, in capturing the essential features of economy–sustainability linkages.

The more detailed analyses which could help to determine the final matrix would depend on planning goals and available data and resources. They may range from the application of conventional sectoral economic analysis methods (appropriately modified in scope to incorporate environmental impacts), to fairly comprehensive system or multisector modelling efforts. The former approach is used in many of the case studies discussed later in this chapter. The latter approach is illustrated by case studies of Costa Rica and Morocco (also described below), where computable general equilibrium (CGE) models were constructed that include both conventional economic, as well as environmental or resource variables. At the moment, data and analytical shortcomings are likely to preclude reliance upon general equilibrium or comprehensive system modelling approaches. Current efforts constitute a first step in this direction – their major contribution being to identify more precisely the information and data required for operational policy purposes, and to test the strengths and limitations of a general equilibrium approach.

Thus far, the more successful attempts to value environmental impacts in the macroeconomic context have been based on their effects on conventional economic output which are priced in the marketplace (supplemented sometimes with shadow-pricing corrections). This approach may be linked quite logically with attempts to modify and improve commonly-used market measures of wellbeing such as GNP (see Chapters 2 to 4 for details). For example, the new United Nations Handbook for the System of National Accounts (SNA), includes a proposal to supplement the conventional SNA with a set of satellite accounts that reflect pollution damage and depletion of natural resource stocks (UNSO, 1993). In certain cases, some environmentally and socially crucial impacts (for example, loss of biodiversity or human health hazards) may be as important as economic effects, which in turn will require the extension or adaptation of conventional economic techniques. One step would be to improve environmental valuation by using a wider range of methods which employ both market and non-market information to estimate indirectly the economic value of environmental assets (for example, travel cost or contingent valuation methods). Such techniques have been used quite widely in project-level applications in the industrial countries (see Freeman, 1993). There is a growing body of case studies on the environmental valuation of project impacts in the developing countries (Munasinghe, 1993b). However, considerable work is required to extend this experience to cover economywide impacts.

Other (non-economic) indicators of environmental and social wellbeing (both micro and macro) also would be helpful in expanding the scope of the AIM-based approach and thereby facilitating decision-making, especially in cases where economic valuation of environmental and social impacts was difficult (see Chapters 6 and 7). Techniques such as multicriteria analysis (MCA) may be used to trade off among different economic, social and environmental indicators, as a supplement to conventional cost–benefit analysis (CBA).

The Sri Lanka case study (described below) explores the MCA approach, in attempting to analyse economic–environmental, as well as environmental–environmental tradeoffs. The essential point is that even when valuation of environmental and social impacts is not possible, if other physical, ecological and social indicators of sustainability are available, then a body of techniques exist that will help to better prioritize such impacts – thereby improving development actions.

In the remainder of this chapter some recent empirical work in the developing world is described, which explores the environmental impacts of economywide policies and methods of quantifying such impacts to make decision-making more effective. The discussion is grouped under five main headings:

- efficiency-oriented policies;
- unaddressed policy, market or institutional imperfections;
- restoring macroeconomic stability;
- short-term adverse effects of recession and government cutback;
- long-term poverty and income effects.

8.3   Efficiency-oriented policies
The main features of most policy reforms directed at various levels of economic decision-making are price changes which are designed to promote efficiency and reduce waste. Programmes which address price-related distortions ('getting prices right') can contribute to both economic and environmental goals. Typically, in many developing countries, misplaced efforts to promote specific regional or sectoral growth and general economic development have created complex webs of commodity, sectoral and macroeconomic price distortions, resulting in economic inefficiency and stagnation. Often, these economic distortions also lead to unanticipated changes in production and input-use that promote resource overexploitation or pollution. Such economic distortions may arise from a macroeconomic policy (such as the overvaluation of the local currency) or from a sectoral policy with economywide implications (such as subsidized energy prices). In either case, economywide policies that are not designed for environmental purposes may have substantial effects on the level and conduct of environment-related activities, suggesting that correcting such price-related distortions will also result in environmental gains. Among the broadest remedies are those correcting the foreign exchange rate and taxes that distort trade. More sector-specific reforms seek to shift key relative prices – for example, setting efficient prices for energy or water (which have pervasive effects), and removing taxes or subsidies on particular commodities or factors of production.

8.3.1 Macroeconomic reforms

At the level of 'macroeconomic' pricing policies, a study of Zimbabwe illustrates how foreign exchange reforms associated with adjustment efforts can support a key environmental sector (see Munasinghe and Cruz, 1994 for details). Wildlife-based economic activities in Zimbabwe, including ecotourism, safaris, hunting and specialized meat and hide production, constitute some of the fastest-growing sectors. Wildlife-based tourism alone grew at the rate of 13 per cent in 1991, comprising 5 per cent of GDP. From the environmental perspective, wildlife-based activities (unlike cattle ranching which competes for limited land resources), are better suited to the country's semi-arid climate and poor soils. Economically viable systems can be maintained with lower stocking rates and a reduced environmental burden, compared with cattle ranching and pastoral activities. Equally important is the indirect environmental benefit associated with wildlife management goals of conserving a natural habitat that appeals to visitors.

There is much interest in wildlife development in Zimbabwe, with emphasis placed on its potential role as a more sustainable land-use system than cattle ranching or conventional agriculture, in semi-arid zones. Wildlife enterprises currently account for 15 per cent of land use on commercial and communal lands. Wildlife on which ecotourism is based competes with beef production – in terms of land use, rather than meat output. Despite its economic and environmental advantages, sectoral land policies have generally discouraged wildlife activities since these are still perceived as 'underutilizing' land. Livestock marketing and pricing policies have also traditionally subsidized cattle ranching. More importantly, for many years, the government's foreign exchange and trade policies severely penalized this sector. The Zimbabwean dollar was overvalued by 50 to 80 per cent from 1981 to 1990. This meant that export-oriented sectors were implicitly taxed, including wildlife and nature tourism concerns. Foreign exchange earnings were diverted to other sectors, depressing incomes and investment in wildlife. In 1990, the government introduced an adjustment package, including measures aimed at boosting the level of exports. The currency was devalued by 25 per cent, and more liberal access to foreign exchange was allowed. These moves were beneficial on both economic and ecological fronts – because exports increased, and at the same time the profitability of the wildlife sector improved, leading to a significant increase of wildlife on commercial farmlands.

While the Zimbabwe study illustrates how relatively straightforward and unambiguous links between macroeconomic reforms and specific environmental effects can be traced and measured, in other cases the effects of policy change are more indirect. Such indirect or system effects of economic policies on the environment have prompted some interest in the use of CGE models. An early study of Thailand (see Chapter 8) illustrated the importance of complementary measures to ensure that successful economic growth policies do not conflict with environmental objectives (Panayatou and Sussangkarn, 1991). For example, in the absence of clear delineation of property rights, increased incentives induced farmers to overexploit fragile lands while industrial growth, unaccompanied by adequate regulatory or economic instruments, was associated with major environmental damage. Although the quantitative results of this exercise should be interpreted with care (because of data constraints), they make a useful contribution and, in conjunction with others (Devarajan, 1990; Robinson, 1990), highlight the kind of information needed to be able to anticipate with greater accuracy the environmental consequences of policy reform.

This general equilibrium approach has been extended in a study of Morocco (Goldin and Host, 1994), which employed a CGE model that linked agricultural water use with trade policies. Low water charges, together with ineffective collection of these charges, had artificially promoted production of water-intensive crops such as sugar cane. Thus, rural irrigation water accounts for 92 per cent of the country's marketed water use. At the same time, irrigation charges cover less than 10 per cent of the long-run marginal cost (LRMC), while the corresponding figure for urban water tariffs is less than 50 per cent. Given these policies, it is not surprising that a water deficit is projected for Morocco by the year 2020, notwithstanding the fact that by the same year, water sector investments would account for 60 per cent of the government budget. The study, however, goes beyond the traditional sectoral remedy of proposing an increase in water tariffs. It links sectoral policy reforms with ongoing macroeconomic adjustment policies, involving the complete removal of nominal trade tariffs, and analyses the overall effects of both sets of reforms.

In the CGE simulation, liberalization of trade alone leads to a modest increase in real GDP. Household incomes and consumption post significant gains as import barriers are reduced, exports become more competitive, domestic purchasing power rises and resources are allocated more efficiently across the economy. The two major drawbacks, however, are that elimination of tariffs leads to budgetary deficits, and domestic water use increases substantially because of the expansionary effects of liberalization. In the second scenario, only water price reforms are considered. The results indicate (as expected) that, other things being equal, doubling water prices reduces water use significantly – by 34 per cent in rural areas and by 29 per cent for the economy as a whole. This static efficiency gain is associated with a small decline (about one per cent) in the incomes and real consumption of both rural and urban households. In the final scenario, trade liberalization continues to stimulate growth, but simultaneously reforming water prices induces substantial reductions in agricultural (and economywide) water use, unlike in the scenario involving price reform alone.

To summarize, the macroeconomic policy reform (trade liberalization) alone resulted in more efficient allocation of resources and expansion of exports, but also led to environmental stress through increased water use. When complementary water price increases were simultaneously undertaken with trade liberalization, the beneficial expansionary economic effects of the latter were largely retained, but now with substantial reductions in water use as well (because of the higher water prices).

Other illustrative examples of the role of macroeconomic policies include the investigation of links between adjustment policy and environment in the agriculture sector in Sub-Saharan Africa (Stryker et al., 1989). Important contributions have also been made by environmental organizations through studies on the environmental impact of the adjustment process in Thailand, the Ivory Coast, Mexico and the Philippines (see Appendix to this chapter) (Reed (ed.), 1992; Cruz and Repetto, 1992). Within the World Bank, a recent study suggests that trade policies which encourage greater openness in Latin America have tended to be associated with a better environment, primarily due to environmentally benign characteristics of modern technologies (Birdsall and Wheeler, 1992).

8.3.2 Sectoral reforms

More specific or restricted policies affecting major sectors, such as industry and agriculture, or key resources, such as energy, are also addressed in programmes of economywide policy reforms. For example, the potential gains from price reform in the energy sector may be enormous. All recent energy projects supported by the Bank have involved careful assessment of the adequacy of institutional arrangements and price efficiency. In each case efforts were made to promote rational pricing policies, improve institutional effectiveness, and achieve greater transparency and accountability in the provision of energy.

Energy sector reforms can contribute to both economic and environmental goals. In Sri Lanka, for example, as in most developing countries, electricity prices have been well below the incremental cost of future supplies. Many studies show that eliminating power subsidies by raising tariffs closer to the LRMC of power generation will encourage more efficient use of electricity (Munasinghe, 1990). In projecting future electricity requirements in Sri Lanka, the Bank study (Meier and Munasinghe, 1993) found that the economic benefits of setting electricity prices to reflect LRMC is supplemented by an unambiguously favourable impact on the environment. In addition, pricing reforms were found to have better economic and environmental impacts than purely technical approaches to demand-side management, such as promoting the use of energy-saving fluorescent lights. Of course, a combination of both pricing and technical measures provided the best results.

This emphasis is reflected in two recent World Bank policy papers for the energy sector (World Bank, 1993b; World Bank, 1993d). As noted earlier, one of these reports estimates that developing countries spend more than $250 billion annually on subsidizing energy (World Bank, 1993d). The countries of the former USSR and Eastern Europe account for the bulk of this amount ($180 billion), and it is estimated that more than half of their air pollution is attributable to such price distortions. Removing all energy subsidies would produce large gains in efficiency and in fiscal balances, and would sharply reduce local pollution and cut carbon emissions by as much as 20 per cent in some countries, and by about 7 per cent worldwide. Similarly, electricity prices in developing countries are, on average, barely more than one-third of supply costs. As a result, consumers use about 20 per cent more electricity than they would if they paid the true costs of supply. Moreover, recent evidence shows that far from correcting this distortion, many governments have been slow to adjust electricity tariffs to reflect higher costs from inflation, fuel and interest charges. A review of electricity tariffs in 60 developing countries has shown that average tariffs declined over the period 1979–88 from 5.2 to 3.8 cents/kWh (1986 US dollars) (World Bank, 1993b). This is particularly troubling as energy demands are expected to grow, and will probably double in the next 15 years.

Achieving commercial pricing policies is, therefore, central to achieving energy efficiency and economic sustainability. Of the 24 energy and power sector loans approved by the Bank in fiscal year 1993, 16 contained specific requirements to adjust energy prices. For example, the Energy Sector Deregulation and Privatization Project in Jamaica aims to expand power supply as well as improve energy sector efficiency, by focusing on creating a regulatory and policy environment favourable to private sector involvement. Among various activities to support this goal, the project will determine appropriate, market-based pricing principles for application to the petroleum sector. Another example, is the Bulgaria Energy Project which has as an objective the realignment of the level and structure of electricity tariffs to rationalize consumption, reduce imports, lessen the pollution associated with generation, and mobilize resources for the national electricity company (NEK). The project also aims to reorient the operations of NEK along more commercial lines, and improve and depoliticize the tariff setting system by establishing an independent regulatory mechanism.

The negative environmental effects of industrial protection policies also suggest the win–win potential of industrial policy reforms. This is illustrated in the experience of Mexico from 1970 to the late 1980s. Between 1970 and 1989, industrial pollution intensity (per unit of value added) in Mexico increased by 25 per cent, induced by government investments and subsidies in the petrochemical and fertilizer industries. The energy intensity of industry also increased by 5.7 per cent in the same period. Aside from the beneficial environmental aspects of removing such subsidies, there will also be direct fiscal implications. Energy subsidies are generally costly, and must be financed from government budgets that are often in deficit. In Mexico, broad subsidies for fuels and electricity absorbed $8–13 billion, or 4 to 7 per cent of GDP, from 1980 to 1985.

Energy subsidies are not the only form of policy-induced inefficiency. Many natural resources are subsidized, leading to distorted investment decisions and removing competitive incentives to use them efficiently. Unfortunately, subsidies tend to create powerful beneficiaries who come to regard their subsidy as a right, creating challenging political and institutional obstacles to full cost pricing. A recent World Bank Operations Evaluation Department (OED) review (Munasinghe and Cruz, 1995) of experience in urban water supply and sanitation projects between 1967 and 1989, for example, found that borrowers often fail to comply with covenants, especially those on pricing and financial performance. Another OED review of completed irrigation projects (ibid.) found that cost recovery was unsatisfactory in 73 per cent of the 107 projects surveyed. The World Bank has taken steps to strengthen cost recovery mechanisms because benefits from removing subsidies can be substantial, economically, environmentally and socially – especially when such subsidies benefit large-scale users of a resource and the funds could be used to alleviate poverty more directly.

Experience in the water and sanitation sector illustrates the limitations of direct government provision and indiscriminate subsidization of household services. Despite progress in developing affordable engineering solutions, the delivery and maintenance of services have been disappointing. Subsidies are often captured by wealthier customers, and in most situations resources are inadequate to maintain a high quality of service or to extend facilities to low-income areas. Subsidies may be justified in specific situations (rural water supplies in low-income areas and sewage treatment in urban areas), but these are most effective when targeted and explicit. Thus, water and sanitation projects approved by the World Bank increasingly place the emphasis on cost recovery.

The Water Quality and Pollution Control Project in Brazil (ibid.) primarily focuses on urban water pollution and supply problems, which will benefit a substantial portion of the 14 million people in the metropolitan areas of São Paolo and Curitiba. Full cost recovery and improved water quality will be achieved through a variety of instruments – essentially tariffs on sewerage services and water use charges, but including park entry fees, increased property taxes and various forms of betterment fees, with a possible tax on pesticide use. The Karnataka Rural Water Supply and Environmental Sanitation Project in India (ibid.) also includes a component to recover operation and maintenance costs, to help ensure the sustainability of the project. Indeed, the project is designed to include a strong emphasis on community participation to increase the willingness of the beneficiaries to pay for the operation and maintenance of water supply services. Finally, in the Changchun Water Supply and Environmental Project in China (ibid.), the World Bank is helping to formalize a policy linking water charges to the marginal cost of water and to improve the collection and treatment of liquid wastes from both industries and households.

The negative effects of underpricing resources can also be seen in the agricultural sector. In Tunisia, the government's concern with ensuring sufficient supply and affordability of livestock products has resulted in a web of pricing and subsidy interventions. A variety of subsidies has promoted livestock production intensification in certain parts of Tunisia, while in other regions they have encouraged herd maintenance at levels beyond rangelands' carrying capacity. Particularly during dry years, subsidized feed imports have substituted for natural pasture, and have averted herd contraction. This failure of herds to respond to diminished feed availability in natural pastures, however, has contributed to significant rangelands degradation primarily in the central and southern regions of the country. This has direct effects on livestock production, and long-term, indirect implications for the entire agricultural sector.

In the Zambia Marketing and Processing Infrastructure Project (ibid.), one of the principal objectives is to restructure public expenditures for agriculture by eliminating maize, fertilizer and transport subsidies. Until November 1991, the government pursued an interventionist agricultural strategy, nationalizing maize mills, establishing parastatals and government-controlled cooperatives, regulating markets and prices, and giving out subsidies. The resulting short-term gains in maize output were not sustainable since continuous cropping, as well as fertilizer and pesticide subsidies, led to soil acidity and declining productivity. The reforms linked with the project address these distortions, setting the stage for improved efficiency in the production and supply of food, together with more sustainable farming practices.

In the past few years, several additional examples of the adverse environmental effects of these types of economywide policies have been examined. World Bank studies on Brazil have demonstrated the role of sectoral policies in subsidizing frontier land clearing and use that have exacerbated deforestation in the Amazon. Mahar (1988) and Binswanger (1989) have analysed the role of subsidies to agricultural and livestock expansion as the key factor leading to deforestation. Schneider (1993) focuses on institutional barriers at the economic frontier that prevent the emergence of land tenure services, such as titling and property rights enforcement, and thus undermine the potential for sustainable land use. Other studies have addressed similar adverse impacts of agricultural policies on the environment in Indonesia (on soil erosion), Sudan (on deforestation), and Botswana (on pasture land degradation) (Barbier, 1988; Larson and Bromley, 1991; Perrings, 1993).

8.4 Unaddressed policy, market or institutional imperfections

While liberalizing policies typically help both the economy and the environment, unaddressed economic distortions may undermine the beneficial environmental effects of economywide reforms. The reform process is typically handled in stages, with the initial adjustment package aimed at the most important macroeconomic issues. Some policy, market or institutional imperfections that policy-makers intend to address later in the adjustment process, or other constraints that have passed unnoticed in the initial screening, often cause environmental harm (Munasinghe, Cruz and Warford, 1993). The remedy generally does not require the reversal of the original reforms, but rather the implementation of additional measures that will remove the offending policy, market or institutional difficulty.

This approach parallels the way in which the social consequences of adjustment (such as increased burdens on the poor) are handled – by introducing targeted social safety nets. Additional complementary environmental measures include both market- and non-market-based policies, as well as specific investment projects. Some of the most frequently-used market-based instruments include effluent charges, tradable emission permits, emission taxes or subsidies, bubbles and offsets (emission banking), stumpage fees, royalties, user fees, deposit-refund schemes, performance bonds, and taxes on products (such as fuel taxes). Non-market-based instruments comprise regulations and laws specifying environmental standards which in essence mandate (or prohibit) certain actions ('dos' and 'don'ts'). Common examples of environmental standards are ambient standards, emission standards and technology standards.

8.4.1 Remaining policy distortions

Environmental gains can be realized by addressing remaining policy failures. Reforms in energy prices will help the environment, but remaining policy distortions elsewhere may reduce the beneficial effect. This is exemplified in a case study of Poland (Munasinghe and Cruz, 1995), where energy intensity and excessive pollution are caused by not only the undervaluation of coal in the centralized price system but also the entire system of state ownership which suppressed market signals and incentives. Previous research has already shown how economywide adjustments, including increases in energy prices, contributed to improvements in energy use and pollution in Poland (Hughes, 1992). However, energy intensity and excessive pollution in Poland are a result not only of the undervaluation of coal in the centralized price system but, more importantly, of the entire system of state ownership that encourages output maximization rather than cost minimization. This means that price responsiveness is blunted, since financial losses are simply absorbed by the public budget, or passed on to consumers in the form of higher output prices.

The Poland study points out the special challenges that the Former Soviet Union (FSU) and other countries of Central and Eastern Europe face as they attempt to restructure their economies and make a rapid transition to a market-oriented system. All of these economies are more material intensive than market economies, and soft budget constraints and centralized plans lead to maximization of output and resource use, rather than cost minimization. The energy intensity endemic to all socialist economies is manifested in Poland's case through excessive reliance on coal. The study also indicates that, especially in the case of economies in rapid transition, reform of regulations and institutions should not be allowed to lag too far behind economic restructuring.

In 1990, Poland initiated an economic transformation programme that led to the privatization of many enterprises. The programme was adversely affected by recession and the collapse of trading arrangements linked to the Council of Mutual Economic Assistance (CMEA). Furthermore, the process of privatization proved to be more complex and lengthy than initially expected. The government has therefore introduced an enterprise and bank restructuring programme to assist in the restructuring of state-owned enterprises (SOEs) and in reducing their debt-servicing constraints.

Despite these changes, SOEs will continue to be major players in the Polish economy, at least in the short term. Of particular relevance is the decision by the government to retain ownership in the energy, mining, steel and defence sectors in the medium term, and to decide on privatization on a case-by-case basis over the next three years. Thus, energy sector restructuring efforts have focused on creating the institutional and legal framework to facilitate competition and greater private sector participation in the future. Coupled with aggressive energy pricing reforms, this strategy appears to be making some headway. For example, a recent survey of large state-owned manufacturing enterprises found that even without privatization, SOEs were already responding to the transformation programme. In particular, the survey found that all firms reduced their consumption of materials and energy per unit of sales (Pinto, Belka and Krajewski, 1993).

The same generic set of issues is encountered in China, with specific reference to sustainable agriculture. Dramatic reforms have included reductions in subsidies for chemical fertilizers and pesticides, increases in energy prices, lifting of quotas for key agricultural products, and reduced intervention in product markets. One component of the study (Munasinghe and Cruz, 1995) focused on farm-level decision-making in Jiangsu Province, where rapid industrialization is occurring and the opportunity cost of labour has increased considerably in recent years. Application of crop and animal residues as fertilizer (a labour-intensive activity) has been discouraged by current trends in labour costs, thereby stimulating excessive demand for chemical fertilizer which may be less environmentally desirable. Increases in commercial energy prices may also result in burning of biomass. Another potential problem arises from the fact that one major agricultural input, namely land, is still subject to command and control and, in some communities, arbitrariness in its allocation. In such circumstances, the uncertainty about land allocation tends to encourage short-run profit maximization and exploitation of land at the expense of sustainability in agricultural production. Land access issues are also relevant in the institutional reforms discussed below.

8.4.2 Market failures

Aside from existing policy distortions, the absence of price signals for environmental services can undermine the contribution of efficiency- and growth-promoting reforms. These failings may lead to environmentally costly patterns of growth. However, recent studies on high-growth economies indicate that addressing environmental concerns early in the transition to growth may allow countries to limit the adverse environmental impacts of expanded economic activity. For example, a recent study on mitigating pollution and congestion impacts in the high-growth economy of Thailand concludes that environmental effects are not solely determined by the scale of economic activity – the 'structure of the economy, the efficiency of input-use (especially in energy and industry) and the types of production technologies in use all matter in determining the environmental impacts' of economic growth (World Bank, 1994d).

The specific role of market failure in influencing the environmental implications of economic reforms is illustrated in the case of liberalization policies and industrial promotion in Indonesia (Munasinghe and Cruz, 1995). In this case, adjustment reforms which are successful in the traditional sense of stimulating industrial growth may have adverse pollution consequences because of market failure – no price signals prevent excessive build-up of pollution. Accelerated industrial growth, while clearly desirable for poverty reduction, could therefore bring with it increased pollution. Changes in incomes and the structure of consumption may also have environmental implications, in terms of demand for both domestic and imported goods.

The Indonesia study shows how reforms can mitigate some of the pollution problems associated with growth. In terms of emissions per unit of output, or pollution intensity, the study found that processing industries (for example, food products, pulp and paper) tend to be dirtier than assembly industries (for example, garments, furniture). Liberalization in the 1980s promoted a surge in assembly industries, thereby reversing the 1970s pattern of more rapid growth in 'dirty' processing sectors. Projections indicate that the share of basic processing industries in total industrial output will fall from 72 per cent in 1993 to about 60 per cent by 2020.

In addition, industry expanded rapidly outside densely populated Java, reducing the health impact of industrial concentration. However, industrial output growth has been so rapid that general pollution levels have nevertheless increased. Thus, while decreases in pollution intensity and industrial decentralization have helped to limit pollution, formal regulations will need to be strengthened also, to avoid health and environmental damage in the future.

8.4.3   Pervasive institutional constraints

The nature of macroeconomic effects on the environment is also contingent upon prevailing regulations or institutions governing resource use. The current case studies indicate that pervasive institutional constraints may undermine potentially beneficial environmental impacts of policy reforms. For example, the eventual impact of economywide reforms (such as those affecting international and domestic terms of trade) on the incentives facing farm households will be influenced by intervening institutional factors (which are themselves determined by cultural, economic and political factors) – especially those affecting access and use rights over agricultural resources such as land and water.

The role of institutional constraints in macroeconomic reform programmes is examined in the Ghana case study (Munasinghe and Cruz, 1995). In this example, trade liberalization, by reducing the taxation of agricultural exports, leads to increased production incentives, while efforts to reduce the government wage bill tend to increase the pool of unemployed. Thus, the adjustment process helps to stimulate production of export crops, and combines with rapid population growth and lack of employment opportunities outside the rural sector to create increasing pressure on land resources, encroachment on to marginal lands and soil erosion. This effect on resource use is influenced by the allocation of property rights. Whether in relation to the security of land tenure of peasant farmers, or to the right to extract timber by logging companies, uncertainty normally results in environmental degradation. In Ghana, as in many regions of Africa, agricultural lands are governed by traditional land-use institutions, and farms are communally owned by the village or tribe. These common property regimes may have been sufficient in allowing sustainable use of agricultural lands when populations were much smaller, and sufficient fallow periods could allow land to regain its fertility. However, such traditional arrangements would be overwhelmed ultimately by economywide forces, resulting in reduced fallowing, loss of soil fertility and environmental decline. The foregoing suggests that better clarification of property rights may help to resist externally induced pressures.

In the China case study discussed earlier, economywide pricing reforms in output markets have not been accompanied by similar reforms on the input side. Land resources are, of course; among the major agricultural inputs, and uncertainty may persist about future rights to farm individual plots of land in many localities, even as agricultural markets in general are being liberalized. This could worsen the incentives for short-term overexploitation of land resources, leading to degradation.

Relevant laws and regulations governing resource access should be reviewed when economywide reforms are planned, especially when there is evidence that key resource sectors such as land, forests, minerals or marine resources will be affected. A useful example of how such programmes could incorporate legal reforms for environmental purposes is the recent adjustment operation undertaken in Peru. In this example, it was determined that economywide reforms to promote economic recovery could potentially increase harvesting pressures on Peru's overexploited fisheries. Thus, the complementary new fishing regulations to protect various fishing grounds were incorporated directly into the adjustment programme (World Bank, 1993c).

Another common institutional problem relates not to the rules and regulations themselves, but rather to the government's capacity to establish and enforce such rules. Regulating large numbers of potentially environmentally degrading activities is especially difficult, even for industrialized country governments. Substantial reductions in institutional and monitoring needs may be achieved with the use of indirect measures or modified pricing-regulation approaches. This is illustrated, for example, by the Mexico City air pollution study (Munasinghe and Cruz, 1995) which shows that while, in principle, pollution taxes are the most accurate means of achieving reductions in pollutants, in practice, administrative feasibility demands that less-refined instruments such as taxes on consumption of fuels may have to be used. While recourse to blunt instruments may help, the magnitude of the institutional capacity-building challenge nevertheless remains clear. Building the relevant institutional capacity in developing countries therefore should be underscored, and appropriate resources should be made available early in the adjustment process to assist country governments in this task.

8.5   Restoring macroeconomic stability

One broad objective of structural adjustment lending is to help restore stability in countries beset by economic crises. A recent example involves the Sub-Saharan countries, where a World Bank study concluded: 'No economy can function well for long if it has rampant inflation, an overvalued exchange rate, excessive taxation of the agricultural sector, scarce supplies of needed inputs, regulations on prices and production, deficient public services, and limited financial services' (World Bank, 1994a, p. 37). The causes of macroeconomic instability often arise from imbalances created by long standing, internal policy failures and are aggravated by adverse external conditions. For example, a history of policies which have allowed increased domestic spending without parallel growth in production eventually leads to inflation or current account deficits or both. When unfavourable external credit or trade conditions arise, the result is macroeconomic instability. Under these conditions, both government budget deficits and international trade balances progressively deteriorate. When an external shock occurs (such as an increase in the prices of imported energy or a decline in the prices of the country's main exports), the result is macroeconomic instability of crisis proportions.

The relationship between environmental issues and policy reforms is fairly straightforward at this general level. Macroeconomic instability is not only disastrous for the economy, but also frequently detrimental to the environment. For example, high interest rates associated with economic crises can severely undermine the value of sustainable production, as resource outputs in the future lose most of their expected value. Thus, to the extent that adjustment policies can help restore macroeconomic stability, their impact will be unambiguously beneficial for long-term natural resource management and environmental concerns.

The above link is illustrated in a case study of Costa Rica, which used a macroeconomic model incorporating timber harvesting activities, to examine the deforestation implications of various macroeconomic factors (Persson and Munasinghe, 1995). Simulation results demonstrate that lower interest rates associated with a stable economy allow the logging sector to correctly anticipate the benefits from future returns to forestry, thereby leading to a decline in current logging activities. The effect of inadequate tenurial security over the resource (and future benefits from it) parallels the results for high discount rates. This corresponds to the well-known result in renewable resource-exploitation models, that the effects on economic behaviour of open-access resource conditions are formally equivalent to those of having secure property rights with infinitely high discount rates.

Other studies have indicated that low and stable discount rates favour the choice of sustainable farming rather than short-term cultivation practices (Southgate and Pearce, 1988). This is important since 'mining' of agricultural land resources is often the prevailing form of resource use in many tropical areas. Frontier farmers have to choose between a sustainable production system with stable but low yields and unsustainable practices which initially have high yields. Using farm models and data from Brazil, a recent World Bank study found that if interest rates are very high, farmers would tend to choose less sustainable methods (Schneider, 1994). For example, at interest rates of 40 per cent (the prevailing real interest rates at the time of the study), farmers would pursue unsustainable agricultural practices that yielded high initial returns but led to subsequent annual declines in productivity of 10 per cent. This explains why agricultural land 'mining' is so prevalent in the Amazon – since most sustainable farming technologies available to Brazilian farmers cannot provide such high incomes. The critical macroeconomic implication of this result is that attempts to resolve the land degradation problem solely by focusing on providing better agricultural technologies would probably be ineffective. To arrest land degradation, macroeconomic reforms which reduce the real interest rate would be needed.

The issue of high debt levels (often associated with sustained periods of government budget deficits and macroeconomic instability) and its implications for environmental degradation have been raised some time ago. However, the available evidence indicates that the linkage is neither clear-cut nor significant.

8.6 Short-term adverse effects of recession and government cutbacks

To the extent that economywide policy reforms promote new economic opportunities and employment for the long term, they will clearly alleviate poverty and reduce pressures that encourage unsustainable exploitation of fragile resources by the unemployed (see Section 8.7 on these long-term effects). In the first place, worsening poverty and income distribution result from the very economic distortions that stabilization and adjustment reforms seek to remedy. However, in the transition period when fiscal austerity is required to arrest deteriorating economic conditions, short-term distributional problems may arise, linked to the recessionary aspects of reforms. One issue concerns the relationship between short-run recessionary effects of adjustment reforms and their potentially adverse impacts on employment, poverty and the environment. The second focuses on the decline of environmental services associated with the government spending cuts mandated by many stabilization and adjustment programmes.

Early views on the environmental implications of adjustment-related reforms, paralleled concerns raised about the social impacts of adjustment. Work on the social aspects of adjustment was motivated by the concern that adjustment programmes would focus on growth, at the expense of distributional objectives (Cornia et al., 1992). A major issue was that the poor, who would be most vulnerable to the effects of macroeconomic contraction, also might be deprived of 'safety nets' – especially if governments unwisely cut social services. Many of the price-related policies would have differential implications for various sectors, and in some cases the poor would be badly affected unless special programmes were introduced to buffer such effects and protect them. At the same time, since unemployment and poverty might be exacerbated by short-term contractionary effects of stabilization programmes, there would be correspondingly important increases in population pressure on fragile resources.

Reduced government spending and its potential adverse impact on environmental protection services have been the subject of criticism from environmental groups. In a study performed by ECLAC (1989), it was concluded that adjustment policies pursued in Latin America during the 1980s led to cutbacks in current expenditure allotments for managing and supervising investment in sectors such as energy, irrigation, infrastructure and mining. This limited the funds available for environmental impact assessments and the supervision of projects to control their environmental impacts. Miranda and Muzondo (1991), in an IMF survey, recognized this problem and suggested that high levels of government expenditure in other areas may lead to reduced funding of environmental activities. Recent case studies attributed increases in air pollution problems in Thailand and Mexico to reductions in expenditures for adequate infrastructure (Reed (ed.), 1992).

While the argument sounds reasonable enough that government cutbacks undertaken as part of adjustment austerity efforts may undermine the funding for environmental initiatives, empirical assessment of its true importance is difficult. Usually, only general categories of expenditures can be identified in most government budgets, so that detailed assessments of environmental programmes normally cannot be initiated. In one effort that was undertaken to assess the social consequences of adjustment lending in Africa, it was found that although there have been declines in government expenditures, the budget proportion going to social expenditures and agriculture actually increased during the adjustment period (Stryker et al., 1989).

The results of studies focusing on social safety nets during adjustment programmes confirm that pursuing fiscal discipline and macroeconomic stability need not take place at the cost of increased hardship for the poor. In much the same way, specific environmental concerns can be incorporated in stabilization efforts. For example, it has been reported that in many countries in Sub-Saharan Africa, forestry departments and their activities have always been severely underfunded (World Bank, 1994a). Thus, targeted efforts to support forestry management activities could, with modest costs, be included in reform packages as part of a proactive environmental response. In brief, both critical environmental and social expenditures could be protected if government budget cuts are made judiciously.

8.7   Long-term poverty and income effects

In addition to the short-term concerns discussed earlier, the crucial long-term links between poverty and environmental degradation in developing countries are increasingly being recognized. For example, the *World Development Report 1992* noted that the growing evidence of the relationship between reducing poverty and addressing environmental goals points to the need to undertake poverty and population programmes as part of environmental efforts (World Bank, 1992e). The need to break the 'cycle' of poverty, population growth, and environmental degradation has also been identified in a recent report of the International Development Association (1992) as a key challenge for sustainable development.

An important result of examining the general equilibrium effects of macroeconomic policy is that indirect resource allocation effects are important and may dominate the more direct effects of some price or income policy changes. In the Costa Rica study, the economic and environmental implications of wage restraints in structural adjustment are examined with the use of a CGE model which highlights the economic activities and factors affecting deforestation in Costa Rica (Persson and Munasinghe, 1995). The model differs from standard approaches in two important respects. First, it can simulate the effect of introducing property rights on forest resources, thus allowing the private valuation of future forestry returns to contribute to sustainable management. Second, it also includes markets for logs and cleared land – loggers deforest to sell timber to the forest industry and squatters clear land for agricultural production and for sale to the agriculture sector (as the latter expands and requires more land).

The importance of indirect effects in Costa Rica is demonstrated in the analysis of economywide policies beyond pricing and intersectoral environmental linkages that can be identified in general fragile environments. This effect can be analysed in conjunction with the assessment of large migration episodes. These may occur as part of direct resettlement programmes or may be induced by inappropriate policies, such as land colonization programmes.

Similar issues have been considered in the World Bank's recent forest sector policy paper, which identified the relationship between *deforestation* and *poverty and population pressure* as a priority resource management concern. The need for correct economic incentives regarding timber harvesting, agroecological zoning and regulations, and the role of public investment and research were the other priorities identified in the policy paper.

With regard to sustainable agriculture concerns, work explicitly links the related problems of rapid population growth, agricultural stagnation and land degradation in Africa (Cleaver and Schreiber, 1991). The study found that shifting cultivation and grazing in the context of limited capital and technical change cannot cope with rapid population growth. At the same time, the traditional technological solution of relying on high-yielding crop varieties is not available. Thus, the study identified the need for a mix of responses in terms of reforms to remove subsidies for inappropriate land uses, improve land-use planning, recognize property rights, provide better education, and construct appropriate rural infrastructure to promote production incentives.

Among current World Bank research studies, the Philippines case study (Munasinghe and Cruz, 1995) evaluates the policy determinants of long-term changes in rural poverty and unemployment that have motivated increasing lowland to upland migration. This process has led to the conversion of forest lands to unsustainable agriculture and has been identified as a key mechanism contributing to the deforestation problem. The inability of the government to manage forest resources is an important direct cause of deforestation, but there is increasing recognition that economic policies, both sectoral and economywide, also significantly contribute to the problem. For example, the study links lowland poverty to agricultural taxation, price controls and marketing restrictions, and uses an econometric model to demonstrate that the poverty contributes significantly to migration pressures on forest lands.

Trade and exchange rate policies have also played important roles in the Philippines and have been dominated by an urban consumer and industrial sector bias. The agricultural sector was implicitly taxed by an average of about 20 per cent for most of the 1970s and early 1980s. In addition, because the industrial sector did not provide an alternative source of growth, poverty generally has worsened and rural incomes in particular have suffered. The study results indicate that the main mechanism by which these economic problems affect the environment is through migration and the conversion of forest lands to unsustainable agriculture. Population pressure already evident in the 1970s worsened during the 1980s. The net upland migration rate grew from 3.4 to 9.4 per cent between 1970–75 and 1978–80, and increased substantially to 14.5 per cent between 1980 and 1985. Consequently, upland cropped area grew at annual rates exceeding 7 per cent from 1971 to 1987. These results suggest that while forestry-specific conservation programmes are needed, economywide policy reforms could be as important in arresting the process of deforestation.

8.8   Conclusions

Although economywide policies (both sectoral and macroeconomic) are not directed explicitly towards influencing the quality of the natural environment, they may affect it for good or bad. This chapter underscores not only the importance of improving our understanding of such economic–environmental links, but also the difficulties of developing a general methodology to trace all the environmental impacts of policy reform. However, it also offers evidence that careful case-specific work on important environmental impacts may help in identifying better ways to deal with them, and sets out several practical steps for implementing the results in operational work. In particular, an approach based on the action impact matrix (AIM) helps to first articulate the range of development actions (policies and projects), and then mesh them with key sustainability impacts (economic, social and environmental). The identification, analysis and prioritization of sustainable development issues, and the formulation and implementation of remedial measures will be facilitated even further by using the action impact matrix – supplemented with appropriate sustainable development indicators (at the economywide level).

The results of empirical, country-specific studies help to examine the links between economywide policies and the environment. The case studies utilize a variety of analytical methods and approaches for identifying such links. The specific findings are: (1) removal of price distortions, promotion of market incentives, and relaxation of other constraints (which are among the main features of adjustment-related reforms), generally will contribute to both economic and environmental gains; (2) unintended environmental harm occurs when economywide reforms are undertaken while other neglected policy, market or institutional imperfections persist. The remedy does not generally require reversal of the original reforms, but rather the implementation of additional complementary measures (both economic and non-economic) that remove such policy, market and institutional difficulties; (3) measures aimed at restoring macroeconomic stability will generally yield environmental as well as economic benefits, since instability undermines sustainable resource use; (4) the stabilization process also may have unforeseen adverse short-term impacts on the environment; and (5) economywide policies will have additional longer-term effects on the environment through employment and income distribution changes, while environmental policies also have income distributional implications.

These findings stress the importance of improving economic–environmental coordination, and have special relevance for decision-making. Proper recognition of the generally positive environmental consequences of economywide policy reforms would help to build additional support for such programmes. At the same time, broader recognition of the underlying economic and policy causes of environmental problems can enhance support for environmental initiatives – in terms of both environmental policies and projects. The following are immediate steps that can be taken by decision-makers: (1) more systematic efforts are needed to monitor environmental trends and anticipate emerging problems, when policy reform proposals are being prepared; (2) serious potential environmental impacts of proposed economywide reforms identified earlier should be carefully assessed, to the extent that data and resources permit; (3) where potential adverse impacts of economywide reforms can be identified and analysed successfully, targeted complementary environmental policies or investments need to be implemented – to mitigate predicted environmental damage, and enhance beneficial effects; and (4) a follow-up system for monitoring the impacts of economic reform programmes on environmentally sensitive areas (identified earlier) should be designed, and resources made available to address environmental problems that may arise during implementation.

More systematic and in-depth work is required in tracing the environmental implications of economywide policies, especially through the application of the AIM-based approach and use of more effective sustainable development indicators. Further work should examine links between the longer-run structure of growth, poverty alleviation and environmental protection. Such studies also need to relate packages of macroeconomic and sectoral policy reforms to a fuller range of priority environmental concerns, in a variety of countries. Some areas of current interest, such as trade reform and privatization policies, are receiving early attention. At the same time, emphasis should be placed on developing more practical models and analytical tools which can be applied in a variety of situations.

Distributional, political economy and institutional issues need to be addressed in future work, with greater attention being paid also to the identification, evaluation and mitigation of the social impacts of economywide policies. The nature of environmental and social problems is heavily dependent on the allocation of political and institutional power, and policy reforms may have substantial implications for the distribution of income and welfare. Thus, there are obvious obstacles to overcoming what might be very powerful vested interests when environmental reforms are recommended. Implementation issues such as asymmetries in the incidence of environmental costs and benefits (especially health impacts), consultation and empowerment of disadvantaged groups, timing of reforms and the role of environmental conditionalities, are especially important. Overall distributional incidence will depend not only on the distribution of costs of environmental policy, but also on the distribution of benefits of those policies. Unfortunately, little is known about the distributional incidence of environmental benefits. Much hinges on the magnitude of the income elasticity of demand, that is, the percentage increase in demand for environment quality arising from a given increase in income. In an early paper, Pearce (1980) challenged the hypothesis that environmental quality is a 'luxury good', that is, a good which would primarily benefit the wealthy relative to the poor. This hypothesis states that the relevant elasticity is greater than 1, thus implying that the share of income devoted to environmental goods rises as income rises. Pearce's analysis was inconclusive, as there were comparatively few studies that permitted quantification of the income elasticity at that time. Kristrom and Riera (1996) has also challenged the luxury good argument in the European context, showing that very few studies support the view that the income elasticity is greater than 1 and that a number of studies suggest income elasticities of the order of 0.3, that is, a 10 per cent increase in income leads to a 3 per cent increase in the 'demand' for environmental quality. This is consistent with the observation that the poor suffer most from environmental degradation. Thus, environmental policy is generally 'pro-poor', and could serve distributional goals, depending on how the programme is financed.

Finally, the need for a more systematic way of monitoring the environmental implications of reform programmes suggests that better economywide indicators of sustainability should be developed, along the lines already discussed in the earlier chapters. For example, recent work has focused on methods of incorporating environmental aspects into national income accounts. However, severe data constraints limit the applicability of such a comprehensive approach in many developing countries. 'Short-cut' methods therefore need to be developed. Thus, more easily applicable rules of thumb (calibrated by well-chosen national studies) could be used to devise baseline estimates of national wealth in the form of natural resources, human capital and produced assets. A useful starting point would be the identification of selected indicators (both physical and economic value based), which can contribute to the more effective monitoring of economywide conditions of sustainability.

Appendix   Structural adjustment and the environment

8A.1   Introduction
The economic situation of developing countries in the 1980s was characterized by the so-called 'debt crisis', which forced most of them to undertake drastic changes in the way economic policy was being conducted. Public austerity, privatization and openness to foreign investment and trade became essential to obtain financial aid. However, the overall changes in the economy did not mean an automatic return to growth, or a solution to increasing social problems. Critics have said that the structural reforms went too far, defenders have said that reforms needed to go even deeper. At the same time, the sustainable development literature was concluding that the development pattern followed by developing countries was not consistent with long-run sustainability. By the end of the 1980s, some authors started linking one problem to the other claiming that developing countries were pressured into adopting unsustainable ways of increasing economic production. As we show, finding evidence for either side is a complex issue.

8A.2   Adjustment programmes: alternative definitions
The balance of payment crisis of the early 1980s forced highly indebted developing countries to look for financial assistance from the international monetary agencies. The international agencies asked for reforms in the way the economy was being managed in such countries. The reforms involved two different sets of policy recommendations, namely *stabilization* and *structural adjustment*, both identified with the expression 'adjustment' (World Bank, 1988, p. 1). They share some common objectives, such as an improvement of the trade balance and changes in government influence in the economy, restraining the range of its activity and making it more efficient. Also, the implementation of stabilization and structural adjustment programmes tends to be complementary rather than exclusive. Nevertheless, they have different assumptions about the timing required for adjustment and the extent of reforms required to modernize the economy.

Structural adjustment   Slow recovery of export growth combined with overall recession showed that medium- and long-term measures indicated a need for structural change on the supply side of indebted economies. These measures included changes in relative prices and institutions, as well as specific lending operations for sectoral improvements. This approach was called structural adjustment, and its aim was to give more flexibility and efficiency to the economy, in order to restore growth after the short-run recession caused by stabilization programmes. It is important to note that stabilization (demand-side) objectives were not abandoned; the new issue was that reforms at the sectoral level – for example, correct distortions to agricultural–industry terms of trade – were also necessary and would require more time to achieve their objectives. Reduction of the public sector's role in the economy was also part of this process: for example, efficiency improvements in public enterprises; reduction of state intervention (privatization and decrease of the public deficit).

8A.3   Criticisms of reform policies

Since their inception, adjustment policies have always been the subject of controversy. Non-environmental critiques focused on: (a) the economic consequences of adjustment policies; and (b) the social costs of adjustment.

Economic consequences   The economic consequences of adjustment policies have not been uniform or unequivocal in ensuring long-term economic growth for developing countries. Low-income countries' economic performance has been much less satisfactory performance in terms of both conventional economic growth and export promotion. In contrast, middle-income countries witnessed a significant increase in the ratio of exports to GDP (World Bank, 1992b). In regional terms, Latin American and Asian countries performed better than those in Africa. Regarding exports, matters have not been helped by the historic trend of falling prices of the resources that they trade with other countries. To ensure a positive trade balance the volume of exports (in physical units) would have had to have increased more than export values declined, in a global economic environment of disguised protectionism and overall recession.

On the import side, immediate and undifferentiated reductions in import tariffs have not provided time to allow national industries to improve their competitiveness, causing deindustrialization and erosion of the fragile industrial base of many adjusting economies, especially in Africa (United Nations, 1989; Reed (ed.), 1992).

Fiscal policy measures have also been considered to be detrimental to growth of the average ratio of investment to GDP. Nor did domestic private finance or foreign capital fill this gap. In fact, empirical work by Mosley et al. (1991) suggests a negative relationship between adjustment and aggregate investment.

Social and political consequences   Social or distributional impacts of adjustment programmes have been particularly stressed because of the absence of social objectives and mechanisms to protect the most vulnerable groups of society: for example, the urban poor experienced a combination of increased food prices, decreased wages and public spending cuts (Cornia et al. (eds), 1987). Yet, since their impact varies widely Bourguinon and Morisson (1992) argue that adjustment policies do not *automatically* increase inequality or produce negative effects on the poor. Indeed, improvements in social conditions have been identified in Indonesia, Malaysia and rural areas of Ghana and Morocco. In these countries some mitigating social expenditure was safeguarded. Nevertheless, recent adjustment programmes have become more concerned about their social consequences, noting poverty relief as a policy priority.

The need to establish a broader domestic coalition of decision-makers has also been recognized. Such a group could act to support policies which were the most unpopular in the short run.

8A.4   Environmental consequences

Agriculture   Policy reforms resulting from adjustment objectives are expected to have direct positive impacts on agricultural production through increases in output prices, tax reductions on production, and exchange rate devaluation (in the case of tradable crops). The literature suggests that this overall increase in agricultural production tends to present an immediate negative impact on the environment, due to more intensive use of soil and higher demand for marginal land (Southgate, 1988). For example, Josserand (1989, quoted in Reardon and Vosti, 1992) associates increasing grain prices with the expansion of cropped area and the removal of native vegetation in the Sahel over the last few decades.

Forestry   Empirical studies suggest that forestry activities in developing countries follow a boom-and-bust pattern. Initially, logging and processing industries are very profitable, stimulating the expansion of their activities. However, harvesting may not be accompanied by appropriate management of secondary forests, and the industry collapses when primary forest reserves become exhausted (Vincent, 1994). It is also argued that the main relationship between forestry and deforestation is not direct, but indirect. Paths opened to remove logs are a stimulus for farmers to settle in forested areas, where they usually practice slash-and-burn cultivation, sometimes followed by cattle ranching. Finally, empirical studies show that timber harvesting, when not properly managed, opens a huge canopy area, with high waste and affecting many more species than just those with commercial value (Veríssimo et al., 1992; Uhl et al., 1991).

The main causes of the boom-and-bust pattern are identified as the undervaluation of stumpage values and the effects of international trade (Barbier et al., 1994a, 1994b; Vincent, 1994). The former less controversial cause reflects widespread recognition of the failure of timber concession policies in charging realistic stumpage fees; creating perverse incentives by basing fees on timber harvested, not including the other trees cut or damaged in the extraction process; and encouraging short time horizons. The extension of concessions and establishment of property rights is usually included in adjustment programmes, but there are practical problems in its implementation such as the actual definition of property rights. Policies to increase stumpage values have the advantage of increasing public revenue. This measure is also more simple to implement, and results can be expected in the short term. However, its effectiveness will depend on the capacity of the public sector to enforce higher fees and the scope for such increases given the international price of logs (Vincent, 1994).

With regard to the timber trade, econometric work (see Barbier et al., 1994b) suggests that it is not the major cause of deforestation. Developing countries produce mainly tropical timber, which suffers from competition with temperate timbers (whenever substitution is feasible) and international prices may not reflect the increasing scarcity of timber in a specific developing country. Furthermore if future prices are expected to rise at a rate less than the opportunity cost of capital, increased, not less, harvesting may be encouraged (Vincent, 1994). Indeed, adjustment programmes have often stimulated the growth of the forestry sector as a source of foreign exchange and government revenues. The main solution adopted to increase the revenues from timber extraction is to stimulate domestic-based wood industries with higher value-added products (for example, by discouraging the export of raw logs), despite evidence at the high opportunity costs of these actions (Barbier et al., 1994a; Vincent, 1994).

Industry and energy   Reform policies favour export sectors, which are expected to grow relative to domestic-based industries. Since adjusting countries have a greater comparative advantages in natural resource-based activities, critics say that adjustment programmes stimulate the overexploitation of these assets, particularly in mining sectors. There is also the question of capital inflows being associated with the migration of pollution-intensive industries. However, the evidence for this is ambiguous (for a review of these arguments, see Leonard, 1988 and Weil et al., 1990). Recent empirical evidence shows that polluting industries have in fact expanded faster in developing countries than the average rate for all industries (Lucas et al., 1992; Low and Yeats, 1992) but that it is far from clear that there exists a migration process of dirtier industries from developed countries (Leonard, 1988) as pollution abatement and control expenditures are small in comparison with total costs. Other reasons for this can be listed (Low (ed.), 1992), such as the costs of 'unbundling' technology. Hence it would appear that open developing economies became less pollution intensive than closed economies in the 1970s and 1980s (Lucas et al., 1992; Birdsall and Wheeler, 1992).

Public sector reform   Environmental protection services are usually provided by the state in developing countries. Drastic reductions in public expenditures affect the quality of such services: sanitation and other urban infrastructure investments, emissions control, national parks protection, and so on. Therefore, it is possible that the quality of these services will decline during adjustment, with negative environmental consequences, even if the economy as a whole is recovering. Yet, empirical evidence from the Brazilian Amazon supports the idea that migration to marginal land is linked to public expenditure on infrastructure (such as roads which open up the hinterland), resulting in deforestation and related resource depletion (Binswanger, 1989; Mahar, 1988). Privatization is another crucial aspect of adjustment programmes. Critics argue that the withdrawal of the state from certain infrastructure activities, such as water and energy supply, does not mean that the private sector will automatically invest in them, or that the poorest will benefit from more expensive services.

8A.5   External debt, structural adjustment and the environment

Debt and the environment   Capistrano (1990) and Capistrano and Kiker (1990) included the debt service ratio as an explanatory variable for deforestation, measured by industrial roundwood removal from broadleaved forests, in 45 developing countries between 1967 and 1985. On the one hand, their results suggest that international debt was not a significant cause of deforestation, contrary to the claims of many environmental organizations. On the other hand, devaluation of the exchange rate, one of the most important policies in the adjustment programme, was found to be a significant cause of deforestation. Combined, these two results imply that indebtedness itself is not a main cause of deforestation, but the adjustment measures adopted as a consequence of indebtedness can be (for useful caveats to this assertion see Burgess, 1992). The role of increased public external in stimulating deforestation has also been proposed by Kahn and McDonald (1992, 1994). They consider that the existence of high levels of debt may cause countries to behave in a myopic fashion, with resulting higher levels of deforestation than would have occurred with lower levels of debt.

Adjustment and the environment   Independent of the controversy about whether or not external debt is relevant to natural resource degradation, it seems that the most relevant aspect is the link between indebtedness and economic policy. The World Bank has sponsored two reviews of the environmental consequences of its lending operations. Sebastian and Alicbusan (1989) and Warford et al. (1993) conclude that adjustment policies appear to have a bias, on balance, actually in favour of the environment. These studies review the economic and institutional components of selected structural adjustment loans (SALs) and sectoral adjustment loans (SECALs) in 43 countries, covering 83 per cent of the World Bank adjustment loans between the fiscal years of 1979 and 1987. Such policy reforms were then analysed in terms of the potential environmental effects they could have. The authors claimed evidence for: increased soil conservation (via increased agricultural prices); decreases in polluting agricultural inputs (via rising prices of fertilizers, pesticides, insecticides and herbicides); and increased energy conservation (increased energy prices). Yet, both studies were based on intended objectives suggesting a need for the *ex post* evaluation of environmental impacts. The World Wide Fund for Nature (WWF) sponsored three country studies, for the Ivory Coast, Mexico and Thailand (Reed (ed.), 1992). In each case, adjustment programmes appear to have had ambiguous impacts on the use of natural resources. On one hand, stabilization programmes tend to have deflationary impacts, at least in the short term, often slowing resource depletion and emissions increases. On the other hand, poverty increases with recession resulting in more pressure to deforest marginal land, or migrate to urban areas with no infrastructure (for example, slums), where the environmental conditions tend to deteriorate quickly (see, also Cruz and Repetto, 1992).

8A.6   Conclusions
Structural adjustment policies have ambiguous effects on the environment. Reform policies (trade reform and pubic sector restructuring are the most important) can lead to more efficient use of resources. But to the extent that they are effective in restarting economic growth, they may lead to more depletion. In any case, the implementation of structural adjustment reforms can be impeded by the contractionary effects of stabilization. As discussed before, the review suggests that non-growth scenarios tend to give rise to worse results than growth situations because of the link between poverty and environmental degradation. Hence, the best scenario seems to be the successful implementation of adjustment policies, with growth recovery, combined with the adoption of specific environmental programmes, in order to alleviate the problems caused by economic expansion. Indeed, some of the studies speculate that the implementation of such measures would help the economic recovery, since business would profit more in a healthy environment (Reed (ed.), 1992; Sebastian and Alicbusan, 1989; Warford et al., 1993).

9 Policies for sustainable development

9.1 Policy-making and indicators

Chapter 1 suggested a general interpretation of 'sustainable development' as a policy goal for nations and the international community. Failure to account for environmental degradation erodes the capital base for future development. However, the main theme of this book has been the ways in which sustainable development might be measured. It was shown that the burgeoning literature on sustainability measurement tends to produce indicators that address some but not all of the ingredients of sustainability: that is, some are focused on development or 'wellbeing' but omit the environmental dimension, while others include the development and environment dimensions but neglect the poverty aspect that was stressed by the Brundtland Commission. Yet others are specifically poverty oriented without adequately addressing the environmental dimension or the temporal sustainability issue. These various inadequacies are often not the fault of the compilers of the indicators: as we have seen, measuring the environmental dimension of sustainable development is beset with conceptual and empirical difficulties. All this suggests that, for the time being, we will need several sets of indicators. Those favoured here are some version of the 'savings rule' introduced in Chapter 4; a resilience measure perhaps based on output variability (Chapter 6) or, perhaps in the future, some biodiversity measure over time; and some fairly simple poverty indicator, perhaps an improved integrated poverty index discussed in Chapter 7.

In terms of policy, governments are increasingly concerned with the extent to which the current path of economic development, including the exploitation of the natural environment, affects the potential for the future welfare of their country. Moreover, governments have been charged with considering and promoting the sustainability of development, in response both to the Brundtland Commission and to the United Nations Conference on Environment and Development's Agenda 21.

The policy process cannot begin, however, unless we have some idea of *why* unsustainable development occurs. This leads to a number a questions such as why are natural resources being depleted too rapidly or why does environmental degradation occur at its present rates? In the remainder of this chapter, we begin to examine the economic factors giving rise to environmental degradation, by considering the policy implications that emerge from Chapters 3 and 4. In addition, we consider how stronger criteria for sustainable development can serve as complementary policy goals.

Chapter 9 introduced the action impact matrix as a tool for the formulation and implementation of sustainable development policies and showed the key role that indicators play in this process. The chapter also summarized the results of a number of case studies involving the links between economywide policies and the environment. In many cases unaddressed market, policy and institutional constraints interact with expansionary economic policies to cause environmental harm. In these instances sustainability requires the introduction of complementary measures to correct the imperfections that gave rise to the environmental damage. The Appendix examined the impacts on sustainability of past structural adjustment policies against the backdrop of increasing indebtedness.

9.2 Policy implications of environmental and resource accounting

The promise of resource and environmental accounting is that it can provide the measurement instruments required for sustainable development policy. The various forms of satellite accounts outlined in Chapter 3 – resource stock accounts, resource and pollutant flow accounts and environmental expenditure accounts – have a wide array of policy applications, including:

- assessment of physical resource scarcity;
- resource sector financial analysis;
- productivity measurement;
- valuing depletion;
- measuring the incidence of taxes and regulations;
- estimating emission tax rates;
- linking to macro models;
- estimating pollution abatement costs; and
- measuring the economic burden of environmental protection.

National accounts aggregates adjusted to reflect resource depletion and environmental degradation are the most comprehensive and integrated of the categories of accounts considered in Chapter 3. These aggregates therefore promise to be superior indicators to guide policies for sustainable development. But the choice of which green accounting aggregate to concentrate upon turns out to be important.

Many people would argue that obtaining measures of Hicksian or sustainable income – that is, a 'green NNP' – is intrinsically important. However, this is not the same thing as saying that green measures of income have direct relevance with regard to policies for sustainable development.

Part of the problem is that producing a new figure for the *level* of national income does not readily translate into a policy signal about the sustainability of development. The fact that a green national income series is, say, 10 per cent lower than the traditional measure does not, in itself, tell you what policy decisions should follow, particularly since green income is necessarily lower than the standard income measure where exhaustible resources are concerned. Most finance (or treasury) departments and development planners use rates of change to indicate where the economy is going and whether it is responding to policy stimuli. Whether the growth rate of green national income can provide a useful policy signal is open to question. For example, if we imagine a country with a fixed growth rate of standard gross domestic product and no depreciation of produced assets, then for the growth rate of green national income it follows that: (i) if the value of resource and environmental depletion is constant each year, green national income will grow faster than GDP; and (ii) if the value of resource and environmental depletion is a constant proportion of GDP, the growth rate of green national income is necessarily the same as that of GDP. So a divergence in growth rates in the two-income measures does not automatically translate into a message about sustainability.

Green NNP measures *potentially* sustainable income. It does not in itself answer the question of whether the rate of saving is sufficient to maintain this income indefinitely. There is the additional difficulty that green NNP represents the amount that could be consumed while leaving the rate of change of utility *instantaneously* constant (Hamilton 1996). As a sustainability indicator, therefore, green NNP is not particularly satisfactory because it typically does not measure the amount that could be consumed if the economy were actually on a constant-utility path.

If the greening of national accounts includes the expansion of the measure of national wealth (as proposed in Scott, 1956 and Hamilton, 1991) – including the value of stocks of living and non-living resources – then total wealth per capita becomes a useful indicator of sustainability. If this ratio is non-decreasing, then development is sustainable (or *weakly* sustainable, since it is assumed that produced assets are highly substitutable for natural assets). That is, for total wealth W and population P, the sustainability criterion is:

$$\frac{\frac{d}{dt}\left(\frac{W}{P}\right)}{\frac{W}{P}} \geq 0$$

This measure has several desirable properties, including the possibility of separately accounting for the changes in the level of natural assets for which substitution possibilities are low. It is also possible to decompose the measure to show the distinct effects of growth in wealth and growth in population. Assuming that $W = W(P, t)$ and $P = P(t)$, we obtain:

$$S = \frac{(dW/dt)}{W} - \frac{(dP/dt)}{P} \cdot (1-e)$$

where, $e = (dW/dP)/(W/P)$. Clearly, the first term is positive if $(dW/dt) > 0$; that is, S rises as total wealth increases over time, holding population constant. However, the sign of the second term depends on the signs of both (dP/dt) and $(1-e)$. Thus, a fall in population (that is, $dP/dt < 0$) will increase sustainability S, only if $e < 1$. The opposite condition $e > 1$ is more likely to prevail if (W/P) is low to begin with, and (dW/dP) is relatively high – for example, if mild population growth stimulates greater efforts towards wealth creation.

To summarize, while trends in national income per capita (using either green or traditional measures) may say something about economic performance in the short run, measuring trends in wealth per capita gives a much clearer picture of how the confluence of wealth creation and population growth influences the potential for future income per capita.

One of the key conclusions from Chapter 3 is that genuine savings is a one-sided indicator of sustainability, in the sense that persistent negative genuine savings must lead to declines in utility. If genuine savings is a superior sustainable development indicator, what policy implications follow from its measurement? To answer this question we will concentrate on the situation of developing countries because, on the empirical evidence, this is where issues of sustainability are most urgent.

The standard model of economic development – for example, the World Bank's RMSIM model – is a so-called 'two-gap' model: developing countries typically have a savings–investment gap, with investment exceeding savings, which is matched by an export–import gap, with imports exceeding exports. The role of development lending and grants as provided bilaterally and by agencies such as the World Bank has been to finance levels of investment that exceed the limited savings of developing countries.

At the heart of this model is a concern with gross levels of saving and investment, since it is the gap between these two quantities that must be financed. The effect of calculating genuine savings levels for developing countries is therefore not to deflect attention from this fundamental issue in development finance, but rather to give a new focus to the question of how much net wealth is being created and, critically, how domestic savings levels compare with the depreciation, depletion and degradation of a country's assets.

As Hamilton and O'Connor (1994) point out, Figures 4.4 and 4.5 from Chapter 4 can be interpreted in terms of how investment is financed. Starting with gross investment in East Asia in, say, 1981 as a benchmark, we see that the 29 per cent of GNP that was invested was financed by a small amount of foreign borrowing, by a larger depreciation allowance, by a still larger depletion allowance (including, as argued previously, the amount that should be set aside to compensate other countries for East Asia's contribution to global warming damages), and by a substantial amount of genuine savings – nearly 11 per cent of GNP. By analogy with a private firm, the depreciation and depletion allowances represent funds that a firm that wished to be sustainable would set against the erosion of its capital base. Thinking of the development problem in this manner clarifies exactly in what sense genuine savings are 'genuine'.

An important determinant of genuine savings rates for developing countries is the value of resource depletion. However, it would be wrong to conclude that the policy response regarding savings and natural resources is to boost genuine savings by restricting resource exploitation – this is clearly incorrect since it ignores the lessons from growth theory alluded to earlier, that the discovery of a natural resource, properly managed, leads to a permanent increase in the sustainable stream of income for a country. The question with regard to natural resources is therefore one of what constitutes 'proper management'. Part of this concerns the investment of resource rents and is therefore an element of the broader question of saving discussed below. But an important policy concern is the achievement of efficient levels of resource exploitation.

The basic components of natural resources policy, royalty regimes and tenurial arrangements, are therefore relevant to the genuine savings issue. If government royalties on natural resources are set too high, then this will be a significant disincentive to resource exploitation, with less than optimal extraction/harvest rates; if royalties are set too low then natural resource firms will have an incentive to overexploit resources in order to capture rents. With regard to tenure and property rights, the issues are well known: open access to a resource such as a fishery where property rights are not established will lead to overexploitation, generally leading to the requirement for second-best policies regarding restrictions on exploitation effort; similarly, resource leases that are too short will lead to overexploitation because extracting firms will either have an incentive to exhaust more quickly than the efficient level, in the case of an exhaustible resource, or will lack an incentive to manage a resource for its efficient sustainable yield in the case of renewable resources.

Consideration of resource depletion within the genuine saving framework also casts a somewhat different light on resource exports. When a natural resource is sold at the border price in international markets, the full value of this sale shows up in the conventionally measured national income of the exporting country. However, a part of this income is in fact the liquidation of an asset, as measured by the value of depletion. This suggests that investment policies (in terms of investing resource rents) should also form a component of policies aimed at trade expansion and that the foregoing concerns about efficient exploitation rates for resources need to be considered as well. The bottom line is that the net benefit of exporting a natural resource commodity is not as great as conventional accounting implies (see also chapter 5).

The treatment of pollution in the genuine savings calculation raises issues that are similar to the exploitation of natural resources. First, because increments to pollution stocks have some analogues with depletion of natural resources, there is the need to see that investments in produced assets offset these increments. Second, there is the issue of achieving efficient levels of pollution emissions. Part of this involves the design of policies that attempt to equate pollution damages and abatement costs at the margin, and part of it is the cost-effectiveness of the policies themselves, with market-based approaches being the instruments of choice.

The generation of royalties from natural resources raises the question of public investment, since the 'rule of thumb' for sustainable development is to invest resource rents. Prudent government policies would aim to ensure that public investment, in education, infrastructure or other assets, at least matches the value of depletion of natural resources (assuming, of course, the usual situation of resource ownership lying with government, and the government then leasing resources for exploitation). If the arguments in Chapter 4 about the treatment of current educational expenditures are accepted, then these expenditures should be considered to be investment. These sorts of considerations reinforce the notion that it is important to distinguish between current and capital expenditures by governments when judging their fiscal stance and role in the economy. Questions of the appropriate scale of public versus private investment in the economy, and the effectiveness of public investments, are difficult to deal with, but necessarily part of the considerations in this domain.

Thinking about government expenditures raises the broader issue of consumption levels. Negative genuine savings rates imply, by definition, excessive consumption whether by governments or households. Extreme poverty plays a role in this picture, because at the margin the poor have little option but to consume all their income and, often, to run down their assets. So policies that promote growth and the alleviation of poverty will, in general, lead to a more favourable climate for generating private savings.

Reducing consumption expenditure by governments is one policy approach to boosting genuine savings. The government's fiscal stance is therefore a legitimate concern in this regard – deficit financing of public consumption, for instance, has the effect of both boosting overall consumption and crowding out private investment. But the lessons from the structural adjustment literature suggest that indiscriminate cutting of government expenditures, for example, on primary health care and education, is likely to be harmful. The question, as always, is one of the appropriate role for the public sector and its appropriate scale. The situation with respect to the redistributive effects of government taxation is more complex. If redistribution is based on a progressive income tax system then it necessarily involves transferring income from households with high marginal propensities to save to ones with low propensities, reducing savings in the aggregate. However, redistribution may contribute to the *social* aspects of sustainable development, not discussed here, in that equity is increased and redistribution may also aid in the alleviation of poverty, with positive effects on saving in the longer run.

Promoting private savings is a complex affair, involving both the creation of a viable financial sector that can attract savings and mediate between savers and investors, and the establishment of a macroeconomic policy climate that encourages savings. One essential feature of this macroeconomic climate must be positive real interest rates, which governments can set through their monetary policies.

Gross savings ratios differ across countries for many reasons. For example, it might be expected that savings ratios are lower in poorer countries because there are fewer resources available for saving after subsistence needs are met (Gillis et al., 1992). Yet, differences in per capita income are not the only reason for these observed differences. Savings ratios can also significantly differ between countries with more-or-less similar per capita incomes – for example, Japan and the USA. A plausible explanation for this is that households in these countries face different incentives to save. Indeed, the behaviour underlying household mobilization of saving – that is, the channelling of deferred household consumption to firms through financial intermediaries – is central to economic theories of saving. These theories have attempted to explain the way in which households' 'smooth consumption' over their lifetimes (see, for example, Heertje (ed.), 1993). Theories such as the life-cycle hypothesis predict savings to be zero over the lifetime of individuals and hence, in this basic form, assume no bequests. Nevertheless, significant evidence has been found for a bequest motive in household saving behaviour reflecting, it is argued, a desire to accumulate wealth for the benefit of future generations (Kotilloff and Summers, 1981; Owens, 1993).

In terms of the policy implications of theories of household saving behaviour, significant attention has been given to the degree to which households respond to government saving (see, for example, Barro, 1974; Bernheim, 1989) and government policies regarding say, pension contributions (Heertje (ed.), 1993). Governments can also affect the level of saving via the distributional impact of taxation (for example, between capital and labour taxes), the composition of government spending (for example, between capital and current spending) and interest rate policy. As an example of the latter, negative real interest rates encourage dissaving through capital flight. Hence, governments may be able to raise savings ratios by maintaining positive real rates of interest. However, the degree to which additional savings are encouraged by *changes in positive real interest rates* will be determined by the relative magnitudes of the income and substitution effects associated with this change (Heertje (ed.), 1993). Determining these effects empirically depends largely on the quality of available data – a particular issue in developing countries.

It is through financial policy that Gillis et al. (1992) suggest greater scope for mobilizing saving (as opposed to interest rate policy). A general policy of liberalizing financial markets might lead to increased saving effort by presenting more choices to potential savers (who are often restricted to saving in the form of cash, deposits and durable goods). This may also increase the efficiency of the banking system and stem the tendency towards capital flight suffered by a number of developing countries (Aghevli et al., 1990). Last but no less important, these financial institutions may be poorly evolved in developing countries. If so, these countries could face a constraint on saving in the form of an absorptive capacity (Stewart, 1991). This constraint also applies to the availability of suitable projects, infrastructure and the scarcity of managerial and administrative capacity.

Investment in new assets is not the only way to increase production in the short run – increasing X-efficiency, for example, can lead to significant gains – but it is the classic remedy. More important is the effectiveness of investment. While each unit of savings should be put to its most productive use in principle, in practice many investments, especially in developing countries, have been wasteful. So while the analysis of genuine savings has an important role to play in focusing governments' attention on the net creation of wealth, it should also encourage increased concentration on the return to investment.

9.2.1 Strong sustainable development

Savings rules of the type considered in this book have been criticized (Victor, Hanna and Kubusi, 1994; Martínez-Alier, 1995) because they are concerned only with *weak* sustainability. One response to this criticism is to suggest that countries that fail by the savings rule, in the sense that they have persistently negative genuine savings, probably are also failing to meet the criteria for *strong* sustainability, in the sense that critical natural assets are being depleted. It would be surprising if this were not the case.

Another response to this criticism is to consider more carefully what the operation of a strong sustainability regime would entail. It clearly cannot mean that *all* natural assets are critical and must be preserved – in this case not only would growth be impossible but so would the maintenance of current consumption. If *some* natural assets are considered to be critical then it is possible to speculate about how sustainability rules would operate.

Consider the classic example of a critical asset – the tropical rainforest. If preserving some quantity of the rainforest is considered to be critical for the long-term wellbeing of humanity, the effect of this preservation is to reduce the quantity of forest that can be considered to be an economic resource. Other things being equal, therefore, the effect of the strong sustainability policy will be to reduce the quantity of harvest that can be carried out sustainably from the remaining stock. This will have the effect, under standard assumptions about the production function, of increasing the price (or, to be more accurate, the unit rental rate) of the resource. A different mix of natural resource and produced capital inputs into production will therefore ensue. But the key point is that the savings rule will still be the determinant of sustainability, because the savings rule is concerned with the *change* in the real value of stocks rather than with the *absolute size* of the stocks. If genuine savings rates are persistently negative for the economy that is preserving its critical natural capital, then this economy will still eventually experience declining levels of welfare: that is, it will be unsustainable.

The key indicators for the economy operating under a strong sustainability regime will be twofold: are stocks of critical natural assets declining and are genuine savings rates persistently negative? A positive answer to either of these questions would be an indication of unsustainability. Independently of whether the policy regime is one of strong or weak sustainability, therefore, savings rules will be key indicators.

Thinking about sustainable development and its measurement inevitably leads to a conception of the process of development as one of portfolio management. Prudent governments will not only consider natural resources as assets, and pollution stocks as liabilities, in the national balance sheet, they will be concerned with the appropriate mix of produced assets and human capital as well. Some preliminary evidence on the composition of wealth, in terms of natural resources, produced assets and human capital, is presented for a wide range of developed and developing countries in World Bank (1995a). A simple model is presented in the Appendix to this chapter which shows that the sustainable level of income can be measured as the return on produced assets, where human capital is considered to be a produced asset in addition to traditional capital goods.

Questions of the 'appropriate mix' of assets are inherently questions about returns on the marginal investment. This marginal investment may be in better resource management, boosting the value of natural resources in the national balance sheet; it may be in pollution control, decreasing the size of the pollution liability to its efficient level; it may be in infrastructure, as has traditionally been the case; and it may be in primary education, as an essential building block in increasing human capital. Typically, returns to investments in environmental assets will be non-marketed and hence it is likely that countries will underinvest in these assets and overinvest in activities such as land conversion. Hence, significant attention has been devoted to demonstrating values of services derived from environmental assets at the local, national and the global level, to which we now briefly, turn.

9.2.2   Carbon storage

All forests store carbon so that, if they are cleared for agriculture, there will be a release of carbon dioxide which will contribute to the accelerated greenhouse effect and hence global warming. Table 9.1 shows the scale of land-use change since 1979 while Table 9.2 illustrates the net carbon storage effects of land use conversion from: tropical forests; closed primary, closed secondary or open forests; to: shifting cultivation, permanent agriculture or pasture. The negative figures represent emissions of carbon; for example, conversion from closed primary forest to shifting agriculture results in a net loss of 194 tonnes of carbon per hectare (tC/ha). The greatest loss of carbon involves change of land use from primary closed forest to permanent agriculture. These figures represent the once and for all change that will occur in carbon storage as a result of the various land use conversions. The data suggest that, allowing for the carbon fixed by subsequent land uses, carbon released from deforestation of secondary and primary tropical forest is of the order of 100–200 tC/ha.

Table 9.1   Land conversions, 1979/81–1991

	Cropland	Pasture	Forest	Other	Total
	(million hectares)				
Africa	+9	+8	–26	+11	+1
North and Central America	–2	+4	+2	–4	0
South America	+13	+21	-42	+11	+3
Asia	+6	+ 66	–26	–43	+3
Europe	–2	–3	+1	+ 4	0

Notes: 'Other' land includes roads, uncultivated land, wetlands and built-on land. Rounding errors and data imperfections, especially in Asia and South America, prevent rows and columns summing to zero. In order to derive a value for the 'carbon credit' that should be ascribed to a tropical forest, we need to know: (a) the net carbon released when forests are converted to other uses; and (b) the economic value of one tonne of carbon released to the atmosphere.

Source: World Resources Institute (1994, Table 17.1).

The carbon released from burning tropical forests contributes to global warming, and there are now several estimates of the minimum economic damage done by global warming, leaving aside catastrophic events. Recent work suggests a 'central' value of $20 of damage for every tonne of carbon released (see Fankhauser, 1995 and Chapter 4). Applying this figure to the data in Table 9.2, we can conclude that converting an open forest to agriculture or pasture would result in global warming damage of, say, $600–1,000 per hectare; conversion of closed secondary forest would cause damage of $2,000–3,000 per hectare;

and conversion of primary forest to agriculture would give rise to damage of about $4,000–4,400 per hectare. Note that these estimates allow for carbon fixation in the subsequent land use.

Table 9.2   *Changes in carbon with land-use conversion (tonnes of carbon per hectare)*

	Original carbon	Shifting agriculture	Permanent agriculture	Pasture
Original carbon		79	63	63
Closed primary	283	–204	–220	–220
Closed secondary	194	–106	–152	–122
Open forest	115	–36	–52	–52

Note: Shifting agriculture represents carbon in biomass and soils in the second year of shifting cultivation cycle.

Source: Brown and Pearce (1994a).

How do these estimates relate to the development benefits of land-use conversion? We can illustrate this with respect to the Amazon region of Brazil. Schneider (1992) reports upper bound values of $300 per hectare for land in Rondonia. The figures suggest carbon credit values 2–15 times the price of land in Rondonia. These 'carbon credits' also compare favourably with the value of forest land for timber in, say Indonesia, where estimates are of the order of $1,000–2,000 per hectare. In terms of policy, all this suggests the scope for a global bargain. The land is worth $300 per hectare to the forest colonist but several times this to the world at large. If the North can transfer a sum of money greater than $300 but less than the damage cost from global warming, there are mutual gains to be obtained.

9.3   Population growth

Chapter 1 showed that, however sustainable development was modelled, rapid population change appeared as a basic threat to its achievement. This result appears to be consistent across the theoretical models of optimal economic growth, the modified models dealing with sustainable development, and the practical experience.

Population pressure is clearly a force of some considerable importance. The story about world population change is by now well known. Table 9.3 records World Bank projections for the next 160 years. World population is expected to stabilize at about 12 billion people towards the end of the next century, but this is more than twice the number of people on Earth today. The fastest growth rate is in Africa, currently growing at 2.9 per cent per annum and heading for a population of 3 billion people towards the end of the next century, about five times the population of today. As discussed earlier, excessive population growth rates that exceed the rates of wealth creation will bring about a decrease in overall sustainability.

Table 9.3   World population projections

	1990	2100 (billions)	2150
World Population	5.4	12.0	12.2
Geographical distribution (%)			
Asia/Oceania	59.4	57.0	56.8
North and South			
America	13.7	11.0	10.8
Africa	11.9	23.9	24.5
Europe	15.0	8.1	7.9

Source: Adapted from World Bank (1992a).

9.4   Conclusions

This chapter has focused on policy in terms of securing sustainable development and is intended to augment the policy discussion in Chapter 8 on economywide policies. In particular, we have examined the ways in which genuine saving can be increased, including the possibility for investment in human capital. This emphasizes the importance of the quality of investment. The issue of weak versus strong sustainability has been prominent in the sustainable development debate. In this respect, it has been shown that a strong sustainability constraint could be implemented alongside a genuine saving criterion. The existence of constraints on the loss of critical natural capital does not replace the need for genuine savings to be positive. In addition, given that substantial economic value resides in the environmental assets of the developing world, investments that raise genuine saving could plausibly be in environmental assets. Finally, with regard to population growth the ratio of wealth to population is a useful indicator of (weak) sustainability, and wealth creation and population growth interact to determine sustainability.

Appendix   Sustainability and human capital

One important asset that has not been considered in the models of sustainable development presented so far is human capital. Under some not unduly restrictive assumptions about production and the creation of human capital it is possible to characterize the level of consumption that is sustainable.

As in the analytical models of previous chapters, let F be production, K capital goods, C consumption and R resource extraction. If M is the stock of knowledge (human capital) and w the amount of the composite good that is used in the creation of knowledge, then the basic accounting identity is,

$$F(K, R, M) = C + \dot{K} + w.$$

Knowledge accumulates as,

$$\dot{M} = q(w).$$

Define $n \equiv 1/q_w$ to be the marginal cost of knowledge. The programme that maximizes the present value of utility over an infinite time horizon has the following efficiency condition,

$$\frac{\dot{n} + F_M}{n} = F_K.$$

$$(9A.1)$$

Given this condition and the Hotelling rule for resource rents, the Hartwick rule (HR) for constant consumption is,

$$\dot{K} = -n\dot{M} - F_R\dot{S} = -nq + F_R R$$

where S is the stock of resource.

We assume constant returns to scale (CRS), given by,

$$F = KF_K + RF_R + MF_M.$$

Combining HR and CRS then gives,

$$C = F - \dot{K} - w = KF_K + MF_M + nq - w.$$

Note that $nq - w$ is greater than, equal to, or less than 0 depending on whether the marginal cost of knowledge is increasing, constant or decreasing in w. If n is constant then,

$$C = KF_K + MF_M = (K + nM)F_K, \text{ from expression (9A.1)}.$$

Consumption is then the rate of interest F_K times total produced capital $K + nM$, where n gives the appropriate price of knowledge (as a type of produced capital in this model) relative to physical capital K. Net accumulation of produced capital is exactly offset by depletion of the exhaustible resource, valued at its price F_R – genuine savings are zero. This net accumulation is just sufficient to keep consumption constant as the interest rate declines.

10 Towards new measures of progress

10.1 A general overview

This book has been concerned with sustainable development. We do not elevate sustainable development to be some overriding goal for economic, social and environmental policy. In that we agree with some of the critics of sustainable development (Nordhaus, 1992; Beckerman, 1995). But we part company with these critics by arguing that a focus on sustainability is useful as a corrective measure, given the muddled way in which development policy is taught and, sadly, all too often practised. The critics, such as Beckerman (1995), argue that setting out the technical characteristics of a development path that is sustainable is quite a different exercise to a moral requirement that one should pursue that path. We agree – as Chapter 1 established at the outset – that a sustainable world could be a very undesirable one, especially if current and near-future generations had to suffer privation and infringements of personal liberty in the name of some poorly defined long-run goal. But something has to be wrong with the conventional economic development wisdom if it produces: (a) no improvement at all in the wellbeing of vast numbers of people; (b) increasing threats to future wellbeing; and (c) ever-increasing gaps between the levels of wellbeing of the best and worst off.

Our view is that a focus on 'sustainability' helps to explain what has gone wrong because it reminds us to monitor and evaluate the impacts of development policy on the resource base that will sustain future wellbeing, not necessarily hundreds of years in the future, but in the next few decades. This does not mean that the resource base is sacrosanct – for example, that resources in the ground or in the sea should not be mined. Such a Draconian restriction would be an overreaction, and while we recognize this kind of prescription in some writings on sustainable development, we do not espouse that view. Equally, some resources are depleted at our peril. Even if the science of global warming is still disputed, the science of ozone layer depletion is not. While the epidemiology of air pollution is debated, there is consensus that it harms human beings, and hence the human capital base, more than would normally be required for firm and aggressive action. 'Sustainable development' is not therefore a call for a radical diversion of resources to conserve all resources and all species. It is a call for more humility in the pursuit of development policies, based on the acceptance of our ignorance of what development does to the environment, and in turn, what the environment does for human wellbeing.

We have argued, too, that sustainable development is measurable. The data are poor, but no poorer than when national accounting was first officially recognized. Time will improve both our methods of accounting for resource depletion and pollution damage, and the data required to implement those methods. We have explored a number of ways of measuring sustainability, reflecting different views of the conditions required to achieve sustainability. The most productive approaches, in our view, are to be found in the concept of 'genuine savings' introduced in Chapter 4, and in the ecological analysis of 'resilience'. The former we regard as having firm roots in 'green' accounting procedures. The latter remains open to interpretation and is even more in doubt in terms of measurability. None the less, resilience analysis has barely begun, and there is considerable potential for progress. The savings and resilience approaches are also attractive in capturing the most salient features of the weak and strong sustainability paradigms.

The issue, then, is what have we learned from the analysis of sustainability in the previous chapters? The following sections summarize the lessons.

10.2   Physical indicators

Chapter 2 looked at environmental indicators expressed in both physical and monetary terms. Physical indicators tend to have been dominated by the 'pressure–state–response' framework in which measures of 'stressors' on the environment are linked to measures of the state of the environment and then to policy responses. The chapter argued that, while physical indicators are essential inputs into any measure of sustainability, in themselves they contain inadequate information for appraising whether an economy is or is not on a sustainable path of development. The essential reason for this is that the indicators lack 'weights', that is, measures of importance. Weights could be derived from several sources, including public opinion, implicit market weights, expert judgement or 'distance to goals' measures. Of course, public opinion and expert assessment of what is important are often two very distinct things. Hence, some 'mix' of expert and public assessment is required, with the role of the expert being one of conveying information to individuals as the ultimate arbiters of what they, as the constituents of society, actually want. In our view, such a mix is best achieved through the monetization of preferences – although this has acknowledged limitations. In the dose–response function approach, for example, the dose–response relationship is assessed by experts. Individuals' valuations of the effects (for example, ill-health), then permit the final link between stressor and measure of importance to be derived. Chapter 2 illustrated this with measures of air pollution damage to human health, showing that the resulting social costs in both developing and developed economies could be very large.

The pressure–state–response (P–S–R) framework is also inadequate in taking an overly mechanical view of the causes of environmental degradation. Chapters

8 and 9 show clearly that much of the cause of degradation lies within the distortionary functioning of economies at all levels. Yet these market and government 'failures' rarely figure in the P–S–R framework.

The two attractions of physical indicators are that: (a) they tend to be more 'objective' than weighted indicators; and (b) they have an obvious link to the strong sustainability paradigm which stresses the importance of some environmental assets (and hence the need to know whether they are increasing or decreasing in size and quality). However, this appeal is purely superficial unless underpinned by a satisfactory theory of strong sustainable development (that is, providing the rationale for interest in the change in physical indicators). Nevertheless, physical indicators are an essential input into any measurement of sustainability. The overall judgement must therefore be that physical indicators are necessary but not sufficient for sustainability analysis. Frameworks such as the P–S–R framework are also helpful, but could well be misleading in obscuring the need to get at the underlying causes of environmental degradation.

Hence, we conclude that any approach based on physical indicators needs to be augmented by a focus on socioeconomic impacts of environmental change. In particular, we provided some examples of how health impacts could be evaluated and how such work fits into the P–S–R framework. A major weakness of the air pollution damage work has been the focus on outdoor pollution. Remarkably few studies have measured indoor air pollution. Fewer still make a distinction between ambient concentrations and exposure. The two differ in that exposure depends on human behaviour in the presence of ambient pollution – how long an individual stays in one place, for example. Adding up the total population of the world and expressing it as 'person hours', about 25 per cent of all person hours are in the developed world, and 75 per cent in the developing world (simply reflecting the respective populations). Sixty-eight per cent of all developed-country person hours are spent indoors in urban environments, and 21 per cent are spent indoors in rural environments, leaving only 11 per cent of time in the outdoors. In the developing world the proportions are 70 per cent and 30 per cent. In other words, the major part of an individual's time is spent indoors, not outdoors.

10.3   Green national accounting

Our focus on socioeconomic impacts in turn provides a powerful motivation for what is broadly called 'green national accounting', which consists of two main streams of work: (i) resource and environmental accounts, which are concerned with 'satellite accounts' that augment but do not modify the core components of the System of National Accounts; and (ii) adjusted national accounting aggregates that directly incorporate the value of changes in natural assets. The United Nations integrated System of Environmental and Economic Accounts (SEEA) embodies elements of both approaches.

A useful classification of the various approaches to resource and environmental accounts involves the distinguishing of natural resource accounts, resource and pollutant flow accounts, and environmental protection expenditure accounts. Some of the more important uses of these types of accounts include the following: *Natural resource accounts* – resource management, balance sheet analysis of the resource sectors, productivity measurement and valuation of resource depletion; *resource and pollutant flow accounts* – measurement of the incidence of environmental regulations and taxes, estimation of emission tax rates, emission modelling and macro modelling; and *environmental protection expenditure accounts* – measurement of unit abatement costs.

Where the concern is with the measurement of progress towards sustainable development, however, green national accounting aggregates are the most useful indicators. Considerable progress in laying the conceptual foundations of green national accounting has been made in recent years. The fundamental ideas in the conceptual approach to green national accounting are that: (a) the asset boundary in the national accounts should be expanded to include natural resources and environmental amenities (as well as liabilities in the form of pollution stocks); and (b) the services provided by environmental amenities should be recognized as sources of welfare on a par with the consumption of produced goods and services.

There is a range of general conclusions that comes out of the development of green national accounting aggregates. Expanded measures of net national product (NNP) should deduct the value of resource depletion; add the value of growth of living resources; make no explicit adjustment for discoveries of subsoil resources; deduct the value of pollution emissions; and add the value of dissipation of pollutants in the environment. A natural expansion of these measures is to add the value that households place on the flow of environmental services, in which case the outcome is better interpreted as a measure of economic welfare rather than NNP *per se*. If households make defensive expenditures in order to mitigate the effects of environmental deterioration, then these expenditures should be included in NNP.

The conceptual approach to green national accounting also gives clear guidance regarding the measurement of the relevant resource and environmental flows. Natural resources should be valued at their rental rate, net of any emissions taxes associated with production (the existence of pollution externalities makes resources less valuable than they would otherwise be). Pollution flows should be valued at their marginal social costs. At the optimum, these marginal social costs will equal marginal abatement costs, which in turn are equal to the level of an optimal emissions tax.

While adjusting NNP in the ways noted above certainly provides a truer measure of income, it is not obvious what policy conclusions follow from the measurement of green NNP. Policy-makers are typically concerned with the rate of change rather than the level of GNP, and it is easy to show that the rate of growth of green NNP may give equivocal signals with regard to the condition of resources and the environment. A more promising indicator of sustainability is the rate of 'genuine' saving, or net savings less the value of both resource depletion and the net accumulation of pollutants. If genuine savings are persistently negative, then eventually welfare must decline (that is, negative genuine savings lead to non-sustainability). Concentrating on genuine savings levels leads naturally to a range of policy concerns, including resource management, royalty regimes and the investment of resource royalties, the optimality of pollution levels, and the spectrum of broader macroeconomic policies as they affect savings behaviour.

10.4   Empirical measures of sustainable development
Gross savings are simply the amount of production that is not consumed. Genuine savings represent the amount of saving over and above the value of depreciation of produced assets, the depletion of natural resources and the increment in the value of environmental liabilities in the form of pollution stocks – this is the precise sense in which such savings are 'genuine'.

If all countries were prudent managers of their natural and produced assets there would be little concern with the measurement of genuine savings, except in so far as this represents a more complete measure of saving effort. A broad glance at savings rates in developed and developing countries, however, shows that there were a considerable number of countries which displayed negative genuine savings in the mid-to-late 1980s, while having positive net savings.

The valuation of depletion and carbon dioxide emission damages presented in this study represent the first consistent time series of such estimates with broad country coverage. While some of the estimation methods are necessarily crude (for instance, the use of decadal average rates of deforestation and point estimates of extraction costs), this data set still represents a significant step forward in the measurement of sustainable development.

The plots of genuine savings rates by region group together countries that, to a degree, have similar endowments. The trends from 1980 to 1990 display striking differences. OECD countries and the countries of South Asia all had moderately positive genuine savings rates and correspondingly moderate rates of per capita economic growth. Middle Eastern and North African countries had marginally negative genuine savings, while those of Latin America and the Caribbean were marginally positive. The 'outliers' in this picture are provided by East Asian countries, with substantially positive and increasing genuine savings, and Sub-Saharan African countries with substantially negative and decreasing genuine savings. The rates of per capita economic growth in these two regions mirror the respective savings information.

East Asian countries had extremely high gross savings rates, nearly balanced foreign trade and a decreasing weight of resource depletion in economic activity. In contrast, Sub-Saharan African countries had substantially lower gross savings rates, generally negative current account balances, increasing shares of depreciation of produced assets (as a result of the investments of the 1960s and 1970s) and an increasing share of depletion of natural resources.

A closer look at the savings behaviour in Sub-Saharan Africa seems to paint a picture of 'the curse of the mineral-rich'. This reinforces the points made by Gelb (1988), looking at oil exporters, that only sound micro- and macroeconomic policies combined with the prudent allocation of public resources can turn the discovery and exploitation of natural resources into sustained increases in income.

In one important respect, the calculations presented are pessimistic for countries with large resource endowments. This is because the calculations assume efficient resource pricing over time, so that current rentals correctly value depletion. If that assumption is dropped then some appropriate social rate of discount should be applied in the calculations, leading to valuations of depletion that would be much smaller than those presented for countries with several decades' worth of mineral or energy reserves.

Another respect in which the calculations are pessimistic is that they assume, in concert with standard national accounting practices, that current expenditures on education should be treated as consumption. If the notion of capital is expanded to include human capital, then this would add 2–8 per cent to genuine savings rates by country. Pushing the thinking in this direction leads naturally to the conception of development as a portfolio management, where the aim of development policy is to meet social goals by achieving the appropriate mix of produced assets, natural assets and human resources.

There are gaps in the analysis – soils, gold, diamonds and natural gas, to name just a few. Perhaps the most significant gap is in the valuation of pollution. As countries develop, there has been an accelerating trend towards urbanization and industrialization, with concomitant serious problems for environmental quality. As Chapter 3 demonstrated, the methodologies for bringing pollution into the ambit of green accounting and genuine savings calculations are now well developed. A significant challenge remains, therefore, to value the marginal social costs of pollution emissions in developing countries, and to reflect these amounts in calculations of genuine savings. Such efforts may well show that 'flattening' or 'tunnelling through' the environmental Kuznets curve is the optimal policy as discussed in Chapter 2.

10.5   International trade and sustainability

The claim that international trade in resources is a cause of unsustainable development has been used to support the construction of 'trade-adjusted' indicators of sustainability. In the case of developed countries, these measures are usually said to be indicative of an ecological footprint. Although this has a popular appeal, the lack of any demonstration of a formal link between sustainable development and resource trade does not recommend this approach as a basis for indicator work. However, a separate literature extending the type of models outlined in Chapter 3 has proposed that the genuine savings measures presented in Chapter 4 are altered by terms-of-trade effects as a result of resource trade. This result rests on an assumption regarding the modelling of resource price changes over time. Our interpretation is that this assumption needs to be appraised with respect to its real world relevance. We argue that a plausible inference is that, on the whole, individual countries are price-takers regarding international resource trade and that this implies a resource-extracting country is still to be achieved by reinvesting resource rents regardless of whether for export or not. In other words, the genuine savings approach outlined in Chapter 4 still applies.

Yet, the measurement of the degree to which resource depletion is traded internationally can be motivated by other policy concerns (not unconnected to the question of achieving sustainability). In response to this, our empirical computations have measured the degree to which countries rely on consuming global resources to support domestic final demands. Not surprisingly, these countries turn out to be primarily developed nations such as Japan, the USA and the majority of EU countries. With respect to policy, the extent to which these importing countries are concerned about the sustainability of exporters suggests a possible role for additional bilateral aid in assisting, where needed, the fulfilment of genuine savings requirements.

The issue of transboundary pollution does alter our interpretation of genuine savings as assets in country A are caused by waste emissions in country B. In Chapter 4 we argued that this requires an extension of the polluter pays principle to the domain of national accounting and indicates that the value of these damages should be deducted from the measure of genuine savings in the waste-emitting country. In terms of policy, this should be interpreted as the notional amount of resources to be set aside in order to compensate the recipients of the pollution emitted and transferred across international boundaries.

10.6 Ecological indicators

Chapter 6 showed that ecologists and ecological economists take a rather different approach to sustainability. The clearest and most persuasive approach so far rests with the concept of 'resilience' – the ability of an economic, ecological and social system to 'bounce back' from shocks (such as outbreaks of disease) and to persist despite continuous stresses. Resilience itself appears to be unmeasurable, although Chapter 6 suggested that for some economic systems (for example, agricultural) changes in the coefficient of variation through time do offer some kind of warning signal about future sustainability. Finding out why variability in output should increase through time is the subject of a limited literature and, as yet, it is unclear what role the homogenization of both output and management practice plays. None the less, the approach is promising.

The role of homogenization is clearer in the theory of ecological resilience than in practice. Looked at from its obverse, diversity becomes the clue to resilience. The strength of the diversity–resilience link is in fact disputed in ecology, but, if correct, suggests a way out of the measurability problem. Diversity itself is measurable and there is a flourishing amount of research on biological diversity indicators. As Chapter 6 discusses, however, diversity indicators are problematic in the context of sustainability. Essentially this is because there is no natural origin for such a measure. We can say that diversity has increased or decreased (empirically this is difficult as few measures of diversity have been the subject of time-series data, although bird populations in some countries are one example), but we cannot say what level of diversity is required for sustainability. This may be compared to the savings rule which does have a natural origin – zero genuine savings.

While there are serious doubts about the practical possibilities of seeing diversity indicators of sustainability in the near future, we urge that they be developed and further investigated. First, they come closer to the ecological view of the world, which is required to balance what may be a narrowness in the economic vision. Second, they come closer to the strong sustainability paradigm.

Chapter 6 also investigated the concept of carrying capacity. The problem with carrying capacity is its limited operational use for environmental planning. First, it tends to be computed on the basis of the maximum population that could be sustained at minimum levels of wellbeing, rather than seeking to optimize population and growth rates of consumption. Second, it tends to vary with investment policies. Third, it fails to accommodate trade – national and international – as a mechanism for evening out supply–demand imbalances.

But there are some areas of interest with regard to carrying capacity. First, computing carrying capacity for African nations suggests that some populations are well in excess of it. As a technical statement of a country's current or immediate future prospects this information may be of some interest. We have not investigated the issue here but it would be interesting to know the extent to which those nations with 'excess' populations are also those nations with low economic growth. In fact, Barro and Sala-I-Martin (1995) do find some tentative evidence that growth in per capita GDP was negatively related to population growth and fertility variables for a cross-section of mainly developing countries over the period 1965–85. One fact may then explain the other. However, Barro and Sala-I-Martin (1995) also find evidence of a positive link between GDP and fertility for the lowest-income countries (and a negative relationship past some income level), suggesting the existence of a Malthusian population 'trap' which could have important implications for carrying capacities.

Second, as Chapter 6 showed, focusing on carrying capacity may enable us to single out those resources that are truly constraining. It may, for example, be water or fuelwood rather than food or soil.

Does the ecological approach suggest a much simpler approach to measuring sustainability? Can we not argue that what is being witnessed with global problems such as ozone layer depletion, global warming, tropical forest loss and so on is the ultimate 'limit to growth'? If this is true, then an indicator of non-sustainability might be GNP itself. Again, however, the problem of the origin arises. The measure of economic growth is the change in GNP, not GNP itself. A zero growth rate simply implies a constant GNP, not zero GNP. Since any positive level of GNP is consistent with the using up of resources and with pollution, we have no benchmark for deciding which level of GNP is 'sustainable'. More importantly, in our view, reducing GNP (even if that was something governments could set as an economic goal) in the name of sustainability falls into the very trap set by the critics of sustainability, that is, setting sustainability as an overriding goal, regardless of cost. The value of GNP is not the issue. Unsustainable outcomes arise from excessive consumption of materials and energy. Hence pursuing the growth of GNP while reducing the amount of material throughput has to be the goal of sustainable development. In our view that goal is most efficiently achieved by driving a wedge between the two, and this wedge comprises the price of resource depletion and the price of pollution. Ultimately, there may be a need for genuine 'limits' on critical natural capital – absolute quotas of resource use that, if exceeded, will confer massive social costs on immediate or near-future generations. In such a scenario, quotas and direct controls presumably also have their role to play.

10.7 Social indicators

We saw in Chapter 7 how social indicators had been developed primarily in the 1970s, and largely in response to the perceived inability of conventional indicators of aggregate wellbeing – predominantly GDP, GNP and national income – to capture adequately the social dimensions of economic development, particularly as they pertain to distributional issues. Indeed, in large part, conventional social indicators could be viewed rather as indicators of poverty than of aggregate welfare. This helps to explain the emphasis which has often been placed on the importance of 'basic needs', and latterly 'capabilities', in the construction of social indicators. It also suggests that social indicators could well have relatively more relevance for lower- than higher-income countries. Ideas of 'relative poverty' notwithstanding (for example, Townsend, 1979, 1985), we might also expect an emphasis on absolute, rather than relative, concepts.

It was also evident from our earlier discussion that the most prominent social indicator to be developed so far has been the human development index (HDI), based on a country's relative performance in three areas: national income, education and life expectancy. The HDI has been subject to a number of criticisms, which to a greater or lesser extent have been addressed in the index's many revisions. For instance, the 'relativity' problem – the fact that a country's HDI score could fall because of changes in the situation in other countries, even if domestic conditions were unchanged – has been lessened since 1994 (when the GNP per capita, education and life expectancy limits were 'fixed'). Similarly, the extreme treatment which the income component had received in 1990 – where income above the 'poverty line' was assumed not to contribute to development – has been modified via the addition of a social welfare function (in which the contribution of additions of income to wellbeing is determined by the elasticity of the marginal utility of income). Other problems remain, which to some extent have ushered forth a plethora of rival and complementary social indicators, although some are merely poor imitations of the HDI.

For our purposes, we need to pose the following question: to what extent do any of the social indicators currently proposed, and particularly the HDI, meet our requirements *vis-à-vis* measuring sustainable development? Our broad definition of sustainable development as non-declining welfare clearly suggests that an 'output'-based indicator could be appropriate (and Chapter 3 showed how the 'input'- or 'capability'-based indicator of national income should be extended into a full-blown welfare measure, for the purpose of estimating genuine savings). To the extent that the components of the HDI (and of similar constructs) are at least instruments of human wellbeing, then we might be reasonably hopeful that at least some of our requirements might already have been met by existing measures. A simple extension of the HDI into other areas, most notably the environment, appears to be the next step, and Chapter 7 proposed some candidate physical indicators such as greenhouse gas emissions and habitat preservation.

However, we should remember that our interest in social indicators is the result of a desire to account for the distributional side of sustainability. Our examination of the conceptual aspects of sustainable development in Chapter 1 began with the Brundtland Commission's often-quoted definition: 'development which meets the needs of the present without compromising the ability of future generations to meet their own needs' (WCED, 1987, p. 43). At the same time, the role of the 'essential needs of the world's poor' (ibid.) was also noted, thereby underlining a poverty-oriented approach to measurement. An emphasis on indicators of current social wellbeing suggests that our sustainability criterion ought to prohibit not only current development which was at the expense of the future, but also increases in wellbeing for the better off in society which came at the expense of those who were worse off. This is a rather more specific requirement.

The foregoing considerations might permit us to make the following observations about the HDI and its counterparts. First, it is apparent that desirable indicators of social wellbeing should permit us to make comparisons of absolute conditions over time, so that we can determine whether the situation facing different sections of a community have been improving or worsening. The HDI 'world league' might serve to focus minds (especially those of decision-makers), upon broad issues of development and poverty. However, it is not clear that, save perhaps in the case of 'outliers', the performance of one country can in general tell us anything of particular use about the performance of any other country. The fact that Luxembourg falls 15 places on the HDI scale relative to the GNP scale does little to explain whether the poor in Luxembourg are in any way particularly worse off than the poor in comparable countries. Nor does it necessarily indicate whether Luxembourg's GNP level is being achieved at the expense of the wellbeing of some poorer members of its society. It is not surprising that to a large extent the primary determinant of a country's HDI ranking is its GNP (and the problems of interpreting GNP as a welfare measure have already been emphasized). Conditions in terms of many other indicators are broadly the same for a large number of countries, especially high-income ones. As a result, it is apparent that relative comparisons are of little use in this case, and indeed, indicators which emphasize relativities (such as the Borda count) run the risk of unduly highlighting differences in the relative performance of countries.

The second observation might be that, even if we were able to construct an indicator which did satisfactorily measure the wellbeing of different sections of society, there would be no guarantee that the same indicator would tell us anything about the sustainability or otherwise of that wellbeing. Our definition of dynamic sustainability as non-declining welfare resulted quite naturally in a discussion of the need to maintain the aggregate capital stock intact over time. In turn, this requirement led directly to the concept of genuine savings. Genuine savings as an indicator has the advantage of being theoretically sound and at the same time relatively easy to understand (although we suggested that there may be conceptual problems in integrating the HDI and genuine savings). The question then becomes: is there a corollary to the genuine savings concept for the case of intragenerational sustainability? The answer would appear to have some connection with the nature of capital ownership, or at least, entitlement. From a distributional perspective, this might serve to underline the importance of human capital (and hence education), to sustainable development, especially where human capital is viewed as specific to the individual. Currently, however, it is difficult to say much more. This is undoubtedly a result of the lack of discussion which has so far taken place on the subject of intragenerational sustainability. It might also be the case that distributional issues do not fit so neatly into a formal economic model, precluding the construction of robust and consistent indicators akin to genuine savings. What does seem true, however, is that the sorts of indicators we have examined in Chapter 7 are not sufficient for the purpose of measuring sustainable development.

10.8   Economywide factors

A focus on wider aspects of micro- and macroeconomic policy indicates that any attempt to achieve sustainable development will require an economywide focus in addition to 'traditional' environmental and resource policies. Chapter 8 argues that economywide policies (which are not usually designed for environmental purposes) may have substantial effects on the level and conduct of environment-related activities. However, the linkages between economywide policy reforms and the environment can be complex and ambiguous, while the impact of policy reforms is also indirect. Impacts are often too diverse to be comprehensively traced with precision, and in most cases vary among and within countries. Consequently, the action impact matrix (AIM) is introduced as a practical method to identify, analyse and prioritize key economic–environmental linkages and to formulate and implement remedial measures. An AIM that incorporates key sustainability measures (such as the indicators discussed in earlier chapters), will provide decision-makers with practical benchmarks and trends on which future policies and strategies for sustainable development may be based.

A review of empirical evidence provides important information concerning economy–environment linkages. First, the removal of price distortions, promotion of market incentives and relaxation of other constraints (which are among the main features of adjustment-related reforms), generally will contribute to both economic and environmental gains. For example, reforms which improve the efficiency of industrial or energy-related activities could reduce both economic waste and environmental pollution. Similarly, improving land tenure rights and access to financial and social services not only yields economic gains but also promotes better environmental stewardship.

Second, unintended adverse side-effects occur, however, when economywide reforms are undertaken while other neglected policy, market or institutional imperfections persist. The remedy does not generally require reversal of the original reforms, but rather the implementation of additional complementary measures (both economic and non-economic) that remove such policy, market and institutional difficulties. Such complementary measures are not only generally environmentally beneficial in their own right, but also help to broaden the effectiveness of economywide reforms. Typical examples of potential environmental damage caused by remaining imperfections include:

- *Policy distortions:* Export promotion and trade liberalization, which increases the export profitability of a natural resource, might encourage excessive extraction or harvesting of this resource if it were underpriced or subsidized (for example, low stumpage fees for timber).

*   *Market failures:* Economic expansion induced by successful adjustment may be associated with excessive environmental damage, for example, if external environmental effects of economic activities (such as pollution), are not adequately reflected in market prices that influence such activities.
*   *Institutional constraints:* The environmental and economic benefits of economywide reforms could be negated by unaddressed institutional issues, such as poor accountability of state-owned enterprises, inadequately defined property rights, or weak financial intermediation – which tend to undermine incentives for sustainable resource management.

Third, measures aimed at restoring macroeconomic stability will generally yield environmental benefits, since instability undermines sustainable resource use. For example, stability encourages a longer-term view on the part of decision-makers at all levels, and lower inflation rates lead to clearer pricing signals and better investment decisions by economic agents. These are essential prerequisites for encouraging environmentally sustainable activities. However, the stabilization process also may have unforeseen adverse short-term impacts on the environment. For example, while general reductions in government spending are deemed appropriate, targeting these cutbacks would be desirable to avoid disproportionate penalties on environmental protection measures. Another important issue is the possible short-term impact of adjustment on poverty and unemployment, which may aggravate existing pressures on fragile and 'open access' natural resources by the poor because of the lack of economic opportunities. In this case, appropriate measures designed to address the possible adverse social consequences of adjustment will be justified even further – on environmental grounds.

Finally, economywide policies will have additional longer-term effects on the environment through employment and income distribution changes. Several of the examples confirm one predictable conclusion – that adjustment-induced changes generate new economic opportunities and sources of livelihood, thereby alleviating poverty and reducing pressures on the environment due to overexploitation of fragile resources by the unemployed. However, while growth is an essential element of sustainable development, it will necessarily increase pressures on environmental resources. Increasing efficiency and reducing waste, as well as properly valuing resources, will help reshape the structure of growth and reduce undesirable environmental impacts. Meanwhile, environmental policies themselves could have impacts on income distribution and employment.

Given the foregoing findings, the recognition of the environmental benefits of economywide policies will help build support for economic reforms, and vice versa. That is, broader understanding of the underlying economic–environmental linkages can enhance support for both economic and environmental initiatives, in terms of policies as well as projects. The AIM can play a significant role in the process of devising economywide reforms that promote sustainable development. In this respect, an AIM helps to promote an integrated view, by both linking and articulating the range of development decisions, and then meshing them with priority economic, environmental and social impacts, with the use of effective sustainable development indicators.

The potential use of AIMs in promoting sustainability becomes even more apparent if one considers some past economywide reforms which have been implemented without adequate consideration of their environmental and social, as well as economic impacts. In the case of structural adjustment policies implemented to address the debt crisis faced by many developing countries in the 1980s, partial or piecemeal reforms sometimes pressured countries to adopt methods of increasing economic production which were not only socially harmful, but also environmentally damaging. For example, an unbalanced structure of growth can give rise to excessive pollution and natural resource depletion.

Nevertheless, despite short-term sacrifices, properly managed adjustment facilitates long-term growth without which environmental damage could be worse. More specifically, non-growth scenarios tend to give rise to worse results than growth situations, because of the linkages between poverty and environmental and social decline. Hence, the best approach seems to be the successful implementation of sound economic policies aimed at the recovery or maintenance of growth, combined with the adoption of specific remedial environmental and social programmes. The availability of appropriate sustainability indicators is a crucial prerequisite for improving all such development decisions. Most importantly, sustainable development strategies must be devised on a country-by-country basis, with due regard for local conditions, resource endowments and social needs.

10.9   Role of sustainability indicators in policy

Chapter 9 explained how resource and environmental accounting constitutes an important step towards sustainable development. National accounts aggregates adjusted to reflect resource depletion and environmental degradation are among the most comprehensive and integrated of all such measures, and in this respect, promise to be superior indicators for guiding sustainable development policy. Green NNP is intrinsically important to the extent that it indicates the direction in which the economy is moving and how it is responding to stimuli. However, it does not necessarily provide a policy signal about the sustainability of development. In other words, although green NNP measures *potential* sustainable income, it does not in itself answer the question of whether the rate of saving is sufficient to maintain this income indefinitely. Therefore, green NNP is not particularly satisfactory as a sustainability indicator, because it fails to indicate the maximum amount that could be consumed while maintaining the economy on a constant-utility path.

The greening of national accounts requires an expansion of the measure of national wealth to reflect the value of stocks of living and non-living resources. The resulting indicator of total wealth per capita will be a useful measure of sustainability that has several desirable properties – including the possibility of separately accounting for changes in the level of crucial natural assets for which substitution possibilities are low. It also enables governments to decompose the measure in order to show the distinct effects of growth in wealth and growth in population. Measuring trends in wealth per capita gives a much clearer picture of how the confluence of wealth creation and population growth influences the potential for future income per capita.

The effect of calculating genuine savings levels for developing countries in a two-gap model of economic development should not deflect attention from important conventional issues such as financing the savings–investment and export–import gaps. Instead, it ought to give a new focus to critical questions such as how much net wealth is being created, and how domestic savings levels compare with the depreciation, depletion and degradation of a country's assets. In this context, an important determinant of genuine savings rates for developing countries is the value of resource depletion. However, this does not imply that policies pertaining to savings and natural resources should seek to boost genuine savings by restricting resource exploitation. On the contrary, the sound management of natural resources will lead to a permanent increase in the sustainable stream of income for a country. The question then focuses on what constitutes proper management, rather than mere preservation of natural resources.

Incorporating environmental depletion within the genuine saving framework also casts a somewhat different light on resource exports, because conventional accounting fails to include within the 'full' value of a traded natural resource, the value of depletion of the asset. This suggests that the net benefit of exporting a natural resource commodity is not as great as conventional accounting implies. Moreover, the generation of royalties from natural resources also raises the question of public investment – since the rule of thumb for sustainable development is to reinvest resource rents. Prudent government policies would aim to ensure that public investment at least matches the value of depletion of natural resources. Negative genuine savings rates imply, by definition, excessive consumption whether by governments or households. Extreme poverty plays a role in this, because at the margin the poor have little option but to consume all their income, and often to run down their assets as well. By extension of logic, policies that promote growth and the alleviation of poverty will lead to a more favourable climate for generating private savings.

However, while promoting private savings is a complex affair, important lessons from structural adjustment (see the Appendix to Chapter 8) suggest that the indiscriminate cutting of government expenditure (especially on health care and education), can be harmful. This raises the related issue of the appropriate role of the public sector and its appropriate scale. One view is that the redistributive effects of government taxation, if based on a progressive tax system, may advance the social aspects of sustainable development. In other words, such income redistribution will aid in the alleviation of poverty, and have positive effects on saving in the longer run. At the same time, liberalizing financial markets might not only increase saving efforts by presenting more choices to potential savers, but will also increase the efficiency of the banking system and stem the tendency towards capital flight. In addition, attention should be paid to the effectiveness of investment. That is, while the analysis of genuine savings has an important role to play in focusing government attention on the net creation of wealth, it should also encourage increased concentration on raising the returns to investment.

10.10   Final remarks

Evaluation of the concepts underlying sustainable development has progressed significantly since the expositions of, for example, the Brundtland Commission. Notions of weak versus strong sustainability, while remaining useful for illustrative purposes, have been superseded by a much sharper focus on changes in the real value of assets. For sustainable development, these should not be negative in aggregate. Such insights have allowed first steps to be taken in constructing improved measures of saving and wealth. For these reasons we have devoted consideration to evaluating the theoretical underpinnings for the concept of rates of genuine saving, and its measurement.

Nevertheless, we have also endeavoured to show that the concept of sustainability retains the wide base as envisaged in the Brundtland Report and other policy statements. Hence, the sustainability programme outlined in this book encompasses social, economic and ecological dimensions. Arguably, it is within the economic dimension that most progress has been made *so far* and to reiterate some of this progress has been reflected in our expositions of formal approaches to green national accounting. We argue that the integration of resources and environment into such frameworks has contributed much to the debate on the measurement of sustainability. It is to be hoped that future contributions will strengthen the representation of the social and ecological dimensions.

For example, much of our discussion has identified the measurement of human capital as a crucial dimension of the debate. It remains to be seen how much the emerging *social capital* debate (with its emphasis on factors such as social cohesion) has to offer, but it is already clear that treating current expenditures on education and primary health care as investment would capture at least some of the key points. In this respect, it would be desirable to go beyond simple estimates of the 'costs of provision' to quantify the (discounted) future benefits of these investments. These investments augment wealth in significant ways and their appraisal in terms of the sustainability literature may help to cast light on a related question, namely the link between technological progress and sustainable development.

The scope for investments in human capital and technological progress have often been presented as reasons to be optimistic about future development prospects. In contrast, the ecological dimension has been cited as cause for pessimism. Heavy weather has frequently been made by those who attempt to distinguish between those indicators pertinent to worlds characterized by either weak or strong sustainability. To an extent this debate has been misdirected: sustainability most probably requires both an avoidance of persistently negative genuine savings and declines in stocks of critical natural capital. Determining what actually constitutes critical natural capital and the threshold levels of the stocks that must be held is a crucial test of whether strong sustainability is more than just rhetoric.

If, as we believe, strong sustainability – to retain the distinction – does have much to offer, then, combined with the above-mentioned social and economic dimensions, a coherent and consistent programme for sustainability is emerging from seemingly disparate strands. That said, we believe that important steps towards the measurement of sustainable development have already been made largely on the basis of economic analysis. While it is eminently desirable that this knowledge is augmented, arguably enough is known to *begin* the process of implementing policies for sustainable development.

References

Addison, T. and Demery, L. (1985), *Macro-economic Stabilization, Income Distribution and Poverty: A Preliminary Survey*, Overseas Development Institute, London.

Adelman, M. (1990), 'Mineral Depletion, with Special Reference to Petroleum', *Review of Economics and Statistics*, **72**: 1–10.

Adger, W.N. and Grohs, F. (1994), 'Aggregate Estimate of Environmental Degradation for Zimbabwe: Does Sustainable National Income Ensure Sustainability?', *Ecological Economics*, **11**(2): 93–104.

Adriaanse, A. (1993), *Essential Environmental Information: The Netherlands*, Ministry of Housing, Physical Planning and Environment, The Hague.

Aghevli, B.B., Broughton, J.M., Montiel, P.J., Villanueva, D. and Woglom, G. (1990), 'The Role of National Saving in the World Economy: recent trends and prospects', IMF Occasional Paper 67, International Monetary Fund (IMF), Washington DC.

Agnew, C. and Anderson, E. (1992), *Water Resources in the Arid Realm*, Routledge, London and New York.

Ahmad, Y.J., El Serafy, S., and Lutz, E. (eds) (1989), *Environmental Accounting for Sustainable Development*, World Bank, Washington, DC.

Alam, M. (1990), 'Water Resources of the Middle East and North Africa With Particular Attention to Deep Artesian Groundwater Resources of the Area', *Water International*, **14**: 122–7.

Alexandratos, N. (ed.) (1988), *World Agriculture: Toward 2000 An FAO Study*, FAO, Rome and Belhaven, London.

Alfsen, K. and Saebo, H.V. (1993), 'Environmental Quality Indicators: Background, Principles and Examples from Norway', *Environmental and Resource Economics*, **3**(5): 415–35.

Allen, J. and Barnes, D. (1985), 'The Causes of Deforestation in Developing Countries', *Annals of the Association of American Geographers*, **75**(2) 163–84.

Anderson, J. and Hazell, P. (1989), *Variability in Grain Yields: Implications for Agricultural Research and Policy in Developing Countries*, Johns Hopkins University Press, Baltimore.

Andersson, T., Folke, C. and Nyström, T. (1995), *Trading with the Environment: Ecology, Economics, Institutions and Policy*, Earthscan, London.

Armitage, J. and Schramm, G. (1989), 'Managing the Supply and Demand for Fuelwood in Africa', in G. Schramm, and J.J. Warford (eds), *Environmental Management and Economic Development*, World Bank, Washington, DC.

Aronsson, T., Johansson, P.-O. and Löfgren, K.-G. (1994), 'Welfare Measurement and the Health Environment', *Annals of Operational Research*, **54**: 203–15.

Arrow, K., Bolin, B., Costanza, R., Dasgupta, P., Folke, C., Holling, C.S., Jansson, B.-O., Levin, S., Mäler, K.-G., Perrings, C. and Pimentel, D. (1995), 'Economic Growth, Carrying Capacity and the Environment', *Science*, **268**: 520–21.

Arrow, K.J. and Lind, R.C. (1971), 'Uncertainty and the Evaluation of Public Investment Decisions', *American Economic Review*, **60**: 364–78.

Asheim, G.B. (1986), 'Hartwick's Rule in Open Economies', *Canadian Journal of Economics*, **86**: 395–402.

Asheim, G.B. (1994a), 'Net National Product as an Indicator of Sustainability', *Scandinavian Journal of Economics*, **96**: 257–65.

Asheim, G.B. (1994b), 'The Concept of Net National Product in an Open Economy', paper presented to the International Symposium on 'Models of Sustainable Development. Exclusive or Complementary Approaches of Sustainability?', Université Panthéon-Sorbonne, Paris, March.

Atkinson, A.B. (1970), 'On the Measurement of Inequality', *Journal of Economic Theory*, **2**: 244–63.

Atkinson, G. (1993), 'Carrying Capacity as an Indicator of Sustainability', Centre for Social and Economic Research on the Global Environment (CSERGE), University College, London, and University of East Anglia.

Atkinson, G. (1995), 'Social Accounting, Genuine Saving and Measures of Economic Welfare', Centre for Social and Economic Research on the Global Environment (CSERGE), University College London and University of East Anglia, mimeo.

Atkinson, G. and Hamilton, K. (1996), 'Measuring Global Resource Consumption: Direct and Indirect Flows of Assets in International Trade', Centre for Social and Economic Research on the Global Environment (CSERGE), University College London and University of East Anglia, mimeo.

Barbier, E. (1988), 'The Economics of Farm-Level Adoption of Soil Conservation Measures in the Uplands of Java', Working Paper No. 11, Environment Department, World Bank, Washington, DC.

Barbier, E.B., Bokstael, N., Burgess, J. and Strand, I. (1994a), 'The Timber Trade and Tropical Deforestation in Indonesia', in Brown and Pearce (eds) (1994b).

Barbier, E.B., Burgess, J., Bishop, J. and Aylward, J. (1994b), 'Deforestation: The Role of the International Trade in Tropical Timber', in Brown and Pearce (eds) (1994b).

Barbier, E.B., Markandya, A. and Pearce, D.W. (1990), 'Environmental Sustainability and Cost–Benefit Analysis', *Environment and Planning A*, **22**: 1259–66.

Barnes, D.F. (1990), 'Population growth, wood fuels, and resource problems in Sub-Saharan Africa', Industry and Energy Department Working Paper, Energy Series No. 26, World Bank, Washington, DC.

Barro, R.J. (1974), 'Are Government Bonds Net Wealth?', *Journal of Political Economy*, **82**: 1095–117.

Barro, R.J. and Sala-I-Martin, X. (1995), *Economic Growth*, McGraw-Hill, New York.

Bartelmus, P., Stahmer, C. and van Tongeren, J. (1989), 'Integrated Environmental and Economic Accounting', International Association for Research on Income and Wealth, 21st General Conference, Lahnstein, West Germany, August.

Baster, N. (1972), 'Development Indicators: An Introduction', in N. Baster (ed.) *Measuring Development: The Role and Adequacy of Development Indicators*, Frank Cass, London.

Baumol, W.J. (1968), 'On the Social Rate of Discount', *American Economic Review*, **58**: 788–802.

Beckerman, W. (1995), *Small is Stupid: Blowing the Whistle on the Greens*, Duckworth, London.

Beltratti, A. (1993), 'Sustainable Growth: Analytical Models, Policy Implications and Measurements', paper presented to the Conference of the European Economics Association, Oriel College, Oxford.

Berndt, E. and Field, E. (eds) (1981), *Modelling and Measuring Natural Resource Substitution*, MIT Press, Cambridge, MA.

Bernheim, B.D. (1989), 'A Neoclassical Perspective on Budget Deficits', *Journal of Economic Perspectives*, **3**(2): 55–72.

Binswanger, H. (1989), *Brazilian Policies that Encourage Deforestation of the Amazon*, Working Paper 16, Environment Department, World Bank, Washington DC.

Birdsall, N. and Wheeler, D. (1992), 'Trade Policy and Industrial Pollution in Latin America: Where are the Pollution Havens?', in Low (ed.) (1992).

Bishop, J. (1990), *The Cost of Soil Erosion in Malawi*, Report to Malawi Country Operations Department, World Bank, Washington, DC.

Bishop, J. (1992), *Structural Adjustment and the Environment*, London Environmental Economics Centre, London.

Bishop, R.C. (1978), 'Endangered Species and Uncertainty: The Economics of a Safe Minimum Standard', *American Journal of Agricultural Economics*, **60**: 10–13.

Bishop, R.C. (1992), 'Economic Efficiency, Sustainability and Biodiversity', *Ambio*, **22**: 69–73.

Blum, E. (1993), 'Making Biodiversity Conservation Profitable: A Case Study of the Merck–INBio Agreement', *Environment*, **35**:

Boserup, E. (1981), *Population and Technical Change: A Study of Long Term Trends*, Chicago University Press, Chicago.

Bourguignon, F. and Morrison, D. (1992), *Adjustment and Equity in Developing Countries: A New Approach*, OECD, Paris.

Braden, J.B. and Kolstad, C.D. (eds) (1991), *Measuring the Demand for Environmental Quality*, North-Holland, Amsterdam.

Broome, J. (1978), 'Trying to Value a Life', *Journal of Public Economics*, **9**: 91–100.

Broome, J. (1992), *Counting the Cost of Global Warming*, White Horse Press, Cambridge.

Browder, J. (1985), *Subsidies, Deforestation, and the Forest Sector of the Brazilian Amazon*, World Resources Institute, Washington, DC.

Brown, K. and Pearce, D.W. (1994a), 'The Economic Value of Non-Market Benefits of Tropical Forests: Carbon Storage', in J. Weiss (ed.), *The Economics of Project Appraisal and the Environment*, Edward Elgar, Aldershot.

Brown, K. and Pearce, D.W. (eds) (1994b), *The Causes of Deforestation*, University College Press, London.

Brown, K., Pearce, D.W., Perrings, C. and Swanson, T. (1993), 'Economics and the Conservation of Global Biological Diversity', Global Environment Facility, Working Paper No. 2, Washington, DC.

Bureau of Economic Analysis (1994), 'Integrated Economic and Environmental Satellite Accounts', *Survey of Current Business*, April: 33–49.

Bureau of Mines (1987), *An Appraisal of Minerals Availability for 34 Commodities*, Bulletin 692, Department of the Interior, Washington, DC.

Burgess, J. (1991), 'Economic Analyses of Frontier Agricultural Expansion and Tropical Deforestation', unpublished MSc dissertation, University College London.

Burgess, J. (1992), *Economic Analysis of the Causes of Tropical Deforestation*, Discussion Paper 92–03, London Environmental Economics Centre.

Capistrano, A.D. (1990), 'Macroeconomic Influences on Tropical Forest Depletion: A Cross Country Analysis', unpublished PhD thesis, University of Florida.

Capistrano, A.D. and Kiker, C.F. (1990), 'Global Economic Influences on a Tropical Closed Broadleaved Forest Depletion, 1967–1985', International Society for Ecological Economics Conference, Washington, DC.

Carey, D.I. (1993), 'Development Based on Carrying Capacity; A Strategy for Environmental Protection', *Global Environmental Change*, June: 140–48.

CEC/US (1993), *Externalities of the Fuel Cycles: 'Externe Project'*, Working Documents 1, 2, 5 and 9, Directorate-General XII, European Commission, Brussels.

Cervigni, R. (1993), 'Biodiversity, Incentives to Deforest and Tradeable Development Rights', Working Paper GEC 93–07, Centre for Social and

Economic Research on the Global Environment, University College London and University of East Anglia.

Chemonics International and Associates (1994), *Comparing Environmental Health Risks in Cairo, Egypt*, Vols 1 and 2, Report to US AID, Egypt, September.

Ciriacy-Wantrup, S.V. (1952), *Resources Conservation: Economics and Policies*, University of California Press, Berkeley.

Clark, C.W. (1990), *Mathematical Bioeconomics*, 2nd edition. John Wiley & Sons, New York.

Clarke, M. (1992), *Water: The International Crisis*, Earthscan, London.

Cleaver, K. and Schreiber, G. (1991), 'The Population, Environment and Agriculture Nexus in SubSaharan Africa', Africa Region Technical Paper, World Bank, Washington, DC.

Cleaver, K.M. and Schreiber, G.A. (1992), *The Population, Agriculture and Environment Nexus in Sub-Saharan Africa*, World Bank, Western Africa Department, Washington, DC.

Cohen, J.E. (1995), 'Population Growth and Earth's Human Carrying Capacity', *Science*, **269**: 341–8.

Commission of the European Communities (1994), *Communication from the Commission to the Council and the European Parliament* (COM(94) 640 final), European Commission, Brussels.

Common, M. and Perrings, C. (1992), 'Towards An Ecological Economics of Sustainability', *Ecological Economics*, **6**: 7–34.

Constantino, L. and Ingram, D. (1990), *Supply–Demand Projections for the Indonesian Forestry Sector*, FAO, Jakarta.

Conway, G. (1985), 'Agroecosystem Analysis', *Agricultural Administration*, **20**: 31–55.

Conway, G. (1987), 'The Properties of Agroecosystems', *Agricultural Administration*, **24**: 95–117.

Conway, G.R. (1993), 'Sustainability in Agricultural Development: Trade-offs with Productivity, Stability and Equitability', Imperial College, London, mimeo.

Conway, G. and Barbier, E.B. (1990), *After the Green Revolution: Sustainable Agriculture for Development*, Earthscan, London.

Cooper D., Vellvé, R. and Hobbelink, H. (eds) (1992), *Growing Diversity: Genetic Resources and Local Food Security*, Intermediate Technology Publications, London.

Cornia, G.A., Jolly, R. and Stewart, F. (eds) (1992), *Adjustment with a Human Face, Volume I: Protecting the Vulnerable and Promoting Growth*, Clarendon Press, Oxford.

Crowards, T. (1996), 'Natural Resource Accounting: A Case Study of Zimbabwe', *Environmental and Resource Economics*, forthcoming.

Cruz, W. and Gibbs, C. (1990), 'Resource Policy Reform in the Context of Population Pressure: The Philippines and Nepal', *American Journal of Agricultural Economics*, **72**.

Cruz, W. and Repetto, R. (1992), *The Environmental Effects of Stabilization and Adjustment Programs: The Philippines Case*, World Resources Institute, Washington, DC.

CSERGE/UNC Chapel Hill (1994), 'Economic Values and the Environment in the Developing World', Report to UNEP Nairobi, mimeo.

Cuesta, M., Carlson, G. and Lutz, E. (1994), *An Empirical Assessment of Farmers' Discount Rates in Costa Rica and Its Implication for Soil Conservation*, Environment Department, World Bank, Washington, DC.

Daly, H. and Cobb, J. (1989), *For the Common Good*, Beacon Press, New York.

Dasgupta, A.K. (1989), *Growth, Development and Welfare*, Basil Blackwell, Oxford.

Dasgupta, P. (1982), *The Control of Resources*, Basil Blackwell, Oxford.

Dasgupta, P. (1993), *An Enquiry into Wellbeing and Destitution*, Oxford University Press, Oxford.

Dasgupta, P. and Heal, G.M. (1979), *Economic Theory and Exhaustible Resources*, Cambridge University Press, Cambridge.

de Boo, A.J., Bosch, P.R., Garter, C.N. and Keuning, S.J. (1991), 'An Environmental Module and the Complete System of National Accounts', Occasional Paper No. NA–046, Central Bureau of Statistics, Voorburg.

Deacon, R. and Murphy, P. (1994), 'The Structure of an Environmental Transaction: The Debt-for-Nature Swap', Department of Economics, University of California at Santa Barbara, mimeo.

Department of Energy (1994), *Performance Profiles of Major Energy Producers 1992*, DOE/EIA–0206(92), Washington, DC.

Desai, M. (1994), 'Greening of the HDI?', London School of Economics, mimeo.

Devarajan, S. (1990), 'Can Computable General Equilibrium Models Shed Light on the Environmental Problems of Developing Countries?', paper prepared for WIDER Conference on the Environment and Emerging Development Issues, Helsinki.

Dixit, A., Hammond, P. and Hoel, M. (1980), 'On Hartwick's Rule for Regular Maximin Paths of Capital Accumulation and Resource Depletion', *Review of Economic Studies*, **47**: 551–6.

Dixon, R., Andrasko, K., Sussman, F., Trexler, M. and Vinson, V. (1993), 'Forest Sector Carbon Offset Projects: Near-Term Opportunities to Mitigate Greenhouse Gas Emissions', *Water, Air and Soil Pollution*, Special issue.

Drèze, J. and Sen, A. (1987), *Hunger and Public Action*, Clarendon Press, Oxford.

Dubourg, W.R. (1992), 'The Sustainable Management of the Water Cycle: A Framework for Analysis', CSERGE Working Paper WM 92–07, Centre for

Social and Economic Research on the Global Environment, University College London and University of East Anglia.

Dubourg, W.R. (1996), 'Estimating the Mortality Costs of Lead Emissions in England and Wales', *Energy Policy*, **24**(7): 621–6.

Dubourg, W.R. and Pearce, D.W. (1996), 'Paradigms for Environmental Choice: Sustainability versus Optimality', in S. Faucheux, D.W. Pearce and J.L.R. Proops (eds), *Models of Sustainable Development*, Edward Elgar, Cheltenham.

Economic Commission for Latin America and the Caribbean (ECLAC) (1989), 'Crisis, External Debt, Macroeconomic Policies and Their Relation to the Environment in Latin America and the Caribbean', paper prepared for the Meeting of High-Level Government Experts on Regional Cooperation in Environmental Matters in Latin America and the Caribbean, United Nations Environmental Programme, Brazil.

Ehrlich, P. (1992), 'Ecological Economics and the Carrying Capacity of Earth', paper presented at the 2nd Meeting of the International Society for Ecological Economics (ISEE), Stockholm, 3–6 August.

El Serafy, S. (1989), 'The Proper Calculation of Income from Depletable Natural Resources', in Ahmad et al. (eds) (1989).

Faber, M. and Proops, J.L.R. (1991), *Evolution, Time, Production and the Environment*, Springer-Verlag, Heidelberg.

Falkenmark, M. (1984), 'New Ecological Approach to the Ticket to the Future', *Ambio*, **13**.

Fankhauser, S. (1995), 'Evaluating the Social Costs of Greenhouse Gas Emissions', *Energy Journal*, **15**: 157–84.

Fankhauser, S. and Pearce, D.W. (1994), 'The Social Costs of Greenhouse Gas Emissions', in Organization for Economic Cooperation and Development, *The Economics of Climate Change*, OECD, Paris.

Feder, G., Onchan, T., Chalamwong, Y., and Hongladarom, C. (1988), *Land Policies and Farm Productivity in Thailand*, Johns Hopkins University Press, Baltimore.

Flores, N.E. and Carson, R.T. (1995), 'The Relationship between Income Elasticities of Demand and Willingness to Pay', Discussion Paper 95–31, Department of Economics, University of California, San Diego.

Food and Agriculture Organization (FAO) (1993), *Forest Resources Assessment 1990 (Tropical Countries)*, FAO, Rome.

Freeman, A.M. (1993), *The Measurement of Environmental and Resource Values: Theory and Methods*, Resources for the Future, Washington, DC.

Gámez, R., Piva, A., Sittenfield, A., Leon, E., Jimenez, J. and Mirabelli, G. (1993), 'Costa Rica's Conservation Program and National Biodiversity Institute (INBio)', in Reid et al., (1993).

Gelb, A. (1988), *Oil Windfalls: Blessing or Curse?*, Oxford University Press, New York.

Gillis, M., Perkins, D.H., Roemer, M. and Snodgrass, D.R. (1992), *Economics of Development*, 3rd edition, W.W. Norton & Company, London.

Goldin, I. and Host, D. (1994), 'Economic Policies for Sustainable Resources in Morocco', paper presented to the London Group Meeting, Bureau of Economic Analysis, Washington, DC, 15–17 March.

Goodland, R. (1990), *Race to Save the Tropics: Ecology and Economics for a Sustainable Future*, Island Press, Washington, DC.

Gregory, R. (1986), 'Interpreting Measures of Economic Loss: Evidence from Contingent Valuation and Experimental Studies', *Journal of Environmental Economics and Management*, **13**: 325–37.

Grossman, G.M. (1995), 'Pollution and Growth: What Do We Know?', in I. Goldin and L.A. Winters (eds), *The Economics of Sustainable Development*, Cambridge University Press, Cambridge.

Grossman, G.M. and Krueger, A.B. (1994), 'Economic Growth and the Environment', Princeton University, mimeo.

Grossman, G.M. and Krueger, A.B. and Laity, J.A. (1994), 'Pollution and Growth: Evidence from the United States', Princeton University, mimeo.

Hamilton, K. (1991), 'Proposed Treatments of the Environment and Natural Resources in the National Accounts: A Critical Assessment', National Accounts and Environment Division, Discussion Paper No. 7, Statistics Canada, Ottawa.

Hamilton, K. (1993), 'Greening the Human Development Index', mimeo.

Hamilton, K. (1994a), 'Green Adjustments to GDP', *Resources Policy*, **20**: 155–68.

Hamilton, K. (1994b), 'Estimated Rental Rates for Minerals and Crude Oil', Environment Department, World Bank, Washington, DC, mimeo.

Hamilton, K. (1994c), 'Exhaustible Resources and Net National Product', University College London, mimeo.

Hamilton, K. (1994d), 'Pollution and Pollution Abatement in the National Accounts', University College London, mimeo.

Hamilton, K. (1995), 'Sustainable Development, the Hartwick Rule and Optimal Growth', *Environmental and Resource Economics*, **5**: 393–411.

Hamilton, K. (1996), 'Defining Income and Measuring Sustainability', Centre for Social and Economic Research on the Global Environment, University College London and University of East Anglia, mimeo.

Hamilton, K. and Atkinson, G. (1996), 'Air Pollution and Green Accounts', *Energy Policy*, **24**(7): 675–84.

Hamilton, K. and O'Connor, J. (1994), 'Genuine Saving and the Financing of Investment', Environment Department, World Bank, Washington, DC, mimeo.

Hamilton, K., Pearce, D.W., Atkinson, G., Gomez-Lobo, A., and Young, C. (1994), 'The Policy Implications of Natural Resource and Environmental

Accounting', Working paper, Centre for Social and Economic Research on the Global Environment, University College London and University of East Anglia.

Hamilton, K. and Ulph, D. (1994), 'The Hartwick Rule in a Greenhouse World', University College London, mimeo.

Hammond, A., Adriaanse, A., Rodenburg, E., Bryant, D. and Woodward, R. (1995), *Environmental Indicators*, World Resources Institute, Washington, DC.

Hanna, S. and Munasinghe, M. (1995a), *Property Rights and the Environment: Social and Ecological Issues*, Beijer International Institute of Ecological Economics and World Bank, Stockholm and Washington, DC.

Hanna, S. and Munasinghe, M. (1995b), *Property Rights in a Social and Ecological Context: Case Studies and Design Applications*, Beijer International Institute of Ecological Economics and World Bank, Stockholm and Washington, DC.

Hardin, G. (1991), 'Paramount Positions in Ecological Economics', in R. Costanza, (ed.), *Ecological Economics: The Science and Management of Sustainability*, Colombia University Press, New York.

Harrison, A. (1989), 'Introducing Natural Capital into the SNAP, in Ahmad et al (eds) (1989).

Hartwick, J.M. (1977), 'Intergenerational Equity and the Investing of Rents from Exhaustible Resources', *American Economic Review*, **67**: 972–4.

Hartwick, J.M. (1978a), 'Substitution Among Exhaustible Resources and Intergenerational Equity', *Review of Economic Studies*, **45**: 347–54.

Hartwick, J.M. (1978b), 'Investing Returns from Depleting Renewable Resource Stocks and Intergenerational Equity', *Economics Letters*, **1**: 85–8.

Hartwick, J.M. (1990), 'Natural Resources, National Accounting and Economic Depreciation', *Journal of Public Economics*, **43**: 291–304.

Hartwick, J.M. (1992), 'Deforestation and National Accounting', *Environmental and Resource Economics*, **2**: 513–21.

Hartwick, J.M. (1993), 'Notes on Economic Depreciation of Natural Resource Stocks and National Accounting, in A. Franz and C. Stahmer (eds), *Approaches to Environmental Accounting*, Physica-Verlag, Heidelberg.

Hartwick, J.M. (1994), 'Sustainability and Constant Consumption Paths in Open Economies with Exhaustible Resources', paper prepared for the AERE Conference, Boulder, Colo., 5 June.

Hartwick, J.M. and Hageman, A. (1993), 'Economic Depreciation of Mineral Stocks and the Contribution of El Serafy', in E. Lutz (ed.), *Toward Improved Accounting for the Environment*, World Bank, Washington, DC.

Hartwick, J.M., and Lindsey, R. (1989), 'NNP and Economic Depreciation of Exhaustible Resource Stocks', Department of Economics Discussion Paper No. 741, Queens University, Kingston.

Hazell, P. (1982), 'Instability in Indian Foodgrain Production', Research Report No. 30, International Food Policy Research Institute, Washington, DC.

Hazell, P. (1984), 'Sources of Increased Instability in Indian and US Cereal Production', *American Journal of Agricultural Economics*, 302–11.

Hazell, P. (1989), 'Changing Patterns of Variability in World Cereal Production', in Anderson and Hazell (1989).

Heertje, A. (ed.) (1993), *World Savings: An International Survey*, Basil Blackwell, Oxford.

Herfindahl, O.C., and Kneese, A.V. (1973), 'Measuring Social and Economic Change: Benefits and Costs of Environmental Pollution', in Moss (ed.) (1973).

Hicks, R.J. (1946), *Value and Capital*, 2nd edition, Oxford University Press, Oxford.

Higgins, G.M., Kassam, A.H. and Naiken, L. (1982), *Potential Population Supporting Capacities of Lands in the Developing World*, Food and Agricultural Organization, Rome.

Hill, P. and Harrison, A. (1994), 'Accounting for Subsoil Assets in the 1993 SNA', presented to the London Group on National Accounts and the Environment, London, March.

Hodgson, G. and Dixon, J. (1988), *Logging Versus Fisheries and Tourism in Palawan*, Occasional Paper No. 7, East West Center, Honolulu.

Holling, C.S. (1973), 'Resilience and Stability of Ecological Systems', *Annual Review of Ecology and Systematics*, **4**: 1–24.

Howarth, R.B. and Norgaard, R.B. (1990), 'Environmental Valuation Under Sustainable Development', *American Economic Review*, **82**: 473–7.

Howarth, R.B. and Norgaard, R.B. (1993), 'Intergenerational Transfers and the Social Discount Rate', *Environmental and Resource Economics*, **3**: 337–58.

Hueting, R. and Bosch, P. (1990), 'On the Correction of National Income for Environmental Losses', *Statistical Journal of the United Nations*, ECE **7**: 75–83.

Hueting R., Bosch, P.R. and de Boer, B. (1992), 'Methodology for the Calculation of Sustainable National Income', Statistical Essays M44, Central Bureau of Statistics, Voorburg.

Hughes, G. (1992), 'Cleaning Up Eastern Europe' *Finance and Development*, **29**: 16–19.

International Development Association (IDA) (1992), *IDA's Policies, Operations, and Finance in the Second Year of the Ninth Replenishment (FY92)*, Washington, DC.

International Fund for Agricultural Development (IFAD) (1992), *The State of World Rural Poverty*, Intermediate Technology Publications, London.

Jagannathan, N.V. (1989), 'Poverty, public policies and the environment', Environment Working Paper No. 24, World Bank, Washington, DC.

Jodha, N.S. (1990), 'Rural Common Property Resources: Contributions and Crisis', *Economic and Political Weekly*, 30 June.

Johnson, O. and Salop, J. (1980), 'Distributional Aspects of Stabilization Programs in Developing Countries', *IMF Staff Papers*, **27**: 1–23.

Jones-Lee, M.W. (1976), *The Value of Life: An Economic Analysis*, Martin Robertson, London.

Jones-Lee, M.W. (1989), *The Economics of Safety and Physical Risk*, Basil Blackwell, Oxford.

Jorgenson, D.W. and Fraumeni, B.M. (1992), 'The Output of the Education Sector', in Z. Griliches, (ed.), *Output Measurement in the Service Sectors*, University of Chicago Press, Chicago.

Josserand, H. (1989), 'Impact of non-African meat imports on cattle trade between West African countries', paper presented at Seminar on Regional Cereals Markets in West Africa, CILLS/Club du Sahel.

Juster, F.T. (1973), 'A Framework for the Measurement of Economic and Social Performance', in Moss (ed.) (1973).

Kahn, J. and McDonald, J. (1992), 'Third World Debt and Tropical Deforestation', Department of Economics, SUNY–Binghampton, mimeo.

Kahn, J. and McDonald, J. (1994), 'Investigating the Linkages Between Debt and Deforestation', in Brown and Pearce (eds) (1994b).

Kahnemann, D. and Tversky, A. (1979), 'Prospect Theory: An Analysis of Decisions Under Risk', *Econometrica*, **47**: 263–91.

Katila, M. (1992), 'Modelling Deforestation in Thailand: The Causes of Deforestation and Deforestation Projections for 1990–2010', Finnish Forestry Institute, Helsinki, mimeo.

Katzman, M. and Cale, W. (1990), 'Tropical Forest Preservation Using Economic Incentives: A Proposal of Conservation Easements', *BioScience*, **40**: 827–32.

Kelley, A.C. (1988), 'Economic Consequences of Population Change in the Third World', *Journal of Economic Literature*, **26**: 1685–728.

Keuning, S. (1995), 'Accounting for Economic Development and Social Change', unpublished PhD thesis, Erasmus University, Rotterdam.

Keuning, S. and Timmerman, J. (1995), 'An Information System for Economic, Environmental and Social Statistics: Integrating Environmental Data into the SESAME', paper presented to the London Group Meeting, Bureau of Economic Analysis, Washington, DC, 15–17 March.

Kirchner, J.W., Ledec, G., Goodland, R.J.A. and Drake, J.M. (1985), 'Carrying Capacity Population and Sustainable Development', in D.J. Mahar (ed.), *Rapid Population Growth and Human Carrying Capacity*, Staff Working Paper no. 690, Population and Development Series no. 15, World Bank, Washington, DC.

Klaassen, G. and Botterweg, T.H. (1976), 'Project Evaluation and Intangible Effects: A Shadow Project Approach', in P. Njikamp (ed.), *Environmental Economics*, Vol. I, Martinus Nijhoff, Leiden.

Knetsch, J.L. (1989), 'The Endowment Effect and Evidence of Nonreversible Indifference Curves', *American Economic Review*, **79**: 1277–84.

Knetsch, J.L. and Sinden, J.A. (1984), 'Willingness To Pay and Compensation Demanded: Experimental Evidence of an Unexpected Disparity in Measures of Value', *Quarterly Journal of Economics*, **99**: 507–21.

Kotilloff, L.J. and Summers L.H. (1981), 'The Role of Intergenerational Transfers in Aggregate Capital Accumulation', *Journal of Political Economy*, **89**: 706–32.

Krautkraemer, J.A. (1985), 'Optimal Growth, Resource Amenities and the Preservation of Natural Environments', *Review of Economic Studies*, **52**: 153–77.

Krebs, C.J. (1985), *Ecology*, 3rd edition, HarperCollins, New York.

Kriström, B. and Riera, P. (1996), 'Its the Income Elasticity of Environmental Improvements Less than One?', *Environmental and Resource Economics*, **7**(1): 45–55.

Kumari, K. (1994), 'Sustainable Forest Management in Malaysia', unpublished PhD thesis, University of East Anglia.

Kummer, D. and Sham, C.H. (1994), 'The Causes of Tropical Deforestation: A Quantitative Analysis', in Brown and Pearce (eds) (1994b).

Lal, D. (1983), *The Poverty of 'Development Economics'*, Institute of Economic Affairs, London.

Larsen, B. (1994), 'World Fossil Fuel Subsidies and Global Carbon Emissions in a Model with Interfuel Substitution', Policy Research Working Paper, No. 1256, World Bank, Washington, DC.

Larson, B. and Bromley, D. (1991), 'Natural Resource Prices, Export Policies, and Deforestation: The Case of Sudan', *World Development*.

Leipert, C. (1989), 'National Income and Economic Growth: The Conceptual Side of Defensive Expenditures', *Journal of Economic Issues*, **23**: 843–56.

Lele, U. and Stone, S. (1989), 'Population Pressure, the Environment and Agricultural Intensification: Variations on the Boserup Hypothesis', MADIA Discussion Paper 4, World Bank, Washington, DC.

Leonard, H.J. (1985), 'Confronting Industrial Pollution in Rapidly Industrializing Countries: Myths, Pitfalls, and Opportunities', *Ecology Law Quarterly*, **13**: 779–816.

Leonard, H.J. (1988), *Pollution and the Struggle for the World Product*, Cambridge University Press, Cambridge.

Lewenhak, S. (1989), *The Revaluation of Women's Work*, Earthscan, London.

Little, I.M.B. and Mirrlees, J.A. (1974), *Project Analysis and Planning for Developing Countries*, Basic Books, New York.

Low, P. (ed.) (1992), *International Trade and the Environment*, World Bank Discussion Paper no. l59, World Bank, Washington, DC.

Low, P. and Yeats, A. (1992), 'Do Dirty Industries Matter?', in P. Low (ed.), *International Trade and the Environment*, World Bank, Washington, DC.

Lucas, R.E.B., Wheeler, D. and Hettige, H. (1992), 'Economic Development, Environmental Regulation and the International Migration of Toxic Industrial Pollution: 1960–1988', in Low (ed.) (1992).

Lugo, A., Schmidt, R. and Brown, S. (1981), 'Tropical Forest in the Caribbean', *Ambio*, **10**:

Mahar, D. (1988), 'Government Policies and Deforestation in Brazil's Amazon Region', Environment Department Working Paper No. 7, World Bank, Washington, DC.

Mahar, D. and Schneider, R. (1994), 'Incentives for Tropical Deforestation: Some Examples from Latin America', in Brown and Pearce (eds) (1994b).

Mäler, K.-G. (1991), 'National Accounts and Environmental Resources', *Environmental and Resource Economics*, **1**: 1–15.

Margulis, S. (1992), *Back of the Envelope Estimates of Environmental Damage Costs in Mexico*, Working Paper WPS, Country Department II, Latin America and the Caribbean Regional Office, World Bank, Washington, DC.

Marland, G., Boden, R.A., Griffin, R.C., Huang, S.F., Kanciruk, P. and Nelson, T.R. (1989), 'Estimates of CO_2 Emissions from Fossil Fuel Burning and Cement Manufacturing Based on the United Nations Energy Statistics and the US Bureau of Mines Cement Manufacturing Data', ORNL/CDIAC–25, NDP–030, Oak Ridge National Laboratory, Oak Ridge.

Martínez-Alier, J. (1995), 'The Environment as a Luxury Good or "Too Poor to be Green"?', *Ecological Economics*, **13**: 1–10.

May, R.M. (1973), *Stability and Complexity in Model Ecosystems*, Princeton University Press, Princeton, NJ.

Mehra, S. (1981), 'Instability in Indian Agriculture in the Context of the New Technology', Research Report No. 25, International Food Policy Research Institute, Washington, DC.

Meier, P. and Munasinghe, M. (1993), 'Incorporating Environmental Costs into Power Development Planning: a Case Study of Sri Lanka', in M. Munasinghe (ed.) *Environmental Economics and Natural Resource Management in Developing Countries*, World Bank, Washington, DC.

Miller, M. (1991), *Debt and the Environment: Converging Crises*, United Nations, New York.

Miller, R.E. and Blair, P.D. (1985), *Input–Output Analysis: Foundations and Extensions*, Prentice-Hall, Englewood Cliffs, NJ.

Mink, S.D. (1993), 'Poverty, Population and the Environment', World Bank Discussion Paper No. 189, World Bank, Washington, DC.

Miranda, K. and Muzondo, T. (1991), 'Public Policy and the Environment', *Finance and Development*, **28**: 25–7.

Moran, D., Pearce, D.W. and Wendelaar, A. (1995), 'Investing in Biodiversity Conservation: A Cost-Effectiveness Index for Ranking Priorities', Centre for Social and Economic Research on the Global Environment, University College London and University of East Anglia, mimeo.

Mosley, P., Harrigan, J. and Tage, J. (1991), *Aid and Power: The World Bank and Policy-Based Lending*, Routledge, London.

Moss, M. (ed.) (1973), *Studies in Income and Wealth, Vol 1. 38: The Measurement of Economic Performance*, Columbia University Press, New York.

Munasinghe, M. (1990), *Electric Power Economics*, Butterworth Press, London.

Munasinghe, M. (1992), Water Supply and Environmental Management, Westview Press, Boulder, Colo.

Munasinghe, M. (1993a), 'The Economist's Approach to Sustainable Development', *Finance and Development*, **30**: 16–19.

Munasinghe, M. (1993b), *Environmental Economics and Sustainable Development*, World Bank, Washington, DC.

Munasinghe, M. (1995), 'Making Growth More Sustainable', *Ecological Economics*, **15**: 121–4.

Munasinghe, M. (ed.) (1996) *Environmental Impacts of Macroeconomic and Sectoral Policies*, International Society for Ecological Economics, World Bank and United Nations Environmental Program, Washington, DC.

Munasinghe, M. and Cruz, W. (1994), *Econonywide Policies and the Environment*, World Bank, Washington, DC.

Munasinghe, M., Cruz, W. and Warford, J.J. (1993), 'Are Economywide Policies Good for the Environment?', *Finance and Development*, **30**: 40–3.

Munasinghe, M. and Shearer, W. (eds) (1995), *Defining and Measuring Sustainability*, United Nations University, Tokyo and World Bank, Washington, DC.

Ndulu, B., and Elbadawi, I. (1994), 'Long-Term Development and Sustainable Growth in Sub-Saharan Africa', presented to the colloquium on New Directions in Development Economics – Growth, Equity and Sustainable Development, SAREC, Stockholm, Sweden, March.

Nehru, V., and Dhareshwar, A. (1993), 'A New Database on Physical Capital Stock: Sources, Methodology and Results', *Revista de Analysis Economico*, **8**: 37–59.

Newcombe, K. and de Lucia, R. (1993), 'Mobilising Private Capital Against Global Warming: A Business Concept and Policy Issues', Global Environment Facility, Washington, DC, mimeo.

Ninan, K. and Chandrashekar, H. (1991), 'The Green Revolution, Dryland Agriculture and Sustainability Insights from India', paper presented to the 21st International Conference of Agricultural Economists, Tokyo, August.

Nordhaus, W. (1995), 'How Should We Measure Sustainable Income?', Yale University, mimeo.

Nordhaus, W.D. and Tobin, J. (1972), 'Is Growth Obsolete?', in *Economic Growth, Fiftieth Anniversary Colloquium V*, Columbia University Press, New York.

Organization for Economic Cooperation and Development (1991), *Environmental Indicators: A Preliminary Set*, OECD, Paris.

Organization for Economic Cooperation and Development (1993), *Agricultural Policies, Markets and Trade: Monitoring and Outlook 1993*, OECD, Paris.

Organization for Economic Cooperation and Development (1994a), *Environmental Indicators*, OECD, Paris.

Organization for Economic Cooperation and Development (1994b), *Foreign Trade Statistics by Commodity: Series C*, OECD, Paris.

Owens, J. (1993), 'Taxation and Savings', in Heertje (ed.) (1993).

Ozório de Almeida, A.L. and Campari, J. (1993), 'Sustainable Settlement in the Amazon', Education and Social Policy Department, World Bank, Washington, DC.

Page, T. (1977), *Conservation and Economic Efficiency: An Approach to Materials Policy*, Johns Hopkins University Press, Baltimore.

Palo, M., Mery, G. and Salmi, J. (1987), *Deforestation in the Tropics: Pilot Scenarios Based on Quantitative Analyses*, Metsatutkimuslaitoksen Tiedonantaja No. 272, Helsinki.

Panayatou, T. (1993), *Green Markets: The Economics of Sustainable Development*, Institute for Contemporary Studies Press, San Francisco.

Panayatou, T. (1994), 'Financing Mechanisms for Environmental Investments and Sustainable Development', Harvard Institute for International Development, Harvard University, mimeo.

Panayaotou, T. and Sungsuwan, S. (1994), 'An Econometric Study of the Causes of Tropical Deforestation: The Case of Northeast Thailand', in Brown and Pearce, (eds) (1994b).

Panayatou, T. and Sussangkarn, S. (1991), 'The Debt Crisis, Structural Adjustment and the Environment: The Case of Thailand', paper prepared for the World Wildlife Fund Project on the Impact of Macroeconomic Adjustment on the Environment, Washington, DC.

Parfit, D, (1984), *Reasons and Persons*, Oxford University Press, Oxford.

Pearce, D.W. (1980), 'The Social Incidence of Environmental Costs and Benefits', in T. O'Riordan and R.K. Turner (eds), *Progress in Resource Management and Environmental Planning*, Vol. 2, John Wiley, London.

Pearce, D.W. (1990), 'Population Growth', in D.W. Pearce (ed.), *Blueprint 2: Greening the World Economy*, Earthscan, London.

Pearce, D.W. (1993), *Economic Values and the Natural World*, Earthscan, London.

Pearce, D.W. (1994), 'Joint Implementation: A General Overview', in C.P. Jepma (ed.), *Joint Implementation*, Kluwer, Dordrecht.

Pearce, D.W., Adger, N., Brown, K., Cervigni, R. and Moran, D. (1993), *Mexico Forestry and Conservation Sector Review: Substudy of Economic Valuation of Forests*, Centre for Social and Economic Research on the Global Environment (CSERGE) for World Bank Latin America and Caribbean Country Department.

Pearce, D.W. and ApSimon, H. (eds) (1995), *Counting the Costs of Acid Rain*, Report to the UK Department of Environment, London.

Pearce, D.W. and Atkinson, G. (1993), 'Capital Theory and the Measurement of Sustainable Development: An Indicator of Weak Sustainability', *Ecological Economics*, **8**: 103–8.

Pearce, D.W., Atkinson, G.D. and Dubourg, W.R. (1994), *Annual Review of Energy and Environment*, **19**: 457–74.

Pearce, D.W. and Bann, C. (1993), 'North South Transfers and the Capture of Global Environmental Value', Working Paper GEC 93–24, Centre for Social and Economic Research on the Global Environment, University College London and University of East Anglia.

Pearce, D.W., Barbier, E. and Markandya, A. (1990), *Sustainable Development: Economics and Environment in the Third World*, Edward Elgar, London and Earthscan, London.

Pearce, D.W. and Crowards, T. (1996), 'Particulate Matter and Health in the United Kingdom', *Energy Policy*, **24** (7): 609–20.

Pearce, D.W., Markandya, A., and Barbier, E.B. (1989), *Blueprint for a Green Economy*, Earthscan, London.

Pearce, D.W. and Moran, D. (1994), *The Economic Value of Biodiversity*, Earthscan, London.

Pearce, D.W. and Prakesh, T.R. (1993), 'Sustainability as Resilience', Centre for Social and Economic Research on the Global Environmental, University College London and University of East Anglia, mimeo.

Pearce, D.W. and Ulph, D. (1995), 'A Social Discount Rate for the United Kingdom', Working Paper 95–01, Centre for Social and Economic Research on the Global Environment (CSERGE), University College London and University of East Anglia.

Pearce, D.W. and Warford, J.J. (1993), *World Without End: Economics, Environment and Sustainable Development*, Oxford University Press, Oxford and New York.

Pearson, P. (1995), 'Energy, Externalities and Environmental Quality: Will Development Cure the Ills It Creates?', *Energy Studies Review*, **6**(3): 199–216.

Pemberton, M., Pezzey, J., and Ulph, D. (1995), 'Measuring Income and Measuring Sustainability', University College London, mimeo.

Perrings, C. (1992), 'An Economic Analysis of Tropical Deforestation', Department of Environment and Economic Management, University of York, mimeo.

Perrings, C. (1993), 'Pastoral Strategies in Sub-Saharan Africa: The Economic and Ecological Sustainability of Dryland Range Management', Working Paper No. 57, Environment Department, World Bank, Washington, DC.

Perrings, C. (1994), 'Ecological Resilience in the Sustainability of Economic Development', paper presented at the International Symposium on Models of Sustainable Development, Paris, March.

Perrings, C., Turner, R.K. and Folke, C. (1995), 'Ecological Economics: Paradigm or Perspective?' Paper presented at the European Association of Environmental and Resource Economists Annual Conference, Umeå, June 1995.

Perrings, C., Turner, R.K. and Folke, C. (1995), Paper presented at the European Association of Resource and Environmental Economists Conference, Umeå, July, Working Paper GEC 95–, Centre for Social and Economic Research on the Global Environment (CSERGE), University College, London and University of East Anglia.

Peskin, H. (1989), 'A Proposed Environmental Accounts Framework', in Ahmad (eds) (1989).

Pezzey, J. (1989), 'Economic Analysis of Sustainable Growth and Sustainable Development', Environment Department Working Paper No. 15, World Bank, Washington, DC.

Pezzey, J. (1994), 'The Optimal Sustainable Depletion of Non-Renewable Resources', University College London, mimeo.

Pinto, B., Belka, M. and Krajewski, S. (1993), 'Transforming State Enterprises in Poland: Microeconomic Evidence on Adjustment', Policy Research Working Paper Series No. 1101, World Bank, Washington, DC.

Proops, J.L.R and Atkinson, G. (1997), 'A Practical Sustainability Criterion When There Is International Trade', in S. Faucheux, M. O'Connor, and J. van den Straaten (eds), *Sustainable Development: Analysis and Public Policy*, Kluwer Academic Publishers, Dordrecht, forthcoming.

Proops, J.L.R, Faber, M., and Wagenhals, G., (1993), *Reducing CO_2 Emissions: A Comparative Input–Output Study for Germany and the UK*, Springer-Verlag, Heidelberg.

Pyatt, G. (1990), 'Accounting for Time Use', *Review of Income and Wealth*, **36**(1): 33–52.

Ramsey, F. (1928), 'A Mathematical Theory of Saving', *Economic Journal*, **38**: 543–59.

Randall, A. (1991), 'Total and Non-use Values', in J. Braden and C. Kolstad (eds), *Measuring the Demand for Environmental Quality*, North-Holland, Amsterdam.

Rawls, J. (1971), *A Theory of Justice*, Harvard University Press, Cambridge, MA.

Reardon, T. and Vosti, S.A. (1992), 'Issues in the Analysis of the Effects of Policy Conservation and Productivity at the Household Level in Developing Countries', *Quarterly Journal of International Agriculture*, **31**: 380–94.

Reed, D. (ed.) (1992), *Structural Adjustment and the Environment*, Earthscan, London.

Rees, W.E. and Wackernagel, M. (1994), 'Appropriated Carrying Capacity: Measuring the Natural Capital Requirements of the Human Economy', in A.M. Jansson, M. Hammer, C. Folke, and R. Costanza (eds), *Investing in Natural Capital: The Ecological Economics Approach to Sustainability*, Island Press, Washington, DC.

Reid, W., Sittenfeld, A., Laird, S., Janzen, D., Meyer, C., Gollin, M., Gámez, R. and Juma, C. (1993), *Biodiversity Prospecting: Using Genetic Resources for Sustainable Development*, World Resources Institute, Washington, DC.

Reis, J. and Guzman, R. (1992), 'An Econometric Model of Amazon Deforestation', paper presented at the Conference on Statistics in Public Resources and Utilities, and in the Care of the Environment, Lisbon, April.

Repetto, R., Magrath, W., Wells, M., Beer, C. and Rossini, F. (1989), *Wasting Assets: Natural Resources in the National Accounts*, World Resources Institute, Washington, DC.

Repetto, R, and Gillis, M, (1988), *Public Policies and the Misuse of Forest Resources*, Cambridge University Press, Cambridge.

Robinson, S. (1990), 'Pollution, Market Failure, and Optimal Policy in an Economywide Framework', Working Paper No. 559, Department of Agricultural and Resource Economics, University of California.

Roland-Holst, D.W. and Sancho, F. (1992), 'Relative Income Determination in the United States: A Social Accounting Perspective', *Review of Income and Wealth*, **38**: 311–27.

Romer, P.M. (1990), 'Endogenous Technological Change', *Journal of Political Economy*, **98**(5): 71–102.

Round, J.I. (1994), 'The European Economy: a SAM Perspective', in Round, J.I. (ed) *The European Economy in Perspective: Essays in Honour of Edward Nevin*, Cardiff: University of Wales Press.

Rudel, T. (1989), 'Population, Development, and Tropical Deforestation: A Cross-National Study', *Rural Sociology*, **54**:

Ruitenbeek, J. (1992), 'The Rainforest Supply Price: A Tool for Evaluating Rainforest Conservation Expenditures', *Ecological Economics*, **1**: 57–78.

Ruttan, V.W. (1991), 'Sustainable Growth in Agricultural Production', CREDIT Research Paper No. 91/13, Centre for Research in Environmental Development and International Trade, University of Nottingham.

Sadoff, C.W. (1992), 'The Effects of Thailand's Logging Ban: Overview and Preliminary Results', Thailand Development Research Institute, Bangkok.

Schneider, R. (1992), *An Economic Analysis of Environmental Problems in the Amazon*, Report 9104–BR, Latin America Country Operations Division, World Bank, Washington, DC.

Schneider, R. (1993), 'Land Abandonment, Property Rights, and Agricultural Sustainability in the Amazon', LATEN Dissemination Note No. 3, World Bank, Washington, DC.

Schneider, R. (1994), 'Government and the Economy on the Amazon Frontier', Latin America and the Caribbean Technical Department, Regional Studies Program, Report No. 34, World Bank, Washington, DC.

Schulze, E.-D. and Mooney, H.A. (1993), 'Biodiversity and Ecosystem Functions', *Ecological Studies*, **99**, Springer-Verlag, Berlin, Heidelberg.

Scott, A. (1956), 'National Wealth and Natural Wealth', *Canadian Journal of Economics and Political Science*, **22**: 373–8.

Scott, M.-Fg. (1989), *A New View of Economic Growth*, Clarendon Press, Oxford.

Sebastian, I. and Alicbusan, A. (1989), 'Sustainable Development: Issues in Adjustment Lending Policies', Environment Department Divisional Paper No. 1989–6, World Bank, Washington, DC.

Sedjo, R. (1988), 'Property Rights and the Protection of Plant Genetic Resources', in J.R. Kloppenburg (ed.), *The Use and Control of Plant Genetic Resources*, Duke University Press, Durham.

Sedjo, R. (1991), 'Toward a Worldwide System of Tradeable Forest Protection and Management Obligations', Resources for the Future, Washington, DC, mimeo.

Seldon, T.M. and Song, D.Q. (1994), 'Environmental Quality and Development: Is there an Environmental Kuznets Curve?', *Journal of Environmental Economics and Management*, **27**: 147–62.

Sen, A.K. (1976), 'Poverty: An Ordinal Approach to Measurement', *Econometrica*, **44**: 219–31.

Sen, A.K. (1982), *Poverty and Famines*, Clarendon Press, Oxford.

Shafik, N. (1994a), 'Economic Development and Environmental Quality: An Econometric Analysis', *Oxford Economic Papers*, **46**, Supplementary Issue.

Shafik, N. (1994b), 'Macroeconomic Causes of Deforestation: Barking up the Wrong Tree', in Brown and Pearce (eds) (1994b), 757–73.

Simon, J.L. and Kahn, H. (1984), *The Resourceful Earth*, Basil Blackwell, Oxford.

Sittenfield, A. and Gámez, R. (1993), 'Biodiversity Prospecting in INBio', in Reid et al. (1993).

Smith, K. (1988), 'Air Pollution: Assessing Total Exposure in Developing Countries', *Environment*, **30**(10), 16–20 and 28–35.

Smith, P. (1994), 'The Canadian National Accounts Environmental Component: A Status Report', London Group meeting on National Accounts and the Environment, London, March.

Smith, V.K. (1991), 'Household Production Functions and Environmental Benefit Estimation', in J.B. Braden and C.D. Kolstad (eds), *Measuring the Demand for Environmental Quality*, North-Holland, Amsterdam.

Solow, R.M. (1974), 'Intergenerational Equity and Exhaustible Resources', *Review of Economic Studies*, symposium.

Solow, R.M. (1986), 'On the Intergenerational Allocation of Exhaustible Resources', *Scandinavian Journal of Economics*, **88**: 141–9.

Southgate, D. (1988), 'The Economics of Land Degradation in the Third World', Environment Department Working Paper No. 2, World Bank, Washington, DC.

Southgate, D. (1994), 'Tropical Deforestation and Agricultural Development in Latin America', in Brown and Pearce (eds) (1994b).

Southgate, D. and Pearce, D.W. (1988), 'Agricultural Colonization and Environmental Degradation in Frontier Developing Economies', Environment Department Working Paper No. 9, World Bank, Washington, DC.

Southgate, D., Sierra, R. and Brown, L. (1989), 'The Causes of Tropical Deforestation in Ecuador: A Statistical Analysis', London Environmental Economics Centre, International Institute for Environment and Development (IIED), London.

Squire, L. and van der Tak, H.G. (1975), *Economic Analysis of Projects*, Johns Hopkins University Press, Baltimore.

Srinivasan, T.N. (1988), 'Population Growth and Food', in R.D. Lee, B.W. Arthur, A.C. Kelley, G. Rodgers and T.N. Srinivasan (eds), *Population, Food and Rural Development*, Clarendon Press, Oxford.

Stewart, F. (1991), 'Capital Goods in Developing Countries', in K. Martin, (ed.), *Strategies of Economic Development*, Macmillan, London.

Stiglitz, G. (1979), 'A Neoclassical Analysis of the Economics of Natural Resources', in V.K. Smith (ed.), *Scarcity and Growth Reconsidered*, Johns Hopkins University Press, Baltimore.

Stone, R. (1977), 'Foreword' in G. Pyatt and A. Roe (eds), *Social Accounting for Development Planning with Special Reference to Sri Lanka*, Cambridge University Press, Cambridge.

Streeten, P. and Burki, J. (1978), 'Basic Needs: Some Issues', *World Development*, **6**:

Stryker, D. (1989), 'Linkages Between Policy Reform and Natural Resource Management in Sub-Saharan Africa', unpublished paper, Fletcher School, Tufts University, and Associates for International Resources and Development, MA.

Swanson, T. (1994), *The International Regulation of Extinction*, Macmillan, London.

Townsend, P. (1979), *Poverty in the United Kingdom*, Penguin, London.

Townsend, P. (1985), 'A Sociological Approach to the Measurement of Poverty', *Oxford Economic Papers*, **37**: 659–88.

Trabold-Nübler, H. (1991), 'The Human Development Index: a New Development Indicator?', *Intereconomics*, September/October: 236–43.

United Nations (1975), *Towards a System of Social and Demographic Statistics*, Studies on Methods, Series F, No. 18, United Nations, New York.

United Nations (1989), *Statistics and Policies: ECA Preliminary Observations on the World Bank Report: Africa Adjustment and Growth in the 1980s*, United Nations, Addis Ababa.

United Nations (1991), *World's Women 1970–1990: Trends and Statistics*, United Nations, New York.

United Nations (1992), *National Accounts Statistics: Main Aggregates and Detailed Tables 1990*, United Nations, New York.

United Nations (1993), *Integrated Environmental and Economic Accounting*, Series F, No. 61, United Nations, New York.

United Nations Conference on Environment and Development (UNCED) (1992), *Agenda 21*, UNCED, New York.

United Nations Development Programme (UNDP) (1990), *Human Development Report 1990*, Oxford University Press, Oxford

United Nations Development Programme (UNDP) (1991), *Human Development Report 1991*, Oxford University Press, Oxford

United Nations Development Programme (UNDP) (1992), *Human Development Report 1992*, UNDP, New York.

United Nations Development Programme (UNDP) (1993), *Human Development Report 1993*, Oxford University Press, Oxford.

United Nations Development Programme (UNDP) (1994), *Human Development Report 1994*, Oxford University Press, Oxford.

United Nations Development Programme (UNDP) (1995), *Human Development Report 1995*, UNDP, New York.

United Nations Statistics Office (UNSO) (1993), *System of National Accounts 1991*, United Nations, New York.

Varian, H. (1993), *Microeconomic Analysis*, 3rd edition, W.W. Norton, New York.

Veloz, A., Southgate, D., Hitzhusen, F. and MacGregor, R. (1985), 'The Economics of Erosion Control in a Subtropical Watershed: A Dominican Case', *Land Economics*, **61**: 145–55.

Verissimo, A., Barreto, P., Mattos, M.M., Tariffa, R. and Uhl, C. (1992), 'Logging Impacts and Prospects for Sustainable Forest Management in an Old

Amazonian Frontier: The Case of Paragominas', *Forest Ecology and Management*, **55**: 169–99.

Victor, P., Hanna, H.E. and Kubusi, A. (1994), 'How Strong is Weak Sustainability?', paper presented at the International Symposium on Models of Sustainable Development, Paris, March.

Vincent, J. (1994), 'The Tropical Timber Trade and Sustainable Development', in Brown and Pearce (eds) (1994b).

Vitousek, P., Ehrlich, P., Ehrlich, A. and Matson, P. (1986), 'Human Appropriation of the Products of Photosynthesis', *Bioscience*, **34**: 368–73.

Warford, J. (1994), 'The Evolution of Environmental Concerns in Adjustment Lending: A Review', Working Paper No. 65, World Bank, Washington, DC.

Warford, J.J., Schwab, A., Cruz, W. and Hansen, S. (1993), 'The Evolution of Environmental Concerns in Adjustment Lending: A Review', paper presented at the Committee of International Development Institutions on the Environment (CIDIE) Workshop on Environmental Impacts of Economywide Policies in Developing Countries, World Bank, Washington, DC, February.

Weale, M. (1991), 'Environmental Multipliers from a System of Physical Resource Accounting', *Structural Change and Economic Dynamics*, **2**(2): 297–313.

Weil, D.E.C., Alicbusan, A.P., Wilson, J.F., Reich, M.R. and Bradley, D.J. (1990), *The Impact of Development Policies on Health: A Review of the Literature*, World Health Organization, Geneva.

Weitzman, M.L. (1976), 'On the Welfare Significance of National Product in a Dynamic Economy', *Quarterly Journal of Economics*, **90**: 156–62.

White, G.H. (1984), 'Water Resource Adequacy: Illusion and Reality', in Simon and Kahn (1984).

Wilson, E.O. (1988), *Biodiversity*, National Academy Press, Washington, DC.

World Bank (1984), *World Development Report 1984*, Oxford University Press, Oxford.

World Bank (1988), *Adjustment Lending: An Evaluation of Ten Years of Experience*, World Bank, Washington, DC.

World Bank (1990), *World Development Report 1990*, Oxford University Press, Oxford.

World Bank (1991a), *Malaysia: Forestry Subsector Study*, Report 9775–MA, World Bank, Washington, DC.

World Bank (1991b), *Restructuring Economies in Distress*, World Bank, Washington, DC.

World Bank (1992a), *The Third Report on Adjustment Lending: Private and Public Resources for Growth*, World Bank, Washington, DC.

World Bank (1992b), *World Bank Structural and Sectoral Adjustment Operations: The Second OED Overview*, World Bank, Washington, DC.

World Bank (1992c), *World Development Report 1992*, Oxford University Press, Oxford.

World Bank (1993a), *Commodity Trade and Price Trends*, 1989–91 edition, Johns Hopkins University Press, Baltimore.

World Bank (1993b), *Energy Efficiency and Conservation in the Developing World*, World Bank, Washington, DC.

World Bank (1993c), *Peru: Privatization Adjustment Loan*, Report No. P–5929–PE, World Bank, Washington, DC.

World Bank (1993d), *The World Bank's Role in the Electric Power Sector*, World Bank, Washington, DC.

World Bank (1993e), *World Development Report 1993*, World Bank, Washington, DC.

World Bank (1993f), *World Tables 1993*, World Bank, Washington, DC.

World Bank (1994a), *Adjustment in Africa: Reforms, Results and the Road Ahead*, A World Bank Policy Research Report, Washington, DC.

World Bank (1994b), *Indonesia Environment and Development: Challenges for the Future*, Environment Unit, Country Department III, East Asia and Pacific Region, World Bank, Washington, DC, March.

World Bank (1994c), *Social Indicators*, World Bank, Washington, DC.

World Bank (1994d), *Thailand: Mitigating Pollution and Congestion Impacts in a High Growth Economy*, Country Operations Division, Country Department I, East Asia and Pacific Region, World Bank, Washington, DC, February.

World Bank (1994e), *World Development Report 1994*, World Bank, Washington, DC.

World Bank (1994f), *Chile: Managing Environmental Problems. Economic Analysis of Selected Issues*, Environment and Urban Development Division, Country Department I, Latin America and Caribbean Region, World Bank, Washington, DC.

World Bank (1995a), *Monitoring Environmental Progress*, World Bank, Washington, DC.

World Bank (1995b), *World Development Report 1995*, Oxford University Press, Oxford.

World Commission on Environment and Development (1987), *Our Common Future*, Oxford University Press, Oxford.

World Conservation Monitoring Centre (1992), *Global Biodiversity: Status of the Earth's Living Resources*, Chapman & Hall, London.

World Resources Institute (1986), *World Resources 1986*, World Resources Institute, Washington, DC.

World Resources Institute (1992), *World Resources 1992–3*, World Resources Institute, Washington, DC.

World Resources Institute (1994), *World Resources 1994–5*, World Resources Institute, Washington, DC.

Young, C.E.F (1993), 'Economywide Policy Effects on Rural Poverty and the Environment', Department of Economics, University College London, mimeo.

Index

abatement costs 39, 48–9, 50, 51, 57, 59–60, 61, 66–8, 85, 86, 87, 188, 192, 204

action impact matrix (AIM) 18, 155–6, 157–62, 178, 179, 188, 212, 214

Adelman, M. 61, 83

Adger, W.N. 102

Adriaanse, A. 24–7, 119, 153

Afghanistan 134

Africa 104, 107–10, 123–6, 176, 177, 196, 198, 208
  see also Africa, North; Africa, Sub-Saharan

Africa, North 76, 77, 97, 124, 205
  see also Africa

Africa, Sub-Saharan 2, 77, 78–81, 98, 125, 165, 173, 176, 205–6
  see also Africa

Agenda 21 (UNCED, 1992) 1, 33, 187

aggregate physical environmental indicators 24–7, 119

Aghevli, B.B. 194

Agnew, C. 123

agricultural carrying capacity 121–2

agricultural productivity 128–30, 131, 168

agricultural reforms 170–171, 177, 183

agricultural subsidies 168, 170, 177

air pollution
  economywide policies and 158–9, 160, 166, 173, 175–6
  health cost of 29–31, 88, 89, 202, 203
  indoor 31, 203
  transboundary 87, 89, 100–101
  valuing air pollution in OECD Europe *see* empirical measures of sustainable development

Alam, M. 125

Alexandratos, N. 125

Alfsen, K. 34

Algeria 82, 97, 107, 109, 112, 113, 126, 135

Alicbusan, A. 185, 186

America, Central 104, 108, 110, 124, 196
  see also Latin America

America, North 124, 196, 198
  see also Canada; United States

America, South 104, 108, 110, 124, 196, 198
  see also Latin America

Anderson, E. 123

Anderson, J. 129

Andersson, T. 100

ApSimon, H. 89

Argentina 97, 108

Armitage, J. 125, 126

Aronsson, T. 64

Arrow, K.J. 5, 119, 127, 130

Asheim, G.B. 62, 101, 116

Asia 104, 109, 110, 124–5, 196, 198
  see also Asia, East; Asia, South

Asia, East 77, 78–9, 96, 190–191, 205–6
  see also Asia

Asia, South 76, 77, 98, 205
  see also Asia

Atkinson, A.B. 136

Atkinson, G. 10, 54, 64, 69, 70, 100, 103, 111, 112, 113, 126

Australia 106, 134, 140, 143

Austria 93, 94, 106, 140

avertive expenditures *see* defensive expenditures

Bahamas 108, 110

Bahrain 108, 110

Bangkok 30

Bangladesh 98, 147

Barbier, A.B. 15, 127, 168, 183, 184

Barro, R.J. 10, 193, 208

Bartelmus, P. 43, 59

basic needs approach 133, 137–8, 209

basic needs index (BNI) 143, 145

Baster, N. 132

Baumol, W.J. 5

Beckerman, W. 201

Belgium 93, 94, 106, 140
Belize 97
Belka, M. 170
Beltratti, A. 14
Berndt, E. 11
Bernheim, B.D. 193
bilateral aid 113–14, 207
Binswanger, H. 168, 185
biodiversity 13, 14, 15, 74, 90, 161
    indicators 18, 120, 127–8, 129,
        131–31, 150, 187, 208
biogeochemical cycles 14, 15
Birdsall, N. 165, 184
Bishop, J. 75
Bishop, R.C. 15
Bolivia 97, 108
Borda rank 139–41, 211
Bosch, P.R. 43, 59, 102, 119
Boserup, E. 11
Botswana 135, 137, 147, 168
Botterweg, T.H. 15
Bourguignon, F. 182
Braden, J.B. 61
Brazil 97, 108, 110, 167, 168, 174, 185,
    197
Bromley, D. 168
Broome, J. 8, 89
Brown, K. 197
Brundtland Commission 12, 33, 148,
    187, 210, 216
Brunei 109, 110, 111–12
Bulgaria 107, 166
Bureau of Economic Analysis 44
Bureau of Mines 72
Burgess, J. 185
Burki, J. 137
Burkina Faso 107, 126, 134, 147
Burundi 80, 98

Cairo 30
Cameroon 98, 107, 110, 112, 113
Canada 106, 134–5, 140, 143
Capistrano, A.D. 185
capital
    constancy of critical natural capital 16,
        17–18, 121, 194–5, 198, 209, 217
    constancy of natural capital stock
        14–15, 16, 17–18, 120–121
    constancy of overall stock of 9, 14, 16,
        17, 62

depreciation of *see* depreciation of
    produced assets
diversity of 127
human *see* human capital
marginal productivity of 5, 7, 8, 11, 58
social 216–17
substitution of produced for natural
    8–9, 11, 12–13, 14, 16, 18, 44,
    62, 64, 120–121, 130
carbon dioxide emissions 2, 9–10, 25–6,
    49–50, 57, 58–9, 100–101, 150,
    154, 196–7
    valuing marginal social costs of 71,
        74, 76, 78, 88, 90, 93, 205
carbon storage 13–14, 74, 89, 196–7
carbon tax 9, 38, 50, 57, 58–9, 74
Caribbean 77, 78, 97, 205
carrying capacity 99–100, 114, 119–26,
    130, 150, 208–9
Carson, R.T. 23
CEC/US 88–91
CES functions 11
CFC gases 25–6
Chad 107, 126
Chandrashekar, H. 129
Chemonics International and Associates
    30
Chile 84–5, 97, 108
China 96, 109, 110, 135, 137, 167–8,
    170–171, 172
Ciriacy-Wantrup, S.V. 15
Clark, C.W. 5
Clarke, M. 123
Cleaver, K. 177
Cobb-Douglas production function 9, 11
Cohen, J.E. 120, 121
Colombia 97, 108, 135
commercial natural resources 40, 41, 44
Commission of the European
    Communities 52
Common, M. 127
computable general equilibrium (CGE)
    models 161, 163–4, 176–7
Congo 80, 82, 98, 107, 109, 112, 113
constant elasticity of substitution (CES)
    production functions 11
consumer rate of time preference 5–6, 7,
    62, 82, 83, 115
consumption rate of interest 62, 81–2
contingent valuation 14, 61, 89, 161

Conway, G. 127
Cooper, D. 129
Corniak G.A. 175, 182
Costa Rica 97, 108, 110, 161, 174,
    176–7
Council of Mutual Economic Assistance
    (CMEA) 170
crop yields 128–30, 131, 168
Crowards, T. 89, 92, 102
Cruz, W. 160, 163, 165, 167, 169, 170,
    171, 172, 173, 177, 186
CSERGE/UNC Chapel Hill 87
Czechoslovakia 107, 135

Dasgupta, P. 4, 6, 15, 62, 83, 132, 133,
    139–41
de Boer, B. 102, 119
de Boo, A.J. 52
debt, international 185–6, 188, 214
defensive expenditures 41, 42, 50–51,
    57, 59, 64, 89, 204
deforestation 2, 49, 158, 160, 168, 174,
    176–8, 183–4, 185, 186, 209
    value of 71, 73–4, 78, 79, 88, 89,
        196–7, 205
Denmark 93, 94–5, 106, 140
Department of Energy 72
depletion of resources, valuation of 37,
    40, 41, 42, 43, 60–62, 63, 71–5, 188
    estimates of resource depletion and
        genuine saving 75–85, 190–192,
        205–6, 215
    exported resources 103–14
    marginal social costs of carbon
        dioxide emissions 71, 74, 76, 78,
        205
    price-taking resource exporter model
        101–2, 114–16, 207
    reattributing resource depletion
        117–18
    soil erosion 43, 74–5
    tropical forests 71, 73–4, 78, 79,
        196–7, 205
    valuation of resource rents for non-
        renewable resources 71–3
deposit-refund schemes 159, 169
depreciation of produced assets 75, 79,
    102, 112–13, 152, 189, 190–191,
    206
Desai, M. 150

Devarajan, S. 164
Dhareshwar, A. 75
discount rate 4–7, 8, 45, 61–2, 81–3,
    115, 174, 206
discoveries, resource 41, 42, 43, 47–8,
    56, 58, 204
dispersion and impact models 38
diversity indicators 18
    see also biodiversity
Dixit, A. 9
Dominican Republic 97
dose-response studies 27, 61, 89, 202
Drèze, J. 122
Dubourg, W.R. 15, 89, 123
Dutch Central Bureau of Statistics (CBS)
    52, 102

Earth Summit (Rio de Janeiro, 1992) 1,
    33
ecological economics, definition of 119
'ecological footprints' 99–100, 114, 131,
    207
ecological indicators 17, Ch.6, 207–9
    see also carrying capacity; resilience
Economic Commission for Latin
    America and the Caribbean
    (ECLAC) 175
economywide policies 18, Ch.8, 212–14
    action impact matrix (AIM) approach
        18, 155–6, 157–62, 178, 179,
        188, 212, 214
    efficiency-oriented policies 162–8,
        212
        macroeconomic reforms 163–5
        sectoral reforms 165–8
    improving economic-environmental
        coordination 179–80
    integrating environmental concerns
        into economic decision-making
        156–62
    long-term poverty and income effects
        176–8, 179, 213
    range of 155
    restoring macroeconomic stability
        173–5, 179, 213
    short-term adverse effects of recession
        and government cutbacks 175–6,
        177, 213
    structural adjustment policies 18, 165,
        175–6, 181–6, 188, 214, 216

unaddressed policy, market or
    institutional imperfections
    168–73, 178–9, 188, 212–13
  institutional constraints 172–3, 213
  market failures 171, 213
  policy distortions 169–71, 212–13
Ecuador 97, 108, 110, 112
educational attainment 135–6, 139–40,
    141, 142, 153, 210
educational expenditures 83–5, 152, 206,
    217
efficiency-oriented policies 162–8, 212
effluent charges 159, 169
Egypt 97, 107, 113
Ehrlich, P. 120
Elbadawi, I. 80
El Serafy, S. 42, 58, 62, 81
emission banking 159, 169
emission permits 41, 64, 159, 169
emission taxes *see* taxation
empirical measures of sustainable
    development Ch.4, 205–6
  estimates of resource depletion and
      genuine saving 75–85, 190–192,
      205–6, 215
  genuine savings by country 96–8, 205
  genuine savings by region 76–81,
      205–6
  human capital and genuine saving
      83–5, 206
  user cost versus net price 81–3
  resource depletion: measurement
      issues 71–5
  savings rule 70–71, 120, 187, 194–5,
      198, 205, 208
  valuing air pollution in OECD Europe:
      empirical estimates 88–96
  air pollution damage in United
      Kingdom 92–3, 94–5
  genuine savings in OECD Europe
      76–7, 93–6
  genuine savings in United Kingdom
      91–2, 93–4
  valuing air pollution in OECD Europe:
      preliminary concepts 85–7
  measurement 86–7
energy pricing policies 158, 160, 162,
    165–7, 169–70, 212
environmental accounting *see* resource
    and environmental accounting

environmental assessments 157–60, 175
environmental damage 41, 42, 43, 58, 64
  valuation of 59–60, 85–96
environmental efficiency indicators 23,
    38, 150
environmental expenditure accounts 34,
    39, 204
environmental quality indicators 141,
    148–50
environmental resources, measurement
    of, in national accounts 40–41
environmental services 41, 42, 48–51,
    54, 55, 56, 58, 60–61, 63, 64–8, 70,
    204
environmental standards 159, 169
Ethiopia 98, 126
Europe 76–7, 93–6, 124, 196, 198
  see also Europe, Eastern; European
    union; Organization for
    Economic Cooperation and
    Development (OECD)
Europe, Eastern 104, 106, 107, 124, 166
European Union 52, 112–13, 114, 207
  see also Europe
exchange rate policies 158, 160, 162,
    163, 177–8, 185
exhaustible resources 62
  with discoveries 47–8, 56, 58, 204
  heterogeneous deposits of 46–7, 56,
    57–8, 60
  valuation of resource rents for 71–3
existence value *see* non-use value
extraction costs 46, 47, 50, 55, 56, 57,
    60, 72–3, 81, 115, 118, 205

Faber, M. 11
Falkenmark, M. 123, 124
Fankhauser, S. 74, 88, 90, 196
fertilisers 129–30, 166, 170
Field, E. 11
Finland 93, 94, 106, 140
fisheries 173, 191
Flores, N.E. 23
Folke, C. 100, 119
Food and Agriculture Organization
    (FAO) 74, 125
food security index (FSI) 143, 145
forests *see* carbon storage; deforestation;
    fuelwood; reforestation; timber
    resources

fossil fuels 9–10, 15, 49–50, 57, 58–9, 74, 102
see also carbon dioxide emissions; oil resources
France 93, 94, 106, 134–5, 140, 143
Fraumeni, B.M. 84
freedom indicators 139–40, 141
Freeman, A.M. 69, 161
fuel taxes 159, 169, 173
fuelwood 125–6, 148, 209
see also timber resources

Gambia 126
Gelb, A. 80, 206
genetic diversity 129
genuine savings *see* savings, genuine
Germany 93, 94–5, 106, 107, 140
Ghana 98, 107, 147–8, 172
Gillis, M. 193, 194
global warming 6, 10, 15, 25–7, 49, 60, 88, 90, 101, 150, 191, 196–7, 201, 209
see also greenhouse gas emissions
Goldin, I. 164
government expenditure cutbacks 175–6, 184–5, 192, 213, 216
Greece 93, 94–5, 106
greenhouse gas emissions 2, 9–10, 25–7, 49–50, 57, 58–9, 60, 71, 74, 76, 78, 88, 90, 93, 100–101, 150, 154, 196–7, 205
see also global warming
green national accounts *see* resource and environmental accounting
Gregory, R. 14
Grohs, F. 102
gross domestic product (GDP) 135, 136–7, 139–40, 141–3, 189, 208
green 42–3
Grossman, G.M. 23
gross national product (GNP) 54
'green' adjustments to 56–7, 58, 67, 70–71, 161
growth rates by region 77, 78
as indicator of development 33, 39, 49, 54, 56, 134–5, 143, 209, 210, 211
net saving versus depletion share of 75–6

sustainable development and optimal growth of 4–8, 11–12, 137–8, 209
Guatemala 97, 108, 147
Guinea 134
Guyana 97, 108

Hageman, A. 43, 62
Haiti 97
Halon gases 25–6
Hamilton, K. 8, 9, 10, 44, 45, 49, 54, 55, 64, 69, 70, 83, 91, 100, 103, 105, 111, 112, 113, 189, 190
Hammond, A. 25, 119
Hammond, P. 9
Hanna, H.E. 194
Harrison, A. 42, 70
Hartwick, J.M. 9, 43, 44, 45, 46, 47, 57, 58, 62, 64, 69, 73, 101, 114, 116
see also Hartwick rule
Hartwick rule 9–11, 44, 64, 101, 114, 116, 199
Hazell, P. 128, 129
headcount index (HDI) 144–5
Heal, G.M. 4, 6, 62, 83
health cost of air pollution 29–31, 88, 89, 202, 203
hedonic pricing 61
Heertje, A. 193, 194
Herfindahl, O.C. 42
Hicks, J.R. 40
Higgins, G.M. 122
Hill, P. 70
Hoel, M. 9
Holling, C.S. 127
Honduras 97, 108
Hong Kong 109, 110, 139–40
Host, D. 164
Hotelling efficiency rule 8, 36, 43, 47, 58, 61, 62, 77, 81, 101, 115–16, 199
Howarth, R.B. 5
Hueting, R. 43, 59, 102, 119
Hughes, G. 169
Humana index 141
human capital 37, 64, 80, 83–5, 149, 152, 195, 198, 199–200, 206, 211, 216–17
human development index (HDI) 3, 18, 133–43, 153–4, 209–11
criticisms of 138–43, 210

environmental information integrated
into 146, 148–50, 154, 210
genuine savings and 151, 154, 211
Human Development Report (UNDP,
1990) 134, 136, 137, 141, 149
Hungary 106, 107, 135

Iceland 107, 140
import coefficients 104, 117
income elasticity of demand 180
income gap index (IG) 144–5
income tax 5, 192–3, 216
India 98, 109, 128–9, 147, 167
Indonesia 82, 96, 109, 110, 111, 152,
168, 171, 197
infant mortality rate 133, 139, 141, 145
input output analysis 103
institutional constraints 172–3, 213
integrated environmental index 33
integrated poverty index (IPI) 143–5,
146, 187
interest rates 62, 81–2, 174, 193–4,
199–200
see also discount rate
International Development Association
176
International Fund for Agricultural
Development (IFAD) 143–8 *passim*
international trade 17, Ch.5
'ecological footprints' 99–100, 114,
131, 207
liberalization of 164–5, 172, 212–13
measuring direct and indirect flows of
resources 103–14
global trading economy (1985)
104–10
impact on individual countries
111–14, 207
price-taking resource exporter model
101–2, 114–16, 207
reattributing resource depletion
117–18
resource and pollutant flow accounts
38, 103
and sustainable development 100–103,
206–7
international trade in natural
resources 101–3, 191–2
transboundary pollution 17, 87, 89,
100–101, 207

investment, financing of 190–194, 198,
215
see also rents, resource
investment projects 158–9, 160, 167–8,
175
Iran 81, 82, 97, 108, 110, 137
Iraq 108, 110, 113
Ireland 93, 94–5, 106
irreversibility 15, 150
irrigation 164, 167, 175
Israel 109
Italy 93, 94, 107, 140
Ivory Coast 98, 107, 110, 113, 147, 165,
186

Jakarta 30
Jamaica 97, 108, 112, 166
Japan 101, 105, 106, 111–12, 114, 134,
140, 143, 207
Johansson, P.-O. 64
Jones-Lee, M.W. 89
Jordan 109
Jorgenson, D.W. 84
Josserand, H. 183
Juster, F.T. 42, 67

Kahn, H. 120
Kahn, J. 185
Kahnemann, D. 14
Kellog, A.C. 11
Kenya 80, 98, 126, 148
Keuning, S. 151, 152
Kiker, C.F. 185
Kirchner, J.W. 125
Klaassen, G. 15
Kneese, A.V. 42
Knetsch, J.L. 14, 61
Kolstad, C.D. 61
Korea, Republic of 96, 109, 137
Kotillof, L.J. 193
Krajewski, S. 170
Krautkraemer, J.A. 14
Krebs, C.J. 127
Kriström, B. 23, 180
Krueger, A.B. 23
Kubusi, A. 194
Kuwait 109, 110, 113
Kuznets curves, environmental 23–4, 96,
206

Laity, J.A. 23

Lal, D. 137
land
    carrying capacity of 121–2
    degradation 158–9, 160, 168, 172,
        174, 177, 183
    protected 150, 154
    rights to *see* property rights
Larson, B. 168
Latin America 77, 78, 97, 165, 175, 205
    see also America, Central; America,
        South
lead pollution 30–31
Leipert, C. 67
Lele, U. 11
Leonard, H.J. 184
Leontief function 11
Lewenhak, S. 148
Libya 107, 109, 112, 113
Liebig's Law 120–121, 130
life-cycle hypothesis 193
life expectancy indicators 132–3, 135,
        139–40, 141, 144–5, 210
Lind, R.C. 5
Lindsey, R. 47
Lithuania 135
Little, I.M.B. 72
living natural resources 45–6, 56, 58, 60,
        63, 204
Löfgren, K.-G. 64
Low, P. 184
Lucas, R.E.B. 184
Luxembourg 93, 94, 106, 135, 139–40,
        211

macroeconomic models 38
Madagascar 98, 107, 126
Mahar, D. 168, 185
maintenance cost approaches 59, 70
Malawi 107, 126
Malaysia 96, 109, 110, 111, 137
Mäler, K.-G. 9, 45, 51, 69
Mali 98, 107, 126
marginal productivity of capital 5, 7, 8,
        11, 58
marginal social cost 9, 28, 49, 52, 57,
        59–60, 61, 65, 66, 70, 71, 74, 76,
        78, 85, 86–7, 88, 90, 91, 92, 93, 95,
        204, 205, 206
Margulis, S. 30
Markandya, A. 15

market based policies 158, 159, 169
market failures 171, 213
Marland, G. 74
Martínez-Alier, J. 194
materials and buildings damage 88, 90
Mauritania 98, 107, 111, 112, 113
McDonald, J. 185
Meier, P. 165
methane gases 25–6
Mexico 30, 82, 97, 108, 110, 112, 165,
        166–7, 173, 175–6, 186
Middle East 76, 77, 97, 104, 108–9, 110,
        124, 205
migration 158–9, 177, 178, 185, 186
mineral resources 72–3, 83, 85, 110
Miranda, K. 175
Mirrlees, J.A. 70
Mooney, H.A. 14, 131
Moran, D. 128, 129, 130
morbidity rates 29–31, 89
Morocco 97, 108, 126, 161, 164
Morrison, D. 182
mortality rates 29–31, 89, 133, 139, 141,
        145
Mosley, P. 182
Mozambique 108, 145, 147
multicriteria analysis (MCA) 161–2
Munasinghe, M. 2, 24, 123, 157, 159,
        160, 161, 163, 165, 167, 169, 170,
        171, 172, 173, 174, 177
Muzondo, T. 175

National Accounting Matrix including
        Environmental Accounts (NAMEA)
        52, 56
national accounts
    green *see* resource and environmental
        accounting
    measurement of natural resources in
        conventional accounts 40–41, 44,
        57–60
    see also System of National Accounts
        (SNA)
National Environmental Action Plans
        157–60
national wealth (NW), green 42, 43–4,
        189–90, 215
natural resource accounts 34, 36–7, 204
Ndulu, B. 80
Nehru, V. 75

neoclassical production function 45, 64, 115
Nepal 147–8
net domestic product (NDP), green 42, 43, 101
net environmental product (NEP) 54–5
net financial assets 41, 42, 43–4
Netherlands 24–7, 52, 93–4, 106, 107, 119, 134, 139–40, 143
net national product (NNP) 54, 57
    green 45–8, 50, 51, 57–60, 62, 63, 64, 67, 70, 188–9, 204–5, 214–15
net price, versus user cost 81–3
net resource product (NRP) 54–5
New Zealand 106
Niger 80, 98, 134, 148
Nigeria 78, 79, 80, 82, 98, 108, 109, 113, 126
Ninan, K. 129
nitrogen oxides 25–6, 30–31, 37, 88, 93
non-market based policies 158, 159, 169
non-use value 13
Nordhaus, W.D. 10, 12, 54, 201
Norgaard, R.B. 5
Norway 93–4, 106, 107, 134, 140, 143
Nyström, T. 100

Oceania 104, 109, 198
O'Connor, J. 55, 190
oil resources 46–7, 77, 85, 106, 126, 206
    'oil republic' model 114
    prices 92, 94, 102
    user cost and net price estimated for producers 81, 82
    value of depletion of 72, 73, 77, 103, 105, 109, 110
    windfalls 80
Oman 97, 109, 110, 111
option value 13
Organization for Economic Cooperation and Development (OECD) 21, 22, 29, 33, 88, 105
    genuine savings in OECD countries 76–7, 93–6
    international trade in natural resources by OECD countries 104–7
    valuing air pollution in OECD Europe *see* empirical measures of sustainable development

Organization of Petroleum-Exporting Countries (OPEC) 43–4, 102
Our common future (WCED) 1
overconsumption, definition of 100
Owens, J. 193
ozone gases 30–31
ozone layer depletion 201, 209

Page, T. 3, 4, 8
Pakistan 98, 109, 147
Panama 97
Panayatou, T. 23, 164
Papua New Guinea 96, 109
Paraguay 97, 108
Parfit, D. 8
particulate matter 10, 30–31, 88, 89, 92, 93, 94–5
passive use value *see* non-use value
Pearce, D.W. 15, 44, 54, 62, 69, 82, 89, 92, 100, 121, 126, 128, 129, 130, 174, 180, 197
Pearson, P. 23
performance bonds 159, 169
Perrings, C. 119, 127, 129–30, 168
Persson 174
Peru 97, 108, 110, 147–8, 173
Peskin, H. 42, 58, 64
pesticides 129–30, 167, 170
Pezzey, J. 4, 62
Philippines 96, 109, 135–7, 147, 165, 177–8
physical environmental indicators Ch.2, 202–3
    aggregate 24–7, 119
    basic model of environmental information 22–4
    definition of 21
    demand for 20–21
    desirable characteristics for 21
    environmental efficiency indicators 23, 38, 150
    environmental Kuznets curves 23–4, 96, 206
    health cost of environmental damage 29–31, 202, 203
    priorities for information needs 31–2
    and socioeconomic impacts 27–9
Pinto, B. 170
Poland 107, 169–70

policies for sustainable development
    Ch.9, 214–16
    policy implications of environmental
        and resource accounting 188–97,
        215–16
    policy-making and indicators 187–8,
        214–15
    population growth and 189–90, 197–8,
        215
policy-based loans 114
policy distortions 169–71, 212–13
polluter pays principle 87, 101, 207
pollution
    economywide policies and 158–9,
        160, 166, 171, 173, 175–6, 184
    persistent 150
    taxes on *see* taxation
    transboundary 17, 87, 89, 100–101,
        207
    see also abatement costs; air pollution;
        resource and pollutant flow
        accounts; water resources; *and
        under names of individual
        pollutants*, e.g. carbon dioxide
        emissions; particulate matter
population, human 10–11, 95, 176–8,
        189–90, 197–8, 208, 215
    see also carrying capacity
Portugal 93, 94–5, 107, 137
poverty, and environmental degradation
        176–8, 214
poverty indicators 143–8, 187, 210
poverty line 133, 136, 144, 210
Prakesh, T.R. 128, 129
pressure-state-response (P-S-R)
        framework 22–3, 202–3
price-taking resource exporter, model of
        101–2, 114–16, 207
production possibility frontier 5, 6–7
productivity
    agricultural 128–30, 131, 168
    increases 63, 138
    measurement 36, 188
Proops, J.L.R. 11, 103
property rights 146–7, 164, 168,
        170–174 *passim*, 177, 183, 191,
        212, 213
public expenditure cutbacks 175–6,
        184–5, 192, 213, 216
public opinion 21, 202

Pyatt, G. 152

Qatar 109, 110, 111, 113

Ramsey, F. 8
Rawls, J. 8
Reed, D. 165, 176, 182, 186
Rees, W.E. 99, 100, 120, 121, 131
reforestation 159, 160
regulations, environmental 37
relative welfare index (RWI) 143, 145–6
rents, resource 40–58 *passim*, 60–64
        passim, 70, 71–3, 81–3, 101–2, 114,
        115–16, 118, 191, 192, 195, 204,
        206, 207, 215
Repetto, R. 43, 47, 57, 58, 74, 81, 165,
        186
resilience 119, 120, 127–31, 187, 202,
        207–8
resource and environmental accounting
        Ch.3, 203–5
    formal approaches to green national
        accounts 44–51
    carbon dioxide problem 49–50, 57,
        58–9
    defensive expenditures by
        households 50–51, 57, 59, 64,
        204
    exhaustible resources with
        discoveries 47–8, 56, 58, 204
    heterogeneous deposits of
        exhaustible resources 46–7, 56,
        57–8, 60
    living natural resources 45–6, 56,
        58, 60, 63, 204
    measurability 60–62
    as measure of sustainability 62–3,
        204–5
    model of formal approach 64–8
    pollution emissions and
        environmental services 48–9,
        57, 58, 60–61, 63, 64–8, 204
    social accounting matrices (SAMs)
        51–6, 60, 151–3, 154
    policy implications of *see* policies for
        sustainable development
    varieties of environmental accounts
        33–44
    environmental expenditure accounts
        34, 39, 204

green national accounts 34, 39–44, 204–5
natural resource accounts 34, 36–7, 204
resource and pollutant flow accounts 34, 37–9, 103, 204
resource and pollutant flow accounts 34, 37–9, 103, 204
Riera, P. 23
Robinson, S. 164
Roland-Holst, D.W. 152
Romania 106, 107
Romer, P.M. 10
Round, J.I. 52
royalties 41, 159, 169, 191, 192, 205, 215
Ruttan, V.W. 14
Rwanda 80, 98

Sadoff, C.W. 74
'safe minimum standards' rule 15, 16
Sala-I-Martin, X. 10, 208
Sancho, F. 52, 152
Santiago 30
Saudi Arabia 109, 110, 111
savings, genuine 9, 17, 18, 52–3, 55–6, 62–3, 64, 67–8, 69–70, 74, 85, 100, 101, 102, 113–14, 119, 128, 138, 202, 207
    by country 96–8, 205
    estimates of resource depletion and genuine saving 75–85, 190–192, 205–6, 215
    human capital and 83–5
    and human development index (HDI) 151, 154, 211
    in OECD Europe 76–7, 93–6
    and policies for sustainable development 187, 190–195, 198, 215–16
    by region 76–81, 205–6
    savings rule 70–71, 120, 187, 194–5, 198, 205, 208
    in United Kingdom 91–2, 93–4
savings ratios 193–4
scarcity, physical, measurement of 36, 188
Schneider, R. 168, 174, 197
Schramm, G. 125, 126
Schreiber, G. 177

Schulze, E.-D. 14, 131
Scott, A. 44, 189
Scott, M.-Fg. 10
Sebastian, I. 185, 186
sectoral policies 158, 162, 165–8
Seldon, T.M. 23
Sen, A.K. 122, 144–5
Senegal 98, 126, 147–8
shadow prices 60, 65, 67, 70, 72, 115, 161
shadow projects 15
Shafik, N. 96
Shearer, W. 24
Sierra Leone 98, 134
Simon, J.L 120
Sinden, J.A. 14
Singapore 109, 110, 135
Smith, P. 34
Smith, V.K. 51
social accounting matrices (SAMs) 51–6, 60, 151–3, 154
social capital 216–17
social costs 27–9
    health costs *see* health cost of air pollution
    by industry 56
    marginal 9, 28, 49, 52, 57, 59–60, 61, 65, 66, 70, 71, 74, 76, 78, 85, 86–7, 88, 90, 91, 92, 93, 95, 204, 205, 206
social indicators Ch.7, 209–12
    composite indicators 133–46
        human development index (HDI) 3, 18, 133–43, 153–4, 209–11
        poverty measurement 143–6
    incorporating environment and resources 146–51
        genuine savings and HDI 151, 154, 211
        poverty and environment indicators 146–8, 187, 210
        sustainability, environment and HDI 146, 148–50, 154, 210
    nature and rationale 132–3
    social accounting matrices (SAMs) 151–3, 154
social rate of return on investment 62, 81–2
social welfare function 136, 210
soil erosion 43, 74–5, 122, 168, 172

Solow, R.M. 8, 11, 45
Song, D.Q. 23
South Africa 108, 135
Southgate, D. 174, 183
Soviet Union 104, 106, 107, 124, 166
Spain 93, 94–5, 107
Squire, L. 72
Sri Lanka 135, 147, 162, 165
Srinivasan, T.N. 122
state-owned enterprises (SOEs) 169–70,
    182, 213
stationary equivalent of future
    consumption 45
statistical life value 29–31, 89
Stewart, F. 194
Stiglitz, G. 9
Stone, R. 152
Stone, S. 11
Streeten, P. 137
strong sustainability 12–15, 16, 17–18,
    194–5, 198, 203, 208, 217
    see also carrying capacity; resilience
structural adjustment policies 18, 165,
    175–6, 181–6, 188, 214, 216
Stryker, D. 165, 176
stumpage fees 159, 169, 183–4, 213
subsidies 159, 162, 166–8, 169, 170,
    177, 213
Sudan 108, 126, 168
sulphur oxides 9, 10, 30–31, 37, 88, 93,
    94, 100
Summers, L.H. 193
Suriname 97, 108
Sussangkarn, S. 164
sustainability constraints 120
sustainable development Ch.1
    conditions for 8–12
    definition of 3, 16, 148–9, 210
    and human capital *see* human capital
    and optimal economic growth 4–8,
        11–12, 137–8, 209
    policies for *see* policies for sustainable
        development
    strong sustainability 12–15, 16, 17–18,
        194–5, 198, 203, 208, 217
    time horizon for 3–4, 150
    weak sustainability 16, 17–18, 44, 62,
        119, 130, 194
Sweden 107, 134, 139–40, 143
Switzerland 93, 94, 107, 134, 140, 143

Syria 97, 109, 110, 137
System of Environmental and Economic
    Accounting (SEEA) 34–5, 59, 203
System of National Accounts (SNA) 33,
    34, 36, 39–40, 58, 64, 69, 70, 161,
    203
System of Social and Demographic
    Statistics (SDSS) 152

Taiwan 109, 110
tangible assets 41, 42, 44
Tanzania 126, 148
taxation
    income 5, 192–3, 216
    pollution 9, 37, 38, 41, 49, 50, 57,
        58–9, 64, 65–6, 70, 74, 159, 160,
        167, 169, 173, 188, 204
    product 159, 169, 173
technological progress 8, 10–11, 120,
    122, 129–30, 217
terms of trade 114, 116, 122, 207
Thailand 96, 109, 137, 147, 163–4, 165,
    171, 175–6, 186
timber resources 89, 101, 110, 125–6,
    159, 160, 169, 172, 174, 177,
    183–4, 213
    see also deforestation; fuelwood
time horizon 3–4, 150
time preference, consumer rate of 5–6, 7,
    62, 82, 83, 115
Timmerman, J. 153
Tobin, J. 54
total economic value (TEV) 13
Townsend, P. 209
Trabold-Nübler, H. 142
transboundary pollution 17, 87, 89,
    100–101
travel cost models 61, 161
Trinidad and Tobago 97, 108, 110, 112
Tunisia 97, 108, 126, 137, 168
Turkey 107, 137
Turner, R.K. 119
Tversky, A. 14

Uganda 126
Uhl 183
Ulph, D. 62, 82
uncertainty 14–15
United Arab Emirates 82, 97, 109, 110,
    111, 112, 140

United Kingdom 82, 91–5, 106, 107, 134, 140, 143
United Nations 43, 70, 93, 133–4, 147, 182
  System of Environmental and Economic Accounting (SEEA) 34–5, 59, 203
  System of National Accounts (SNA) 33, 34, 36, 39–40, 58, 64, 69, 70, 161, 203
  System of Social and Demographic Statistics (SDSS) 152
United Nations Conference on Environment and Development (UNCED) 1, 187
United Nations Development Programme (UNDP) 3, 133–4, 136, 137, 140, 141, 142, 149
United States 105–6, 112, 114, 134, 140, 142–3, 207
Uruguay 135
user cost, versus net price 81–3
user fees 159, 169
use value 13
Uzawa 6

van der Tak, H.G. 72
van Heemst, J.J.P. 152
Varian, H. 11
Venezuela 81, 82, 97, 108, 110, 112
Verissimo, A. 183
Victor, P. 194
Vincent, J. 183, 184
Vitousek, P. 130

Wackernagel, M. 99, 100, 120, 121, 131
wage-risk studies 89
Warford, J.J. 126, 156, 169, 185, 186
water resources
  availability of 147–8

pollution of 92, 95, 96, 167–8
pricing of 164–5, 167–8
scarcity indicators 123, 124
sustainable use of 122–5, 150, 209
weak sustainability 16, 17–18, 44, 62, 119, 130, 194
Weale, M. 152, 153
Weil, D.E.C. 184
Weitzman, M.L. 43, 45, 55, 80
Wheeler, D. 165, 184
White, G.H. 123
willingness to accept (WTA) 14
willingness to pay (WTP) 14, 23, 31, 48, 54, 57, 60, 61, 65, 70, 87, 89, 91, 96
Wilson, E.O. 130
World Bank 2, 11, 30, 71, 74, 75, 77, 85, 93, 100, 126, 132, 144, 156, 165–8, 171, 173, 174, 176, 177, 181, 182, 185, 195, 197–8
  RMSIM model of 190
World Commission on Environment and Development (WCED) 1, 3, 16, 149, 210
World Conservation Monitoring Centre 128
World Resources Institute 122, 123, 124, 125, 196
World Wide Fund for Nature (WWF) 186

X-efficiency 194

Yeats, A. 184
Yugoslavia 107

Zaire 108, 110, 112, 113
Zambia 80, 98, 108, 110, 111, 112, 113, 168
Zimbabwe 80, 98, 108, 126, 163